Edward Hedican is a Professor Emeritus from the University of Guelph, Canada, whose primary field of study is cultural anthropology. For most of his career, he has conducted research among Canada's Indigenous peoples, such as the Anishinaabe of northern Ontario in the subarctic region around Lake Nipigon. He has also studied the history of Irish immigrants to Canada in the post-famine period, which involved an in-depth analysis of various genealogical, census and demographic documents in both Ireland and Canada. He is the author of over a dozen books, such as *Beyond the Beaten Path: 50 Years of Anthropology in Canada* (2023), *When the Spirit Calls: The Killings at Hannah Bay* (2023) and *Ipperwash: The Tragic Failure of Canada's Aboriginal Policy* (2013).

Caroline Yesno, the co-author of this book, is Johnny Yesno's sister. For this reason, she is able to provide valuable pertinent inside family information concerning Mr. Yesno's life that would otherwise not be available in the usual biography. This information is not only based on the observations that other family members were able to make concerning Johnny's life, but also the written communications between the two of them throughout their lives. In addition, Caroline has been employed for many years as an educational coordinator for the Eabametoong (Fort Hope) First Nation which is situated in northwestern Ontario, and so in this professional capacity she has become familiar with the general social, economic and political trends and contexts of the Indigenous community from which Mr. Yesno began his life. There is also a direct connection between Caroline and the other author of this book, Edward Hedican, since his own daughters are also members of the Eabametoong First Nation and have been in contact with Caroline on numerous occasions regarding their educational goals and objectives.

Dedicated to the memory of my son,
Shaun Philip Hedican, an indigenous artist whose passing at such a young
age will forever leave an irreparable hole in all of our hearts

Edward Hedican and Caroline Yesno

JOHNNY YESNO

FROM RESIDENTIAL SCHOOL SURVIVOR TO HOLLYWOOD STAR

AUSTIN MACAULEY PUBLISHERS®

LONDON * CAMBRIDGE * NEW YORK * SHARJAH

Ordering Information
Quantity sales: Special discounts are available on quantity purchases by corporations, associations, and others. For details, contact the publisher at the address below.

Publisher's Cataloging-in-Publication Data
Hedican, Edward and Yesno, Caroline
Johnny Yesno

ISBN 9798895431566 (Paperback)
ISBN 9798895431573 (Hardback)
ISBN 9798895431580 (ePub e-book)

Library of Congress Control Number: 2025904649

www.austinmacauley.com/us

First Published 2025
Austin Macauley Publishers LLC
40 Wall Street, 33rd Floor, Suite 3302
New York, NY 10005
USA

mail-usa@austinmacauley.com
+1 (646) 5125767

There are several people who made significant contributions to my knowledge of Johnny Yesno's life and character, who knew him as a 'real' person. The most important of these is Caroline Yesno, his sister, who is the co-author of this book, as well as other members of his family. Andrew Yesno provided important details on the Yesno genealogy and family history. Elizabeth Patience (née Yesno) spent many hours with me discussing her early life in Fort Hope (Eabamatoong) on the Albany River.

And finally, I cannot resist adding a personal note to this preface. All my four children (Shaun, Tara, Celeena and Maya) are members of the Eabamatoong First Nation, as is the case with the subject of this book, Johnny Yesno.

Table of Contents

Preface

There are certain people in life who cannot be denied success regardless of the conditions of their birth or the circumstances of their upbringing. They just seem to rise to the top of whatever they are doing, somehow defying the odds and using their innate skills as a pathway to success.

They also have the ability to utilize the fortuitous circumstances that they find themselves to their advantage. All in all, such people just seem destined to rise to the top. This book is about one of these people named Johnny Yesno. While the name Johnny Yesno may not be identifiable among movie buffs, his life is nonetheless worthy of wider recognition for a variety of reasons.

While this book is essentially about his life accomplishments, there are, perhaps, more important details about Johnny Yesno's life that go beyond the general characteristics of his life story. While many people who knew him may not be aware of it, the various circumstances and motivations behind his life story reveal much about the Indigenous history of life in Canada.

As an example, for several years he was the host of a widely popular radio show on the CBC called 'Our Native Land'. This was the first radio show that dealt specifically with the salient Indigenous issues of the day, such as residential schools, poverty on reserves, and racial stigmatization, to name just a few.

Johnny Yesno brought these important issues to the forefront and made them a popular issue of discussion, not only among Indigenous people but among those in the wider society as well.

Obediah Yesno, or Johnny Yesno as he became later known, began life in rather unpromising circumstances. Born the eldest of 11 children in the northern Indigenous community of Fort Hope, now called Eabametoong First Nation, he faced considerable competition for food, clothing, love, and attention. Even his unusual name caused other schoolchildren to pick on him.

Then, at age five, he was sent off to a residential school at Sioux Lookout where he was beaten by the teachers, which caused Johnny and another boy to run away. The police tracked them down and dragged the boys back in handcuffs to suffer further abuse.

Despite these setbacks, Johnny Yesno went on to star in several movies, most notably the Walt Disney classic *King of the Grizzlies*, as mentioned above hosted a popular radio program on CBC Radio entitled *Our Native Land*, and, among other distinctions, was awarded the Order of Canada in 1976.

In the opinion of this author, Johnny Yesno's many achievements in life should not be regarded as a successful adaptation to Euro-American culture, but as a courageous triumph over adversity. His story deserves to be told for no other reason than the inspirational lessons it holds for other disadvantaged people who live in Indigenous cultures.

There are several people who made significant contributions to my knowledge of Johnny Yesno's life and character, and who knew him as a *real* person. The most important of these is Caroline Yesno, his sister, who is the co-author of this book as well as other members of his family.

Andrew Yesno provided important details on the Yesno genealogy and family history. Elizabeth Patience (née Yesno) spent many hours with me discussing her early life in Fort Hope (Eabamatoong) on the Albany River.

And finally, I cannot resist adding a personal note to this preface. All my four children (a son and three daughters) are members of the Eabamatoong First Nation, as is the case with the subject of this book, Johnny Yesno, and the book's co-author and Johnny Yesno's relative, Caroline Yesno.

In the case of my children, they gained status under the Indian Act through Bill C-31, which was passed by the Canadian government in 1985. Their grandmother, also a member of the Eabamatoong First Nation, had lost her status through marriage to a non-status person.

In the case of my children, my son married a status woman and so under the stipulations of Bill C-31, their children have status. However, all my daughters' children, my grandchildren, did not qualify even though their mothers have status. The reason for this inequity is that according to the provisions of Bill C-31, those who gain status are relegated into two categories.

In one category, termed 6 (a), status can be passed onto the next generation, but those in another category, termed 6 (b), are prohibited from doing so. Thus, although the original intention of this amendment to the Indian Act was presumably to end discrimination against Indigenous women by eliminating the loss of status through marriage to non-status males. It nonetheless created further divisions and complications that did not exist previously.

Megwitch to everyone for their help.

Chapter One
Introduction

To do history properly, one must study individuals.

-Marvin Harris (1968: 299)

Social scientists are often fond of postulating large-scale theories of cultural and social change—functionalism, structuralism, evolutionism, to name a few—but what is often forgotten in the process of these formulations is that it has been real live people who are the ones responsible for these changes. There is a *Horatio Alger myth* that a disadvantaged young person can become wealthy through hard work, but this is not entirely accurate.

While in the actual stories, the cause of success, often turns out to be an accident that works to the adolescent's advantage, much depends upon the way this person conducts themselves in life according to traditional virtues that are found in most cultures, such as honesty, charity, and altruism.

As such, the story of Johnny Yesno has a wider lesson in life that we can all learn from, which is to say; that no matter what setbacks one is forced to suffer, people can nonetheless achieve success on their own terms. A disadvantaged birth, then, does not necessarily lead to failure in life. It is no doubt a truism that character and opportunities are important to success, but these are not the sole determinants. What is often disregarded is the indominable life force that some people possess that allows them to overcome what would appear to be insurmountable obstacles to success.

In Johnny Yesno's case, one cannot help but be amazed at the variety of his accomplishments as an actor, engineer, dancer, and politician; any one of which would have no doubt been notable just by themselves. Not every survivor of the Shingwauk Residential School was as fortunate as Johnny Yesno.

In 2021, it came to light that hundreds of Indigenous children's graves were being discovered at former residential schools. As a report in a Sault Ste. Marie newspaper poignantly indicates, "It is impossible to drive by the former Shingwauk Hall grounds without images of children's faces flooding your vision. Their identity was routinely relegated to anonymity with the assignment of numbers in lieu of their given names upon arrival at the schools. While perusing the files on Shingwauk Hall, a yellowed and faded newspaper clipping about a former student's acting career caught [a reporter's] attention" (*Sootday, 5* December 2021).

The news article goes on to indicate that one of Shingwauk's former students, Johnny Yesno, went on to become the star of the Disney film *King of the Grizzlies*. Previous to attending Shingwauk, Johnny Yesno, at the age of 5 had been sent to the Pelican Lake Residential School near Sioux Lookout in northwestern Ontario.

As reported in the *Windspeaker* (7 April 2018) newspaper by reporter Dianne Meili, "Packed with other children into a noisy train, Johnny had an identification tag hung around his neck, and, as he was often heard to say, he had no idea how he survived those awful days. His school memories are hazy, but the sharp edges emerging from the merciful cloud revealed images of physical and sexual abuse."

Later, Johnny and a friend had attempted to escape the Pelican school in the middle of winter, but, the *Windspeaker* article reported, "The pair got lost and found themselves in Kenora, where they were rounded up by police and handcuffed."

In a later article in the *Sault Star* (27 February 1958), the academic accomplishments of the young Johnny Yesno are noted when he was awarded a scholarship in Grade 12 from the Indian Affairs Department to attend further post-secondary education. As the article indicates, "The award was presented before a gathering in the Shingwauk Indian Residential School of which John was a former student, by F.M. Shaw, regional inspector of Indian schools in northern Ontario." This article then goes on to further indicate that when Mr. Shaw presented the academic award to Johnny Yesno, he had also at that time met with the student's father.

The weather was so cold, the article indicated, "On that day there were only four pupils at school, all brothers and a sister of John Yesno" (quoted in *Sootoday*, 5 December 2021).

In summarizing his time at residential school, the *Windspeaker* article notes that Johnny Yesno, "Was often heard to say, he had no idea how he survived those awful years. Some supervisors just like to beat up kids." In a later (1969) interview with reporter Kay MacIntyre of the *Sault Star*, Johnny recalled, "School days at the Soo has rather mixed sentiments with me personally. First, life at the Shingwauk Home was not all that rosy and comfortable as it is purported to be." (*Sootoday*, 5 December 2021)

From the residential school at Sault Ste. Marie, Johnny enrolled at the University of Waterloo to study engineering. Then, in 1963, he competed against 92 other contestants while winning the North American Indian Dancing Championship. It was about this time that Johnny developed an interest in acting. Later, while working for a Toronto engineering firm, he joined a dance group that performed for tourists visiting the city.

During one of his performances, a producer from the CBC (Canadian Broadcasting Corporation) recognized Johnny's undeniable star quality, leading him to secure a role in the premiere episode of the 1966 television drama, Wojeck. In this role, he portrayed an Anishinaabe man whose clashes with the police culminated in a sentence of incarceration. Johnny portrayed Joe Smith, an angry Aboriginal man who committed suicide in a Toronto jail cell.

This initial performance was considered such a success that Johnny was awarded a medal at the prestigious 1966 Monte Carlo Film Festival in France. It was just two years later, in 1968, that he was cast as Moki, a ranch foreman who raised a large bear from a cub, which was the leading role in the Walt Disney movie *King of the Grizzlies* which was released to theaters in July of 1970. The scenes for the movie were filmed in Alberta and BC interior locations as well as other sites.

Now, at age 31, Yesno's career began to take on a spectacular upward momentum. However, he had to overcome some personal obstacles. For one thing, Yesno revealed later in a 1969 interview in the *Sault Star* that, "he was deathly afraid of bears…it goes back to when I was a boy berry picking. I stood up, face to face with a bear. I don't know which was more scared, the bear or me. We both ran, and I met him again, going around the island the other way. Then I found I had to work with a grizzly that stood seven feet high."

Later, when he was living in Thunder Bay, Ontario, Johnny further related to one of his relatives that he believed that he was being followed through a dark city park late at night by a bear. But it turned out to be just a large woman wearing a fur coat.

As the decade of the 1970s emerged, Johnny moved into a significant career change when he began to host and produce his own CBC Radio program called *Indian Magazine*. Now he was becoming a familiar voice in households around the nation.

In this new role Johnny began to become the voice that brought to the forefront issues confronted by the Indigenous people across the country and his radio show became the first-ever program in Canada which focused on the concerns faced by the people of the First Nations, Inuit, and Metis. The program aired on Saturday evenings, a prime-time slot. Later, the show was rebranded and called *Our Native Land*.

In 1971, host Johnny Yesno called *Our Native Land*, "Canada's only national radio program for native peoples. I realize that programs about Indian, Metis, and Eskimo people have been done before, but not with native peoples participating. They were being used, studied, analyzed, and classified like rare butterflies."

Our Native Land was different. It was, as its producers indicated, "All-red, all-the-time" (www.cbc,ca/radio/rewind/our-native-land-holiday-edition, 18 December 2014).

Remembering the bad old days in the residential school-CBC archives 19 November 2017.

According to an article published on *Northernstars.ca*, "His career expanded toward broadcast journalism on the CBC magazine *Take 30*. Yesno became quite vocal about the plight of First Nations people, complaining at one point that the CBC was out of touch and failed to present an accurate picture of Canada Indigenous People (www.northernstars.ca/johnnyyesno/)."

As a follow-up to this commentary, Johnny is quoted, in the *Sault Star* interview previously mentioned, as saying, "One popular misconception about *Indian Magazine* is that most people seem to think it is for native people only. Not true; it's also geared to inform the apathetic Johnny Public to learn more about the Aboriginal people of this great country."

By the mid-1970s, Johnny Yesno, once again found himself in the film business. This time, in 1975, he became involved in a film that depicted scenes reminiscent of his own childhood experience when he attempted to escape his residential school at Sioux Lookout. The film was called *Cold Journey* and starred the legendary Chief Dan George.

The film portrays the story of young Buckley and Yesno, as the school's Indigenous caretaker. Buckley was a boy who longed to return to his home and family. *Cold Journey* is like the 1966 tragedy of Chanie Charlie Wenjack, whose frozen body was found after he tried to escape the harsh conditions of a northern residential school, which Buckley saw more as a prison than a place of learning.

Many readers will probably also be aware that the Chanie Wenjack story was the basis for Tragically Hip's 2017 production of *The Secret Path*, as well as Joseph Boyden's controversial fictional account in his short book entitled simply *Wenjack* in 2016.

Yesno's film and journalism career was given explicit recognition in 1976 when he was made a member of the *Order of Canada*. This recognition was followed by his position as director for the Chiefs of Ontario as well as Aboriginal advisor with the former Ministry of Northern Development in Sault Ste. Marie, a position Yesno held until his retirement in 2002.

When he passed away in 2010, an article in the *Western Star* written by Bryan Meadows credited him with, "helping inspire a generation of Aboriginal people to follow their dreams." In addition, Nishnabe Aski Nation Band Chief Stan Beardy said that "Yesno blazed a trail for us…he pushed our priorities to the forefront [when] he worked to improve satellite communications in far northern communities."

As Beardy went on to indicate, Johnny Yesno, "educated society at a time, when the Lone Ranger and Tonto were on television, about not stereotyping First Nation people" (*Sootday.com*, 5 December 2021).

Johnny Yesno summed up his own life when he participated in the opening of the Rankin Arena on 30 July 1977, in Sault Ste. Marie. In the *Sault* Star, as master of ceremony, Yesno is quoted as stating that, "the arena can help bring both communities together at a crucial time when we seem to be splitting into different ethnic and social entities. We want to promote the acceptance of our unique background," he said. "We aren't looking for integration. We are concerned with understanding and sharing."

Certainly, these are words that we can all profit from and live by.

The Importance of Historical Context

According to the anthropologist Marvin Harris, we cannot study history properly without also investigating the people who created this history. Events do not happen by themselves is the obvious truth that is occasionally forgotten by historians. So, we take it as a self-evident fact that it is the people themselves; the ones who created the actual historical events and situation, that must be the initial starting point of investigations into the past.

One of the earliest proponents of this view—that history is unintelligible without a focus on the individuals who create this history—can be attributable to linguist Edward Sapir who remarked that, "I fail to see how we can deny a determining…cultural influence on a large number of outstanding personalities" (1917: 443).

Of course, this insight does not just belong to Marvin Harris alone, since, as he acknowledges, anthropologist Franz Boas previously stressed studies that focused on *the interaction between individual and society* (1948: 311). Subsequently, one of Boas's students, Paul Radin, published his seminal study entitled *Crashing Thunder; The Autobiography of a Winnebago Indian* (1926), in which he focused on the wider social and inter-cultural trends of an important Indigenous leader in the historical context of his time

Radin explained his approach as follows:

The [historical] task, let me insist, is always the same: a description of a specific period…This can be done only by an intensive and continuous study of a particular tribe, and a thorough knowledge of the language. Also, an adequate body of text and this knowledge can be accomplished only if we realize.

Once and for all, we are dealing with specific, not generalized, men and women, and specific, not generalized events. But the recognition of specific men and women should bring with it the realization that there are all types of individuals. It is this particularity that is the essence of all history (Radin 1933: 184–185).

Thus, with this starting point in mind, we can proceed to investigate not only the individuals who created past events but also their involvement in them. For those who are interested in the Indigenous history of Canada, Johnny Yesno, the subject of this book, provides an ideal opportunity to investigate an important era ranging from the residential school period to later developments of Aboriginal activism in this country. The focus, then, is not so much solely on the life of one individual. Rather, it is on the interaction of historical events and the manner in which they are perceived by those involved in them.

In this study of the life of Johnny Yesno, we do not begin on the day that he was born, but with the historical context of his origins. In this regard, probably the most important factor involved the interaction of the Indigenous Anishinaabe and Cree people of northern Ontario and the European newcomers. By the time that Johnny Yesno was born at Fort Hope, now called Eabametoong First Nation which is situated on the Albany River, there had already occurred at least three hundred years of interaction between the Indigenous people and, principally, the various employees of the British Hudson's Bay Company.

Throughout this period the interaction between the two populations was primarily in the form of economic exchange in the context of the fur trade. There were also many instances of sexual encounter; principally between Indigenous women and the English traders, which resulted in a population that comprised the genetic intermixture of both groups. As time went on, the Europeans attempted to assert their domination over the Indigenous people beyond the fur trade. One might refer to this later domination as a form of *colonial suppression*, however, the Indigenous people were not hapless victims.

The treaty period was initiated when the fur trade began a precipitous decline. One might suggest that the Indigenous people gave up control of their land to the Europeans, however, the Royal Proclamation of 1763 did recognize Indigenous title to their lands:

It is just reasonable and essential to our interest, and the security of our colonies, that several nations or tribes of Indians with who we are connected. Also, those who lived under our protection, should not be molested or disturbed in the Possession of such Parts of our Dominions and Territories as, not having been ceded to or purchased by us, are reserved to them or any of them as their hunting grounds (in Hedican 2013: 24–25).

As the fur trade period continued into decline, especially in the early 20th-century, a new form of suppression was initiated in the form of the residential school system. Few Indigenous communities in northern Ontario had schools prior to the 1950s so it probably seemed reasonable at the time to construct large regional educational centers that would house hundreds of Indigenous students in one place. At the time, few people would probably have anticipated the abuse that Indigenous students would suffer at the hands of the teachers and other hired staff of the residential schools.

While Johnny Yesno was hesitant to reveal the extent of the abuse that he might have suffered personally, it must have been severe enough for him to attempt to escape the confines of the Pelican Lake Residential School situated in Sioux Lookout, near Kenora, in northwestern Ontario.

Later, his father removed him from this school and subsequently enrolled him in the Shingwauk Residential School in Sault Ste. Marie where conditions were apparently less severe. The point here is that Johnny Yesno had personal experience with the residential school system in Ontario.

After he left the residential school system, Johnny Yesno embarked on a multifaceted career in the mass media industry. This activity encompassed films (*King of the Grizzlies* of Hollywood fame, and *Cold Journey* about residential school escapees) and television (principally, the Canadian series *Wojeck* in which Johnny Yesno played the part of a Moosonee man who committed suicide while under police detention).

Moreover, he also starred in the nationally broadcast CBC Radio program *Our Native Land*. In other words, Johnny Yesno was able to share his views about Indigenous life in Canada, and North America broadly, through a variety of existing mass media outlets that would allow him to reach a wide listening and viewing public.

It is one matter to hold certain views about the life that one finds themselves in. However, it is quite another matter to have the capabilities and skills to be able to convey these views to millions of people over a very wide geographical area. Johnny Yesno couldn't control the historical context of his birth, but he learned to use it to share his life experiences with many people. He developed skills to effectively utilize the mass media of his time.

Indigenous Rights in Canada

Our general argument in this book is that the historical context of a person's life is a necessary condition for understanding the situations that play a crucial role in the choices that one makes in his or her life. A subsequent argument is that, as far as Johnny Yesno's role in the film industry is concerned, one must also have a historical comprehension of the course of Indigenous rights in Canada.

The reason that this is such an important factor in understanding the choices that Johnny Yesno made in his life pertains to our characterization of Canada's film industry as primarily concerned with what could be termed *social change-oriented media.*

It is clear that the Canadian Indigenous film industry prioritizes education over entertainment. These films delve into critical issues such as the detrimental impact of the residential school system, the colonial oppression faced by Indigenous peoples stemming from treaties negotiated with British and Canadian authorities, land claims, and a range of other significant historical and contemporary topics related to Indigenous rights.

For this reason, it is important that one gain some understanding of the parameters of these rights through various court cases and other attempts by Indigenous people to counteract the suppression of these rights in everyday life. The following discussion, then, is meant to provide an overview of Indigenous rights issues as a broader introduction to the *social change-oriented media* that tends to characterize the social and political foundations of Indigenous life in Canada.

It is difficult to generalize about definitions of Indigenous rights because of the diversity among First Nations, Métis, and Inuit peoples in Canada. Broadly speaking, however, Indigenous rights are inherent, collective rights that flow from the original occupation of the land that is now Canada, and from social orders created before the arrival of Europeans to North America.

For many, the concept of Indigenous rights can be summed up as the right to independence through self-determination regarding governance, land, resources, and culture. Thus, there is no simple definition of Indigenous rights in Canada because of the diversity among Indigenous peoples. For example, First Nations that have signed treaties with the federal government may enjoy certain privileges (such as annual cash payments) that non-treaty nations do not.

Similarly, Indigenous nations that have won court cases regarding land claims may exercise more control over their lands and populations than others. In general, however, all Indigenous peoples have rights that may include access to ancestral lands and resources, and the right to self-government (*Globe and Mail*, 7 June 2017).

In addition to treaties, which are supposed to enshrine certain rights to land, resources, and more, federal law also protects Indigenous rights, namely the

Constitution Act of 1982. Since 2008, the rights of First Nations people living on reserve have also been covered by the Canadian Human Rights Act. Supreme Court cases have clarified definitions of Indigenous rights and particularly Indigenous rights (or title) to traditional territories. For example, the Delgamuukw case in 1997 showed that Aboriginal title constituted an ancestral right protected by the Constitution.

The *Indian Act*—another federal law—does not enshrine rights (quite the contrary, it has been historically oppressive), but it has impacted Indigenous rights. The *Indian Act* creates legal categories of Status and Non-Status Indians that have caused division among Indigenous peoples. For example, Status Indians have certain rights that Non-Status Indians do not, such as the right to not pay federal or provincial taxes on certain goods and services while living or working on reserves. However, many Indigenous peoples (both Status and Non-Status) refuse to be defined by this federal law (Asch 2014; Borrows 2002, 2010).

Indigenous rights are upheld and challenged at the provincial and local levels as well. Many First Nations have signed land claim agreements with federal and provincial governments. When rights to territory are challenged, relations between these groups become less amicable. For example, the Oka crisis and Ipperwash crisis are but two such instances where provincial and local authorities ignored Indigenous claims to ancestral lands. Since the arrival of Europeans, Indigenous peoples have had to protect their rights, lands, peoples, and ways of life (Hedican 2013: 55–61).

Sources of Indigenous Rights

Indigenous peoples have traditionally pointed to three principal arguments to establish their rights: international law, the *Royal Proclamation* of 1763 (as well as treaties that have since followed), and common law as defined in Canadian courts. On the international stage, Indigenous groups have participated in United Nations working groups concerned with Indigenous populations and minority rights.

Although most nations adopted the UN Declaration on the Rights of Indigenous Peoples in 2007—an agreement that recognizes Indigenous rights to self-government, land, equality, and language, as well as basic human rights. Canada only signed on in May 2016 after a change in the federal government.

Canada initially refused to sign because of issues concerning land disputes and the Declaration's clauses about the duty to consult that could impact resource development. It has yet to be seen how Canada will implement this agreement (Henderson and Bell 2019). On the national stage, the *Royal Proclamation* of 1763 has historically been viewed as the constitutional basis for Indigenous treaties and a source of legal rights. Affirmed by section 35 of the Constitution Act in 1982, the legal principles of the *Royal Proclamation* are still applied in modern-day treaties.

The inclusion of section 35 in the Constitution signaled a new era of judicial and political opinion on the question of Indigenous rights. This section protects a spectrum of different Indigenous and treaty rights, including legal recognition of customary practices such as marriage and adoption.

Also, the site-specific exercise of food harvesting includes other rights that do not involve claims to the land itself and assertions of ownership of traditional lands. The courts, and more specifically, the Supreme Court of Canada, have clarified and guaranteed rights to land and resource activities as well as other issues.

Since governments could not come to a consensus during constitutional negotiations about Indigenous rights, the issue was consequently left to the courts. The rulings become part of Canadian law and may alter the way that the government understands Indigenous rights. As an example, the Calder case helped set the stage for many First Nations in British Columbia to launch their own land claims and cases relating to Aboriginal title (Borrows 2002, 210).

Resource Rights

Historically, Indigenous peoples have had to prove their rights in Canadian courts. For resource rights other than Aboriginal title, the Supreme Court has held that Indigenous people must demonstrate that the right was integral to their distinctive societies and was exercised at the time of first contact with Europeans (see Van der Peet Case and Pamajewon Case).

What this means is that for practices such as fishing and hunting to be enshrined as rights, Indigenous peoples must prove that these activities were practiced before the arrival of Europeans. The courts have seen commercial trade in furs and fish, for example, as the product of European contact rather than integral to Indigenous societies prior to contact. Fishing for food, community, or ceremonial purposes is, however, a protected right and may be exercised in a modern way with modern fishing equipment.

Indigenous peoples have used section 35 of the Constitution Act to support their rights to resource activities, such as fishing. In the Sparrow case (1990)—the first decision by the Supreme Court to interpret section 35—an Indigenous person fished contrary to the provisions of federal law. In his defense, he alleged that the right to fish was an immemorial right protected by treaty by virtue of section 35.

The Supreme Court upheld the right and set out a code of interpretation for section 35. The court did not set limits on the types of rights that can be categorized as Indigenous rights and emphasized that the rights must be interpreted flexibly in a manner *sensitive to the Aboriginal perspective*. The court stated that section 35 only protects rights that were not extinguished (i.e. surrendered) prior to the date the Constitution Act, 1982, came into effect (Asch 2014).

Indigenous peoples have also defended their lands and rights to resources outside the courts. Protests against development companies and the government that seek to infringe on ancestral rights have demonstrated Indigenous resistance and the desire for consultation and open dialogue about matters that affect traditional lands and rights.

Some well-known examples of such demonstrations include Idle No More, the War in the Woods (1984 to 1993), a protest led by the Tla-o-qui-aht and their allies against logging and deforestation in ancient forests, and protests against pipeline developments, such as the Mackenzie Valley and Keystone XL pipelines (*CBC News* 2017).

Aboriginal Title

There have been a few key court cases that have helped to define Aboriginal title. The Calder case (1973) recognized for the first time that Aboriginal title has a place in Canadian law. Additionally, in the Delgamuukw case (1997), the Supreme Court ruled that claims to traditional lands had to show exclusive occupation of the territory by a defined Aboriginal society at the time the Crown asserted sovereignty over that territory.

In the same case, the court ruled that the oral histories of Aboriginal peoples were to be accepted as evidence proving historic use and occupation. The Tsilhqot'in case (2014) further clarified the requirements for establishing

Aboriginal title. The criteria for Aboriginal title are threefold: in short, an Aboriginal group must first prove occupation and then must prove continuity and exclusivity of said occupation.

However, the court has not fully resolved all legal issues concerning Aboriginal title. Serious disputes have arisen over whether or not Aboriginal title carries with it the exclusive right to use and occupy lands. This is an issue in cases where the current occupation is not exclusively Indigenous people and where resource companies and other interests seek to carry on or expand their own uses of the same lands.

Several court cases, including those involving the Nuu-chah-nulth in British Columbia, have already been launched over these issues. In most cases, the rulings ensure that proper administrative requirements are met while permitting resource exploitation and development to continue in the overall public interest. In this regard, the duty to consult was affirmed by the Supreme Court in the Delgamuukw case. It is also a key part of the UN Declaration on the Rights of Indigenous Peoples (Henderson and Bell 2019).

Rights to Self-Government

Although Indigenous rights have yet to be given a comprehensive definition in law, most Indigenous peoples assert that they include the right to self-government. The Supreme Court has not directly addressed that issue. This was, however, a subject extensively studied by the Royal Commission on Aboriginal Peoples, which reported to the federal government in 1996.

The Royal Commission suggested ways to improve the relationship between Indigenous peoples and the Canadian government. These include recognizing self-governance rights, settling land claims, addressing inequities between Indigenous and non-Indigenous Canadians, and establishing Indigenous justice systems.

One of the most well-known examples regarding self-government in Canada is the Nisga'a Final Agreement, signed after 25 years of negotiation following the Calder case in 1973. The content of the treaty and the ratification process were subjected to intense debate and was challenged in court. Upon parliament's passage of the Act in 2000, the treaty became the first modern-day treaty in British Columbia and the 14th modern-day treaty in Canada to be negotiated from 1975–2000.

The Nisga'a Final Agreement gave the First Nation the right to self-government within the 2,019 km2 in the Nass Valley to which the Nisga'a hold title. Since 1973, there have been 26 comprehensive land claims and four self-government agreements (as of 2015).

The Nisga'a Final Agreement was groundbreaking for the British Columbia treaty process because it achieved the aspirations for a negotiated settlement as expressed by the courts in the Delgamuukw case. Other First Nations in British Columbia continue negotiations of their claims. For example, the Tsawwassen First Nation and the Maa-nulth First Nations finalized agreements in 2009 and 2011, respectively. As of July 2017, there were 58 ongoing comprehensive claims negotiations in British Columbia and another seven claims in the implementation process.

Content of Indigenous Rights

No Indigenous right, even though constitutionally protected, is absolute in Canadian law. Fishing rights, for example, are not exclusive in the sense that only Indigenous peoples can exercise them. Also, Indigenous rights are not immune to regulation by other governments.

Additionally, the Aboriginal title may give rise to an exclusive right to use and occupy lands, but that right may be infringed upon by the government for purposes such as economic development, power generation, or the protection of the environment or endangered species.

However, non-Indigenous governments must justify infringement of Aboriginal rights or title based on a legitimate government purpose and recognition of the constitutional protection of the rights being affected. There may also be a requirement for prior consultation with the Indigenous peoples concerned and compensation in some circumstances. The duty to consult, and the issues of what level of government is entitled or required to consult, have been further explored in two 2014 Supreme Court cases, Grassy Narrows and Tsilhqot'in.

In Ontario, the Grassy Narrows case pushed forward the notion that provincial governments may also *take up* treaty lands for development, but in doing so, they also take on the federal government's responsibilities to consult with Indigenous peoples. In the Tsilhqot'in case, the Supreme Court recognized the First Nation's Aboriginal title and authority over 1,750 km2 of their traditional territory in the British Columbia interior.

In taking an expansive view of Aboriginal title, the Supreme Court charted a new course relative to future resource development and the process of consulting with Indigenous groups in areas of Canada that have not been ceded by historic treaties. This suggests that the Crown in the future must do more than fulfill a duty to consult. It must also either obtain consent or meet legal requirements to justify infringing on Indigenous rights (see Henderson and Bell 2019).

Indigenous Women's Rights

During the 1970s and 1980s, Indigenous women launched several cases against the federal government concerning the legal and gender discrimination inherent in the Indian Act. Since 1869, Status Indian women who married Non-Status Indian men lost any treaty and Indigenous rights that they previously enjoyed.

In 1985, Bill C-31 amended the Indian Act to remove discrimination and bring the act in line with the Canadian Charter of Rights and Freedoms. The 1985 amendment allows women who *married out* to apply for the restoration of their status and rights and also allows their children to apply for registration as Status Indians.

The Act no longer requires or allows women to follow their husbands into or out of status, and it allows women to pass status on to their children just as men always have. However, while the amendment addressed much of the former discrimination against women, it also created some problems. As an example, by placing these women, and often their children, onto First Nations band membership lists, the government stretched already limited lands and funds to serve more people. This has at times incited resentment and backlash toward these 'Bill C-31s' by First Nations members (as discussed in Hedican 2008: 182–187, 256–259).

Further, the inclusion of a *second-generation cut-off* rule potentially means a great reduction in the number of people entitled to be registered as Status Indians under the Indian Act. According to Bill C-31, there are two categories of Indian registration. The first, known as sub-section 6(1), applies when both parents are or were entitled to be registered as status Indians under the Indian Act.

The second, known as sub-section 6(2), applies when one only parent is entitled to be registered under 6(1). In this case status cannot be transferred, however, if that one parent is registered under sub-section 6(2). In short, after two generations of intermarriage with non-status partners, children would no longer be eligible for status.

Moreover, for a child to be registered, both the mother's and father's names must be included on the birth certificate. If the father's name is not included, he is assumed to be non-status. In such situations, children born to women registered under sub-section 6(2) are not eligible for status. The amendment therefore significantly limits the ability to transfer status to one's children.

Bill C-31 also did away with the *double mother rule*, which had conferred status on non-married individuals up to 21 years of age whose mother and paternal grandmother were non-status. However, eliminating the effects of this rule created a new inequality that made it difficult to transmit status in certain cases.

In response to the British Columbia Court of Appeal ruling in McIvor v. Canada (2009), Bill C-3 passed in 2010, attempted to ensure parity of status for grandchildren of women who *married out* and those affected by the *double mother* rule. Currently, before parliament, Bill S-3 is attempting to address the disparity in who is entitled to register as a 6(1) and 6(2) Indian. Bill S-3 was a response to the Québec Superior Court ruling in Descheneaux v. Canada in 2015.

Extinguishment of Indigenous Rights

The *extinguishment* of rights means the taking away or surrendering of rights. Historically, treaties or land claims settlements have served to extinguish Indigenous rights. All courts have recognized the power of parliament to extinguish Aboriginal rights and titles up to 1982, but this was never expressly done.

Indigenous rights to hunt and fish, however, have been limited by constitutional amendment, federal legislation, and in some instances provincial laws. In the 1990 Sparrow decision, the Supreme Court ruled that rights could be regulated if the regulation could be justified in the manner described above.

In the Delgamuukw case, the court did not rule out extinguishment after 1982 but made strong statements about consultation and compensation if rights are extinguished. Also, in the Bear Island case, a case appealed to the Supreme Court but dismissed in 1991, it was also held that delay in bringing a court action was sufficient to defeat a claim to Aboriginal title. This alone, if correct in law, would be enough to defeat almost every land claim that is brought to court.

Moreover, the First Nation had signed a treaty in 1850, thereby extinguishing their rights. In the 1995 Blueberry River case, the Supreme Court applied a statutory limitation period to defeat part of a First Nation's claim with respect to a surrender of reserve lands and mineral rights.

Historically, federal laws have also worked to deny the rights of Indigenous peoples. The Indian Act has taken away basic rights over time, such as the right to hold potlatches, dances, and practice Indigenous religions. Willing or forcible enfranchisement (the processes by which Indigenous peoples lost their status under the Indian Act) extinguished Indigenous rights in exchange for others as Canadian citizens.

Other federal legislation has also worked to assimilate Indigenous peoples, and therefore, deny them their rights, such as residential school and the pass system (a policy in which Indigenous peoples who wished to leave their reserve, even temporarily, had to acquire a pass from an Indian agent before leaving).

Métis Rights

Métis rights have largely been defined and clarified by the courts. A particularly important case is R. v. Powley (2003), which affirmed the Métis ancestral right to hunt for sustenance. Powley was the first case in which the Supreme Court affirmed the existence of Métis rights.

The case also established a test to determine Métis rights under section 35 of the Constitution Act of 1982. The Powley test has 10 criteria that determine Métis identity and if a Métis community has an existing right to an activity, such as hunting. The identity part of the test consists of three criteria: to be considered Métis, individuals must identify as Métis, be a member of a modern Métis community, and have ties to a historic Métis community.

This last requirement also asks that individuals prove another set of criteria: that their mixed ancestry group formed a *distinctive* collective social identity, that they lived together in the same geographic area, and that they shared a common way of life. The Powley case therefore confirmed the definition of Métis as one that is specific to a distinct community of peoples rather than anyone who has mixed Indigenous and European heritage.

To those who consider themselves Métis but do not fit this description, namely those living outside the territory as defined by the Métis National Council, including Alberta, Manitoba, Saskatchewan, and parts of Ontario, British Columbia, and the Northwest Territories, they are apt to feel that the Powley decision denies their Indigenous identity. However, to those who can trace their lineage to specific, historic Métis communities, the Powley case validates their long-standing argument that they are a distinct Indigenous community.

The Daniels court case (2016) is also significant to Métis rights. On 14 April 2016, the Supreme Court ruled in the Daniels decision unanimously that the legal definition of *Indian*—as laid out in the Constitution—now, includes the Métis and Non-Status Indians. This ruling will facilitate possible negotiations over traditional land rights, access to education and health programs, and other government services. This ruling did not, however, grant Indian status to any Métis or Non-Status Indian people.

Inuit Rights

The Inuit fall under the category of *Indian* in the Constitution Act of 1982 and are therefore also protected by section 35. However, the Inuit have never been subject to the Indian Act and were largely ignored by the federal government until 1939, when a court decision ruled that they were a federal responsibility, though still not subject to the Indian Act.

Policies of assimilation followed, including forced relocations into sedentary communities and the introduction of disk numbers for administrative purposes. However, various treaties and land claims have subsequently confirmed Inuit rights to land title in northern Canada, including the James Bay and Northern Québec Agreement (1975), the Western Arctic (Inuvialuit) Claims Settlement Act (1984), the Nunavut Land Claims Agreement Act (1993) and the Labrador Inuit Land Claims Agreement (2005).

Together, these four regions cover about 40% of Canada's land mass. An important court case concerning Inuit rights is the Clyde River case (2017). The Inuit living in and around Clyde River, Nunavut, vehemently opposed the plans of the National Energy Board (NEB) to conduct seismic testing for oil and gas deposits near their community since it was first proposed in 2011.

Taking their case to the Supreme Court, the Clyde River Inuit emerged victorious: the judges unanimously decided that the NEB failed to properly consult the Inuit about their plans and did not adequately assess the effect that seismic testing would have on the rights of Indigenous peoples. Quashing the NEB's approval, the Supreme Court put an end to the seismic testing.

While the court did not create guidelines for how to consult with an Indigenous community, this case highlights the importance of consultation. On the international stage, Inuit peoples have had their rights to Arctic lands and waters affirmed by such declarations as the United Nations Declaration on the Rights of Indigenous Peoples.

The content and priority of issues surrounding Indigenous rights and titles continue to evolve judicially and through the negotiation and implementation of self-government agreements between Indigenous peoples and the government of Canada. Over the long term, it is likely that these issues will need to be addressed through negotiated political resolution.

Conclusion

As is aptly illustrated by the previous discussion, the topic of Indigenous rights is a complicated matter for most people. To fully understand the various facets of this topic, one needs to be well-versed in the historical relationships between Indigenous people and Euro-Canadians, legal jurisprudence, as well as a host of other matters.

There are also dozens of books on the subject that outline various cases that have been studied in the court system that stand as legal precedence. Throughout this book, we will continue to stress the importance of linking the historical circumstance that one is born into, with the development of the capabilities and skills that would allow one to reach a wide audience through which one's life experiences can be conveyed.

In other words, this book is not just a biographical account of Johnny Yesno's life but is an attempt to link his life experiences with the wider social and political trends in the society in which he lived. Without a study of this wider historical context, the details of a person's life are hardly intelligible, we contend.

In this regard, we are reminded of Murray Dobbin's study of Métis leaders in his book *The One-And-A-Half Men* in which he states that his book attempts, "to examine history and biography and their intersection with social structure. It is neither strictly biographical nor purely historical" (1981: 9).

Chapter Two
Eabametoong First Nation

Men make their own history, but they do not make it just as they please...but under given circumstances directly encountered and inherited from the past.
-Karl Marx (1978 [orig. 1852]: 9)

As Karl Marx reminded us in his famous quote, we have no control over the time, location, or other circumstantial details of our birth. All of these matters, though, are extremely important factors in how we make our lives. Given this fact of nature, how can one ever hope to write a biographical account of another person's life without taking into account the various historical, personal, social, economic, or political circumstances into which a person is born and lives their life?

This is not to say that personality factors or idiosyncratic twists of fate are not important in how a life turns out, or that one's life is determined only by circumstantial influences. The argument here is that in order to understand a person's life we must be cognizant of the various opportunities, circumstantial situations, or other important factors through which a person must navigate as they play out their life.

It is for these reasons that this book has three primary objectives. The first of these is to provide a biographical account of Obediah Johnny Yesno from his origins in the Eabametoong (Fort Hope) community in northwestern Ontario. This description is followed by an account of his life in the Indian residential school system, and then, on to his multifaceted career as a film star, broadcaster, and politician for which he was awarded the Order of Canada.

The second purpose is to discuss the various social, cultural, and political situations that formed the larger background of his life, such as racial stereotypes in the film industry. Thirdly, to provide contextual information itemized in an abbreviated form in the glossary that would be useful in understanding the circumstances of Indigenous people in Canada, such as issues pertaining to their treaty status or the conditions of reserve life, especially as these apply in the northern areas of Ontario.

In this regard, as a reference work, we feel that it is important that this book includes an extensive supplement of information pertaining to First Nations in Canada. Also, websites and further pertinent data relating to the various reserves and non-status Indigenous communities in Ontario are provided.

In this sense, then, given these three objectives, this book is not a biography in the stricter sense of the term. But one in which an important Indigenous person's life is understood in a wider process of social, cultural, and political context.

Obediah Johnny Yesno was born in 1938 in the remote First Nation community of Eabametoong (meaning *reversing of the water flow*) which is situated on the Albany River in northern Ontario. Eabametoong, also known historically as Fort Hope (Indian Reserve No. 64), is located on the shore of Eabamet Lake which is approximately 300 kilometers (190 miles) northeast of Thunder Bay.

After the retreat of the last ice age, this area of Ontario was left with numerous lakes, rivers, and swamps. As could be expected, the wildlife in such an aquatic environment is populated by beavers, muskrats, and otters, along with a variety of waterfowl such as ducks and geese. Various species of fish are also abundant in this area, such as lake trout, pickerel, and sturgeon.

Such natural resources were an attraction for the Indigenous people as well as fur trapping organizations such as the Hudson's Bay Company which built Fort Albany on the mouth of the Albany River in 1677. Eventually, HBC trading posts were established in more interior locations to lessen the travel by fur trappers to the James Bay coast.

The Fort Hope post on Eabamet Lake was built in 1894 and the Fort Hope Band came into existence in 1905 when Treaty No. 9 was signed by a newly elected chief and eight councilors, who represented about 600 Anishinaabe and Cree people of the surrounding area.

By 1900, the HBC operated a northern post, known as Landsdowne House (Neskatanga) on Attawapiskat Lake. In 1985, the official name of Eabametoong First Nation was adopted which replaced the previous fur trade post designation of Fort Hope.

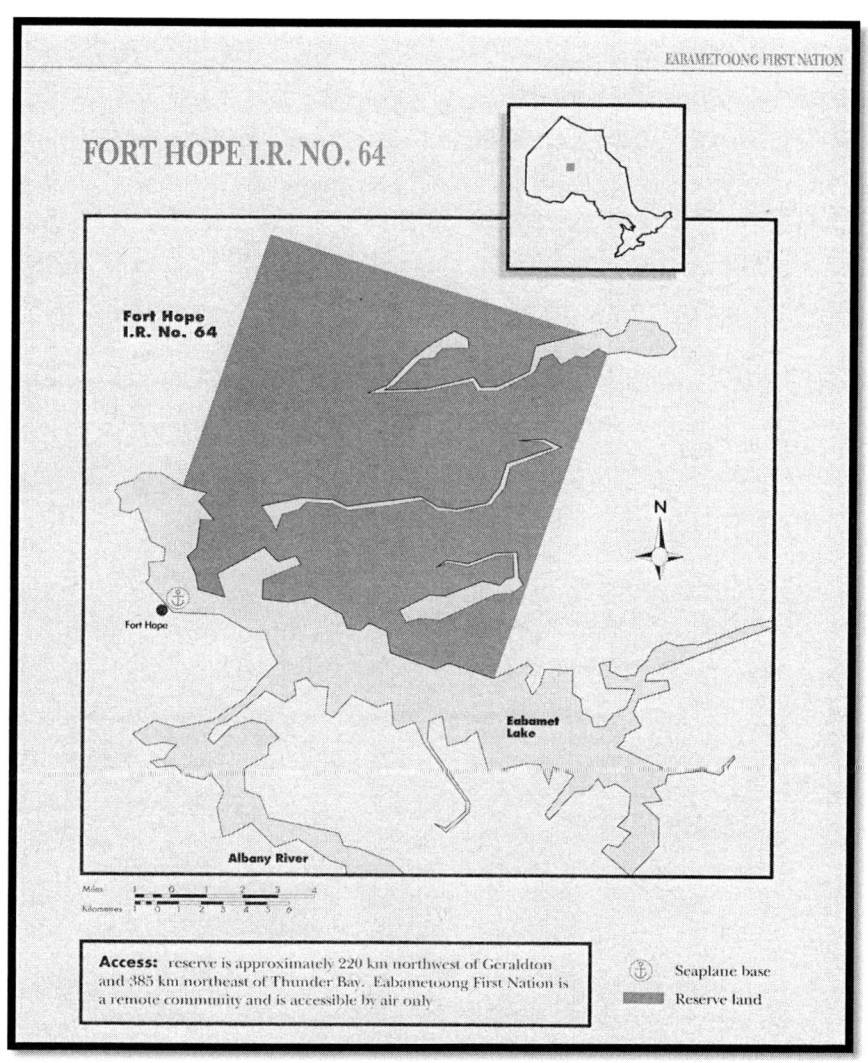

Fort Hope I.R. No. 64

Source: Ontario, Native Affairs Secretariat (1992:87)

At the time, that Johnny Yesno grew up in the 1930s, the Anishinaabe (Ojibway) community of Fort Hope was similar to many other Indigenous communities in this area of northern Ontario. It lacked schools since the people were still engaged in fishing, trapping, and fur trading economy which involved a transitory life in which people moved from one location to the next depending upon their annual cycle of resource extraction.

In this sense, the designation of *Fort Hope community* was a rather imprecise one as people congregated at places such as Eabamet Lake during the warmer summer months to fish and trade furs. After which, they would tend to disperse once again into smaller groups that traveled to their winter trapping territories. The community, then, was characterized by resource cycles of coalescence and dispersal, depending upon the abundance of food resources throughout the year.

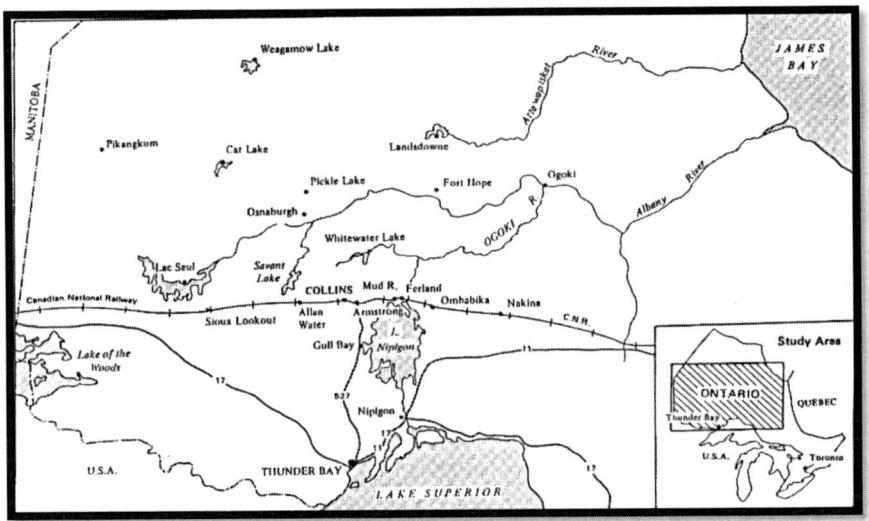

Northern Ontario Settlements and River Systems

Source: Hedican (1986: 24)

With the signing of Treaty No. 9 on 18–20 July 1905, and the payment of annuities, the summer gathering around the fur trading post at Eabamet Lake began to acquire greater significance, both social, economic, and political. The political aspects revolved around a great coherence of band members around an elected chief and council.

This political body then began to make decisions for the Fort Hope Band as a whole, which also tended to enhance the economic importance of the HBC post. This further augmented its fur trade activities with some governmental functions such as a central contact point for such external facilities as the postal service.

Fort Hope Chief Moonias at Treaty No. 9 Negotiations, 1905

Source: Ottawa: Library and Archives Canada (PA-059534)

An important point that should be made, however, is that the term *Fort Hope Band* should not be construed to mean that there existed a unified social unit in the vicinity of Eabamet Lake when the treaty commissioners arrived in 1905. In fact, the term *Fort Hope Band* refers to an artificial construct constituted by the Canadian government according to the terms of the treaty. The term *Fort Hope Band* refers to an artificial organizational unit that did not exist prior to the signing of the treaty.

Even the leadership organization of an elected chief and council was an imposition that did not exist prior to the treaty but was imposed on the Anishinaabe inhabitants to suit the administrative needs of the government.

This is evidenced by the Anishinaabe term *(okima.hka.n)* which can be translated as a *boss-like* among his own people; a surrogate for the real thing, or a *put-up job* (Ellis 1960: 1). Similarly, the same as the term *sheshipkhan* refers to a *duck decoy*, not the real thing (see Rogers 1965).

In order to facilitate administrative control, the Canadian government introduced along with the various treaties a system of elective local government. Via the Indian Act, the election of chiefs and councilors and their duties were specified.

In the existing anthropological and linguistic literature, we are told that the Indigenous people have never fully understood the political system that the federal government of Canada introduced, and therefore, do not recognize (Landes 1937: 2–3). We also learn from this literature that the elected chiefs and councils are the least developed law-enforcing agency in many Indigenous communities (Lips 1947: 475).

One conclusion tends to dominate from the available evidence: in Indigenous communities, "political sovereignty is attenuated, if not controlled ultimately by the Indigenous Affairs administration" (Dunning 1959: 2). Similarly, Rogers concludes that for the Anishinaabe leaders of northern Ontario, "The government asserts that authority be vested in the chief whereby he can carry out his duties. But in the final analysis the chief his lost his former powers and acquired no new ones" (1965: 277).

It has even been said that "some men refuse to accept positions of *authority* for precisely that reason: to accept is to become a target of criticism and ridicule" (Brody 1975: 196). However, one hastens to add that these foregoing descriptions apply more precisely to elected officials. In my study of Anishinaabe leaders, in communities that exist outside of the confines of the Indian Act, more traditional leadership norms are apt to characterize the local political structure (as described in Hedican 1986).

Thus, the caveat here is that not all Indigenous leaders necessarily lack power in their local communities. Even when elective forms of government were introduced with the various treaties, strong traditional leaders were nonetheless still able to operate within their communities.

Anishinaabe Men and Women at Fort Hope Treaty Negotiations in 1905

Source: Ottawa: Library and Archives Canada (PA-059539)

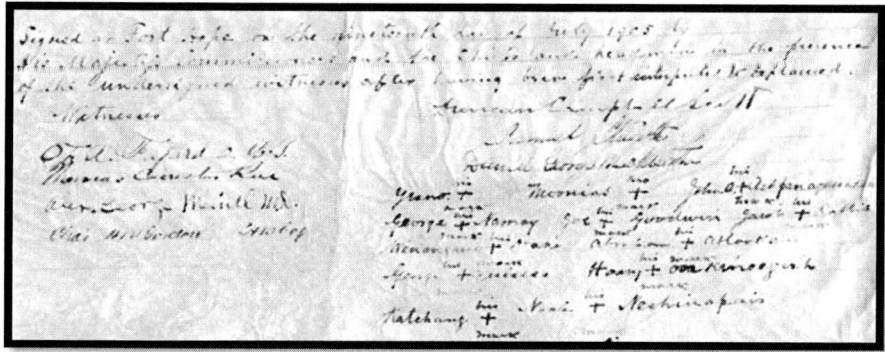

Anishinaabe Signatures to Fort Hope Treaty No. 9

(Top left to Right) Yesno, Moonias, John Ashpanaqueshkum, George Namay, Joe Goodwin, Jacob Rabbit, Wenangasie Drake, Abraham Atlookan, George Quisees, Harry (Benjamin) Ooskineegish, Katchang, Noah Neshinapais

Source: Archives of Ontario, Department of Indian Affairs and Northern Development

41

Another factor is that the so-called Fort Hope *Band* is not comprised of members who live in a single location. In fact, the band members live predominantly in four small villages which are situated between the Albany and Winisk Rivers. Their names are Fort Hope (Eabametoong), Webequie, Lansdowne House (Neskatanga), and Summer Beaver (Nibinamik).

Fort Hope is the only location situated within the band's 160-square-kilometer reserve, and only the community of Fort Hope is located on federal crown land; the others are situated on Ontario Crown Land. As such, it is the government of Ontario that has jurisdiction over the other three communities although all of them receive the same government services. All four communities are geographically dispersed from one another, as Lansdowne House is 80 kilometers distant from Fort Hope, Summer Beaver 160 kilometers, and Webequie about 240 kilometers away (see Driben and Trudeau 1983: 3, 110).

In its heyday (c.1895–1910), Fort Hope was an important Hudson's Bay Company fur trading post but by the time Treaty No. 9 was signed this period of economic activity had passed and the Anishinaabe people began to settle for various periods of time in the vicinity of the trading post.

"By the midpoint of this [20th] century," Driben and Trudeau (1983: 5) state that the Fort Hope trading post, "was surrounded by a tiny collection of makeshift log houses and shacks. The original town site, which was located on the south shore of Eabamet Lake, was moved to its present location in 1962, and following the move the community took on an entirely different appearance…to minimize costs…houses and buildings were erected in tight parallel rows separated by wide dirt roads."

The main terms of Treaty No. 9 were that the Fort Hope Band members were to receive money in the form of an annuity of $4 per annum and a reserve consisting of a tract of land compromising one square mile for each family of five. There were also gratuities presented to the treaty signatories of 355 people.

However, the commissioners estimated that 244 people, or a third of the Ojibwe on the HBC census, did not appear at treaty time (Long 2010: 177). According to one of the treaty commissioners, Mr. MacMartin, the Indians were then asked if they had anything to say.

One of the chiefs, who was named simply "Yesno", replied that he was willing to enter into Treaty and advised the others to act likewise (*ibid*: 183).

It was also noted that Chief Yesno, who received his name from his imperfect knowledge of the English language, which consisted altogether of the use of the words "yes" and "no", made an excited speech in which he told the Indians that they were to receive cattle, implements, seed-grain and tools.

Yesno had evidently traveled and had gathered an erroneous and exaggerated idea of what the government was doing for Indians in other parts of the country. As the undersigned wished to guard carefully against any misconception or against making any promises that were not written in the Treaty itself, it was explained that none of these issues were to be made.

The band could not hope to depend upon agriculture as a means of subsistence; that "hunting and fishing, in which occupations they were not to be interfered with, should for very many years prove lucrative sources of revenue" (ibid: 185–6).

Several years after the treaty negotiations of 1905, anthropologist Alanson Skinner conducted an ethnographic survey of the Cree and Anishinaabe (Saulteaux) populations along the Albany River system in the summers of 1908 and 1909 (Skinner 1911). The Anishinaabe population living around Lake Eabamet was included in this tour which encompassed 2,400 miles altogether mostly by canoe.

He notes that, "the Northern Saulteaux division of the Ojibwa has been steadily encroaching on their (Eastern Cree) southern borders, driving the Cree to seek new hunting grounds to the north and east" (1911: 10). This comment thus indicates a considerable flux of population movement during this period.

During this time period, the Indigenous Cree and Anishinaabe lived in conical lodges constructed of birch bark. Although he comments that, "formerly, many lodges were built of caribou skins," (p. 12). Indicative of cultural change at this time, Skinner notes that, "in 1908, there was not a single birch bark canoe. All of those seen were canvas-covered" (p. 43).

The population of Fort Hope during Skinner's survey was listed as 550 people, similar to the previous census taken in 1905. Skinner also remarks on his journey from Lac Seul to Lake St. Joseph that the Anishinaabe "are expert anatomists and know at once where to cut in order to disjoint the bones" (p. 135).

Regarding social organization, "Their winter camps usually contain several related families, though this does not always follow" (p. 149). Although references to clan organization in Skinner's comments were at the time of his survey not as strong as in previous years, at Fort Hope the moose, sturgeon, loon, raven, goose, and duck clans are still recognized.

Later, Driben and Trudeau (1983: 14) added in their ethnographic account that "on the tribal level the Ojibwas were joined together through patrilineal clans. Each clan was named after an important mythical ancestor who helped create the earth. A person became a member of a clan at birth and regarded his clan mates as lifelong blood relations whom he was obligated to help." Since members of the same clan were regarded as blood relatives, marriage between those of the same clan was prohibited and seen as incestuous. Thus, marriage outside of one's own clan was necessary which also served to unite disparate social groups.

"Men having 13 wives are still remembered," Skinner reported, "though five to seven were more common" (1911: 151). At the time of the treaty signing in 1905, very few marriages would have comprised the number of spouses apparently common in previous times. On the subject of polygynous marriages, ethnohistorian Long (2010: 475) noted that at Fort Hope two hunters each had two wives. It was also noted by Charles Bishop (1974: 13) in reference to his historical research on Osnaburgh House that in earlier times (c. 1821–1890) a mature hunter often had two or three wives. As he notes, "Frequently, a mature hunter had two or three wives (a decline, however, from the previous era when an important trade captain would have to double this number)."

Nevertheless, by 1900, polygyny had virtually disappeared, probably due to missionary influence during the preceding three decades. After 1895, Indigenous people were subject to the same penalties as Whites for practicing plural marriage (Dunning 1959: 11). By 1905, these existing unions were tolerated, but it was expected that the practice, which was discouraged by missionaries and considered bigamy under Canadian law, would come to an end. However, Dunning (1959: 11–12) also noted that, "The policy of the administration throughout Canada was to allow any unions which were extant, but to prohibit any further plural marriages."

In addition, as Alanson Skinner indicated for the Fort Hope population in 1909, clan relationships had lost most of their traditional importance: "The social organization…has been greatly broken up during the past half-century…their winter camps usually contain several related families, clans…now have no importance whatsoever" (1911: 150).

A Missionary's View

One would be remiss for not mentioning the psychological and physical stress that colonialist pressures brought upon the Indigenous inhabitants of northern Canada. For example, Rev. John Horton of Moose Factory made an extensive journey up to Fort Albany on the west coast of James Bay, then on to Rupert's House, East Main, and Fort George on the east side of the Bay, then on into the interior.

This trip caused him to be "torn by sorrow." A description of his journey recounts the following afflictions among the Indigenous Anishinaabe and Cree that he encountered on his journey:

"The hardships and the deaths that he encountered on his visits were almost too harrowing to bear even in the reading of them, as he described them in his letters. Horden would find, in settlement after settlement, that the tribe had been decimated. Also, at times almost wiped out, by hunger, by cold too severe to be endured in their weakened state, by drowning in canoes, and by accidents of various kinds. Added to these were the ravages of the White Man's diseases" (Peterson 1974: 13).

Remember that this assessment of Cree life in the James Bay area was not based on obscure second-hand reports but founded on first-hand observations by Rev. Horton himself. He notes furthermore that, "for the past few years they have suffered greatly from a failure of food, and many have starved…numbers having died of starvation" (ibid 13–14).

It was also noted that "The bodies of both adults and children, weakened by starvation, would be found frozen to death. [In addition], outbreaks of whooping cough, diphtheria, and influenza wrought havoc among them" (ibid:14).

R.J. Renison was born in 1875 in County Tipperary, Ireland. Subsequently, Mr. Renison answered "a call for a missionary to go out and teach the Ojibways around Lake Nipigon in Canada" (ibid: 115). His family consisted of his wife, three boys, and a daughter. "All three boys grew up speaking Ojibway along with the English tongue" Renison noted (ibid: 116).

An arduous journey from Toronto to Fort Hope on the Albany River is described in the year 1898 which provides the reader with a description of travel conditions in northern Ontario at the turn of the 20th-century:

"It was in July of that year when the three [Renison] brothers [Robert, William, and George] set out for Moose Fort. From Toronto, they traveled to

Sault Ste. Marie and Fort William [now Thunder Bay]. Then, boarded a train to Nipigon, where they got themselves outfitted for the long journey to James Bay. At Nipigon, they picked up Michael and Thomas, two Indian guides, and then the five set out in a birchbark canoe on their journey of a thousand miles."

"They would have to live in the wild, uninhabited land through which they passed and live off it as they went. Their route was first across Lake Nipigon, and they reached the Albany River at Fort Hope and made their way down the great river 700 miles. Two weeks after leaving Fort Hope they reached Fort Albany" (ibid: 116).

Later, in 1905, Robert Renison met Rev. Edward Richards (known at the time as "Uncle Ned"), who was an Indigenous priest at Fort Hope who had a Scottish ancestor. According to the Fort Hope baptismal registry, Richards was born at Mattagami (Mattswakumma in the church records) and was of Scottish origins. His wife Jane was of Native and English origin (Long 2010: 477).

The Anglican Church recognized the usefulness of Indigenous missionaries, especially in terms of the use of the Anishinaabe and Cree languages in the proselytizing process. Scottish and English missionaries may develop some proficiency in the Indigenous languages of the James Bay area. However, they probably would never understand the nuances of Indigenous languages in the same manner that a Native speaker would.

In addition, it undoubtedly helped that Indigenous people themselves would aid in the conversion process by outlining the benefits of adopting the Anglican faith. In fact, members of the Anglican Church hierarchy appeared to accelerate the role of Native missionaries in the area.

As an example, Bishop George Holmes noted that the majority of Native ministers were "baptized members of the church." He also lamented that he considered them, "deplorably ignorant. But can we wonder, considering that about one month's instruction in four years is all the poor people have?" Bishop Holmes confirmed 26 of them in a short period of time (see Long 2010: 475).

Rev. Richards was to play a particularly significant role in the negotiations of Treaty No. 9 at Fort Hope. He was a resident of Fort Hope and in charge of the Anglican mission there, while the Roman Catholic church is under the charge of Rev. Father Fafard who visits from the mission at Albany. Rev. Richards, it was noted by treaty Commissioner Stewart, had arrived the previous evening, and we had a conversation with him regarding Indian matters generally.

"As far as the treaty negotiation was concerned, the commissioners had the benefit of the assistance of Reverend Father F.X. Fafard of the Roman Catholic Mission at Albany, whose thorough knowledge of the Cree and Ojibway tongues was of great assistance during the discussion" (Long 2010: 185).

It was further noted by Commissioner Stewart that "Father Fafard, fully explained to the Inds. the nature of the treaty, and the reasons for asking them to surrender the title to their unused lands. They were also informed that by signing the treaty they would acknowledge themselves to be subjects of His Majesty, the King, and their willingness to observe the laws made by him" (ibid: 180).

In addition, according to the notes taken by treaty commissioner MacMartin on 21 July 1905, "Mr. Richards called upon us at the H.B. Company Residence. Had a pleasant talk with him regarding the capabilities of the country as regards agriculture and timber lands, learning that the soil was poor and that the only source from which the Indians and he himself derived means of subsistence…[was] from fish and rabbits" (ibid: 190).

As such, it is obvious then that the treaty commissioners were relying on the missionaries as informants and for information about the Indigenous people in the Fort Hope area. Also, the missionaries appeared to function in the role of intermediaries between the negotiating parties.

Later, in May 1947, when Rev. Renison was 72 years old, and now promoted to Bishop Renison, he described a return visit to Fort Hope, covering the 125 miles by air starting from Sioux Lookout.

At Fort Hope, Bishop Renison indicates that "he would almost certainly be meeting a remarkable Indian trader called John Yesno…John had requested that the bishop baptize his young son Atlee-Bob-Churchill, although he let down the side to some extent by ever afterward referring to the lad as Bob, explaining it is easy. The other names were just for decoration."

"The bishop described him [John Yesno] as a remarkable man with many modern ideas…like a lawyer for the defense, John Yesno stood beside me and interpreted my words to the people. What power and eloquence are lost to the bar! There is no one quite like him" (ibid: 155).

Johnny Yesno's Family Relationships

During the mid-1970s I began my own study of an Anishinaabe community in northern Ontario called Collins (now called Namaygoosisagagun First Nation) which is situated about 30 kilometers west of Lake Nipigon along the Canadian National Rail line (see Hedican 1986). At that time, the community consisted of about 150 people, many of who had once lived in Fort Hope.

In fact, the family who composed the primary leadership structure of this community was directly related to Yesno who was a signatory to the 1905 treaty at Fort Hope and all at one time had lived in Fort Hope. John Patience was a Scottish fur trader who worked for the Hudson's Bay Company as a post manager. While at Fort Hope, he married Elizabeth Yesno who was born in 1910 and a granddaughter of the Yesno who signed Treaty No. 9.

In the late 1930s, John and Elizabeth had four sons (Donald, Peter, and Hamish) as well as a daughter (Sarah). Eventually, in the 1950s, John decided to purchase a store on the CNR line at Collins and the family subsequently moved there. The attraction from a business point of view was that the railway location provided reduced transportation costs for store goods and as such John Patience could compete effectively with the HBC establishments at such places as Fort Hope.

During this time there were many Fort Hope families who had drifted farther south and were attracted to the rail-line stores because they could have received better prices for their furs than was possible at the HBC posts farther north. As a result, the Collins store was able to conduct a profitable business and in time attracted a substantial number of Fort Hope families as well as those trappers from the Lake Nipigon area to the west. During the course of my research, I was able to engage in a variety of discussions with the Patience brothers who now ran the Collins store after their father's passing in 1967.

Collins Store in 1967

Source: Photo Courtesy of Anita Patience

Here is an entry from my Collins research journal:

Collins: Wed. 10 July 1974.

Continued reporting of genealogical material with Don, Peter, and Elizabeth Patience. I have attempted to establish their relationship with chiefs from Ogoki and Fort Hope who participated in the signing of Treaty No. 9 in 1905. The kinship relationships of Collins' Patience family and their wider circle of relatives were then indicated in the following diagram:

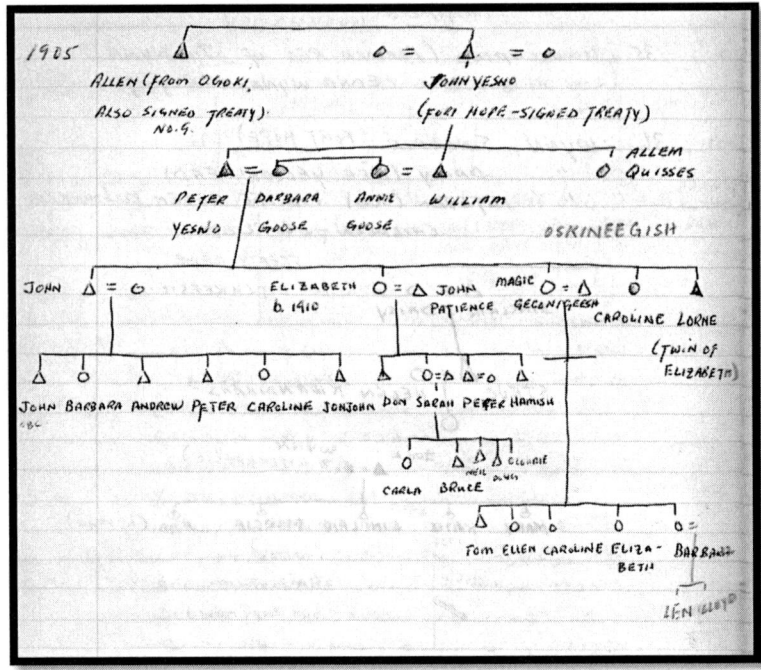

Yesno-Patience Family Diagrams

Source: Edward Hedican Field Notes (1974)

YESNO CLAN

MR. COOPER (HBC) ─┬─ BARBARA ──────────── PETER YESNK
                  (GOOSE)   ├─ LIZZIE (PATIENCE)
        JOHN COOPER   └─ MAGGIE (OSKINEEGISH)

SARA HEAD   KATY SPADE   JANE OKEESE

JOHNNY   NAOMI (CARPENTAR)   ATLEE   CAROLINE

BARBARA   BILL   ANDREW   MARGARET

                              PETER   IDA

                             SYDNEY   RUTH

                             HARVEY

                            JOHN RAY

                             LEWIS

                            EDWARD

MR. COOPER ─┬─ BARBARA   GEORGE OKEESE ─┬─ CLARA

      JOHN C.   JANE OKEESE

            Atlee   Caroline

            Andrew   Margaret

            Peter   Ida

            Sydney   Ruth

            Harvey

            John Ray

            Lewis

            Edward

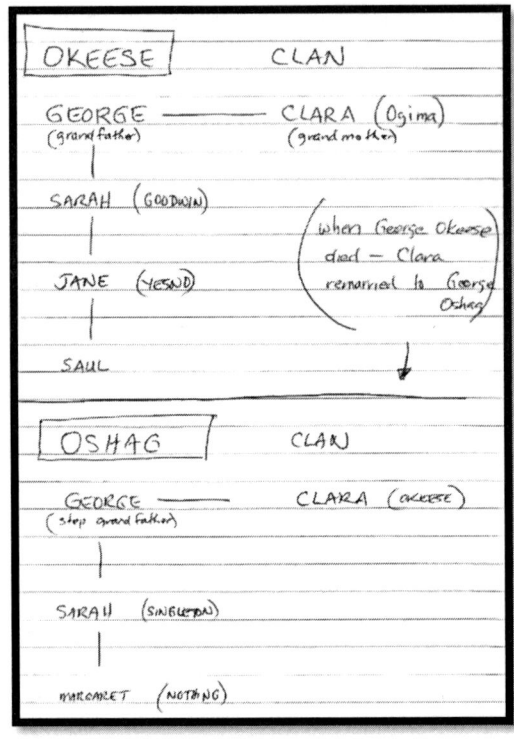

Andrew Yesno's Family Diagrams

Source: Courtesy of Andrew Yesno

In order to assess the various family relationships in the above diagrams I began first to examine the family tree of the Yesno family as reported above by members of the Yesno family. I reasoned that a good place to start would be to investigate the enumeration of Fort Hope families recorded when Treaty No. 9 was signed at Fort Hope in 1905.

Band No.	NAMES.	NUMBER IN FAMILY.					Amount Paid.	Amount returned to Dept. for Absentees.	No. on previous Pay-List.
		Men.	Women.	Boys.	Girls.	Total.			
	Brought forward	64	69	94	88	315	2520 00		
132	Waban Thomas								
133	Wasena								
134	Do David								
135	Whiskey Jack	1	1	4	2	8	64 00		
136	Yesno	1	2		3	6	48 00		
137	Yesno William	1	1	2	1	5	40 00		
138	Do Peter	1	1	1		3	24 00		

Pay-List of Fort Hope Treaty No. 9 Members, 1905

Source: The James Bay Treaty—Treaty No. 9 (gov.on.ca), accessed 25 May 2023.

In the 1905, Pay-List Yesno is enumerated to have two wives, and two adult sons (Peter and William). Apparently, the elder Yesno still has three daughters remaining in his household. Both of his sons are married. William had two boys and one girl, while his other son, Peter, had one boy. As a rough estimate, the elder Yesno was probably around 50 years of age (i.e., born about 1855), and his two sons were around 25 years old (born about 1880). As such, the Yesno population at Fort Hope comprised seven adults and seven children for a total of 14 persons overall.

One aspect of the Yeso family that has intrigued me for some time is that in one of Johnny Yesno's obituaries it is mentioned that when Johnny ran away from the Pelican Lake residential school at Sioux Lookout, his father, John

Cooper arrived to transfer him to Sault Ste. Marie. Thus, the name John Cooper was a puzzle that was not mentioned previously in the recounting of the Yesno family. Later, when I had the opportunity, I asked Caroline Yesno about the Cooper name, and this was her response (1 June 2021):

"My dad's father is George Cooper from Scotland. Hudson's Bay manager. Peter Yesno raised him. My dad used to call him Uncle Peter. My dad took his dad's name, John Cooper Yesno. Andrew Nate is also George Cooper's son. So is Erland Vincent. Erland was taken away and adopted. He was raised in Moose Factory. He came to visit my dad one summer.

There's [also] Allen Vincent who is my dad's half-brother. Son of George Cooper. I know for sure that George had three sons: my dad, Andrew Nate, and Erland (Allen) Yesno Vincent. I wonder where he went from Fort Hope. HBC managers moved around. My sis Ida was telling me that Nayaneekeesics might be related to Yesno.

George may have been in Saugeen. Edward and Erland were not Barbara Goose's sons. This is likely what happened to Aunt Liz' (Elizabeth Yesno-Patience) twin (Lorne) My dad John Cooper Yesno and Andrew Nate are half-brothers. Elizabeth Goose is Edward and Andrew Nate's mom. My grandmother Barbara Goose had a child, my dad, with George Cooper. He must have gone back to Scotland. I really have no idea. He had kids wherever he went, I heard."

The Fur Trader's Wife

Country Marriages in Northern Ontario

The Cree and Hudson's Bay Company employees in the James Bay area were engaged in a serious conflict over the fur trade territory, for at least a century, extending from about 1750 to 1850. There were several important facets to this conflict. One of these concerns is the propensity of HBC employees to take Aboriginal women as wives and then abandon them and their children when the employee left the area.

This discussion of forms of marriage and the establishment of exchange relations is a prelude to the following discussion of marriage between fur traders and Indigenous women; relationships encouraged by Gov. Simpson to increase fur trade profits. His motive apparently was to establish bonds between Hudson's Bay Company employees and Indigenous families as a means of creating more effective trading relationships.

Thus, the use of the term *marriage* in most cases regarding the Cree and Anishinaabe of northern Ontario is misplaced, or in error, since few such unions were solemnized by a Christian church. In addition, the children of such unions were at times given the surname of their European father, but this was probably not usually the case.

Country marriage is a somewhat euphemistic term that connotes a relationship, usually sexual in nature, between an Indigenous woman and a European fur trader (Brown 1980: 62–63, 79–80). Also, when the fur trader retired and returned to Scotland or England, he seldom brought his wife and children of the union with him, but simply abandoned them to their own fate. There are records, though, of small pensions being given by the more affluent traders to their Indigenous spouse upon termination of the relationship, but this was probably a rare occurrence. It is also important to indicate how necessary women were in the fur trade economy.

Kim Anderson points out that "Men worked outside the community as hunters and warriors and women within…These divisions accommodated the work required for a land-based lifestyle" (2000: 59). In addition, Olsen comments further that "The divisions of labor were based on practical needs. Because women are reproducers as well as producers, their labor consisted mainly of work at home. It was the men who procured the necessary items which were then turned into food, shelter, or clothing" (1989: 55).

The involvement of Indigenous women was, therefore, an indispensable part of the northern bush lifestyle. As such, life in a fur trade country would be inconceivable without the participation of women. In the opinion of A.G. Bailey (1969: 102–105), one of the major sources of conflict between Europeans and the eastern Algonkians concerned their divergent concepts of marriage. He based his assessment on Champlain's observations of the pre-marital behavior of Montagnais adolescents, who he thought were promiscuous compared to the youths back in France.

Bailey felt that this period of sexual license was, "taken advantage of by French traders… [such that] the loose morals of the French served as a bad example to the Indians who were accustomed to daily condemnation of these practices by their missionaries" (Bailey 1969: 102).

Bailey (1969: 113) also noted that "there was a custom among the French to sell liquor to these [Indigenous] girls, not only to get them drunk for nefarious purposes, but to make them debtors and, therefore, dependents. If they tried to escape, they were offered violence."

In this context, it is somewhat ironic that those in power in the Hudson's Bay Company, such as Gov. Simpson, whose condescending comments on the "nature and character of the Indians [he found] repugnant to our feelings" (i.e., in Newman 1987: 226). He espoused such a moral high ground when it was the Europeans themselves whose loose morals were a focus at times of censure by the Indigenous people themselves.

One might also conclude, then, that if Gov. Simpson found the "character of the Indians repugnant," then his condescending attitudes about Indigenous people would probably be reinforced by other Hudson's Bay Company employees as well, since they would apparently be approved of by the top person in the organization. One might also presume that if Gov. Simpson should find the customs of the Indigenous people "repugnant," then he would hardly be predisposed to view these customs in a positive manner or seek to understand the behavior associated with these customs.

A further source of conflict with Europeans concerned the fact that the Roman Catholic church never recognized the validity in Indigenous communities of traditional marriage ceremonies which the priests regarded as "worthless and contrary to the laws of God" (Bailey 1969: 103). This problem was exacerbated by a degraded position in which the priests regarded Indigenous women.

As Bailey concluded, "There is no doubt that [Indigenous] women occupied a more degraded position in the settlements of Christians than among the wandering pagans, where divorce was relatively easy." And furthermore, as Bailey states, "Of all the Algonkian customs the missionaries found polygyny the most difficult to eradicate, and in spite of all their arguments against it, the Indians could give reasons for the continuance of the practice" (ibid: 104–105). The priests however could not offer a solution to the question pertaining to the fate of a man's additional wives were they to be abandoned and left to starve in the woods.

As one Algonkian man at Tadoussac stated: "He loved his wife and had sent the others away but they continually returned so that to kill them was the only way to get rid of them" (ibid: 105). However, as Bailey concluded, "There is reason to believe that polygyny continued long after the Jesuits had left the mission among the eastern Algonkians" (ibid). Furthermore, the treatment of Indigenous women by Hudson's Bay Company employees has certainly been the subject of criticism and complaint, especially the practice of abandoning or desertion of "country wives" and their children when fur trade employees returned to their home country, or when they married white women.

Elsewhere in Canada, as far as the maritime fur trade of British Columbia was concerned, Fisher suggests that "there was evidently some concern that Indian women and their children were being deserted by traders, for the Council of the Northern Department passed an order in 1824 requiring all officers and servants to make adequate provision for their Indian women, not only while they were resident in the country but also after their departure" (Fisher 1977: 40; Flemming 1940: 94–95).

However, there was little evidence presented that this order was enforced to any degree, which prompted Fisher to conclude that "there were discrepancies between the ideal of the order, and the reality of its execution" (1977: 40). Of course, there were racist undertones to the country marriage practices such that traders might feel ashamed of their Indigenous wives if they moved to an urban center. In the opinion of HBC employee John Work, "It was out of the question for an Indian wife to join *civilized society*" (Fisher 1977: 40).

Despite this view, some traders did take their Native wives with them when they settled out of the fur trade territory, although how many is unknown (see Lamb 1957:194–195; Cox 1932: 311).

One of the most vociferous critics of this practice of taking country wives and subsequently abandoning them to their own fate was Alexander K. Isbister. He became a spokesperson in England for Indigenous people in fur trade country, especially in terms of his exploitation of British sensitivity to colonial practices.

Isbister, born in 1822, was the grandson of Chief Factor Alexander Kennedy and his Native wife. In 1841, Alexander Isbister left the company because he felt that further advancement was not possible for him. His travels took him to England where he became a teacher, studied medicine, and authored many textbooks on various diverse subjects.

Isbister also maintained an active interest in the affairs of the mixed-blood population and on occasion became their advocate. Isbister, for example, presented evidence for parliamentary investigations and even managed to engage the interest of the Aborigines' Protections Society in the treatment of the Natives by the Hudson's Bay Company (Brown 1980: 184–184). In particular, Isbister was "shocked by the dissolute character of the company's officers, living, as he conceived it, in sin with Indian and half-breed women" (Galbraith 1957: 319).

He also suggested, based on his personal experience, that what the Hudson's Bay Company offered for the Aboriginal people's furs "was outrageously low [and] none of the profits resulting there from were returned to the Indians in the form of services, such as educational facilities" (ibid). "His petition to Westminster's Colonial Office," Newman (1987: 251) asserted, "remains one of the most eloquent and unanswerable indictments of the Hudson's Bay Company's treatment of the Indian Peoples."

Although Isbister's views were largely ignored at the time, his writings were an articulate and persuasive condemnation of the racist attitudes of the British colonial practices in Rupert's Land during his lifetime:

"When we assert that they are steeped in ignorance, debased in mind, and crushed in spirit, that by the exercise of an illegal claim over the country of the forefathers, they are deprived of the natural rights and privileges of free-born men [as the result of] a barbarous and selfish policy, founded on a love of lucre" (ibid).

It is evident, then, that the inter-cultural problems caused by Hudson's Bay Company fur traders who kept Aboriginal women as "wives" at their posts mirrored in macrocosm the larger issues that the company was forced to deal with on a much broader scale (as detailed in Galbraith 1949: 322–335). For example, in the classic work on this topic, Jennifer Brown's *Strangers in Blood* (1980), she notes that "the virtual lack of English and Scottish-born women who would be available for marriage to fur traders was one of the reasons that these men took native-born wives."

However, another important reason was that Indigenous women were well-suited to life in the rugged country in which the fur trade took place. "Imported British wives, on the contrary," according to a statement made by George Simpson in 1848, were unsuitable for country life, "imported wives fancy themselves such great women that there is no possibility of pleasing them" (quoted in Brown 1980: xvi). Thus, Governor Simpson himself became more favorably disposed toward native-born wives (and their children) as the people best adapted to domestic life and work in the fur trade country (ibid: xv).

However, this sentiment was expressed in the late 1840s when the term "native-born" referred principally to women of mixed descent who had been exposed to the so-called "civilizing" (i.e., religious and educational) aspects of European society (see Brown 1976: 92–105). Thus, when Gov. Simpson proposed that fur traders engage in marital relations with the women of Native societies for the purposes of increasing the Hudson's Bay Company's profits, he was in fact utilizing one form of exchange (social) to promote another (economic) type.

The implicit motive behind this suggestion was to instill in the Aboriginal people's mind the idea that through marriage fur traders of the Hudson's Bay Company would thereby become in-laws of their Indigenous trapping relatives. However, from the Indigenous perspective, such a marital relationship implied much more than the fur traders might have expected. Especially, in terms of the reciprocal obligation of helping relatives in need, an idea contrary to the company's profit-oriented attitude. Indigenous trappers also participated in encouraging these arrangements.

"[Hudson's Bay Company] officers faced social pressures from Indian groups," Jennifer Brown remarked. "When Indian traders discovered who was the most important man at a particular post, they sought his favor and friendship by offering him gifts, especially of women" (1980: 62).

The preceding comments about so-called *country marriages* are meant to provide a historical background concerning Johnny Yesno's life and the community in which he grew up. As such, there appears to be some ambiguity concerning his actual parentage, Cooper or Yesno. It must have been a common occurrence when HBC fur traders were sexually interacting with the Indigenous women, but then, did not take responsibility for the resulting children who the traders had a tendency to simply abandon when they left the area of their trading post.

Conclusion

Johnny Yesno's personal history is intertwined with the complex history of marriage among the Anishinaabe who lived, hunted, and trapped along the Albany River in northern Ontario. Until relatively recent times, that is in the early 20th-century, the Anishinaabe lived a migratory life of hunting and trapping.

The Hudson's Bay Company trading posts, such as that of Fort Hope, which was established in 1894, were constructed in an attempt to secure the furs of the Indigenous people who lived inland from the James Bay coastal regions. It was not long after, in 1905, that Treaty No. 9 was signed with the leaders who traded in the vicinity of the Fort Hope region.

Even when Johnny Yesno was born in the late 1930s, Fort Hope did not consist of any sort of settlement that one could call a village community. The area surrounding the trading post apparently consisted of makeshift dwellings. They were inhabited on a seasonal basis as most families lived most of the year on their traplines, only occasionally visiting Fort Hope to trade their furs and visit other relatives.

In other words, the signing of Treaty 9 did not lead to the establishment of a community of residents who consistently inhabited the "village" throughout the year. The various trapping families who lived in the Fort Hope region of the Albany River were united by marriage bonds throughout the area. Since, as the historical records indicate, a trapper might have more than one wife, the social bonds uniting the various families formed a complex web of social and economic interrelationships.

There was also a cultural practice whereby the new husband would live with his wife's family for a certain period of time, usually for a year or two. It was seen as a form of compensation for the loss of the new wife's economic contribution to her natal family.

The result of this complex pattern of marital interrelationships was that one would probably have a multifaceted pattern of relationships with a multitude of relatives. Anthropologists have suggested that these wide-ranging marriage patterns could function to provide a wide web of support in environments such as the Eastern Subarctic where food and other resources were thinly distributed.

In turn, the emergence of the residential school system served to dissociate young people from this multifaceted system of social and economic system of support that had evolved over many centuries. Therefore, the norms and values that had evolved over long periods of time among the Indigenous Anishinaabe and Cree people of northern Ontario would no longer provide support for the young people as they grew into adulthood.

Instead, the norms and values that the young Indigenous students were expected to follow in the residential school system were very much diametrically opposed to those existing in their home communities. Students were punished for using their Native language, for example, and therefore the thought processes that are part of language construction were inhibited. This abrupt change in psychological and cultural processes would have been a matter of grave concern for the young students and resulted in what could be termed *dissociative behavior*, or *cultural dissonance*.

Chapter Three
Pelican Lake and Shingwauk
Residential Schools

I read in an article that John Cooper came and took Johnny out of residential school at Sioux Lookout when he ran away with another boy. Johnny apparently got abused badly but he never talked about it. My brother Andrew went to school there and he doesn't talk about it either.

The only reason I know Andrew was abused is because the Nate girls told me. Quite vivid too. I was at Pelican when I was very young. My sis Barb was working there. Andrew was [also] attending there. I think Johnny was at Shingwauk because I don't remember him.

-Caroline Yesno, 31 May 2021.

As this chapter is being written the most horrific, unimaginable accounts are now emerging about residential school children buried in mass graves without even their names being recorded. The details, if correct, are nothing sort of shocking: priests having babies with Indigenous school girls, and then, burning them in basement furnaces. How could the religious authorities not have been aware of such widespread abuse of the children in their care?

As Ryan Flanagan of CTV News (4 July 2021) asks, "What do we really know about the true history of Canada?"

Apparently, the answer is "not much!"

Back in May 2021, ground-penetrating radar detected the remains of 215 children buried at the site of a residential school in Kamloops first announced by the Tk'emlups te Secwépemc First Nation. Just a few weeks later, the Cowessess First Nation reported finding an estimated 751 unmarked graves outside a former residential school on its territory.

Many Canadians may have been astonished at these findings, but they shouldn't have been. As an example, the Truth and Reconciliation Commission (TRC) had previously identified 4,100 Indigenous children who died while attending residential schools. The overall death toll could be as high as 15,000, according to one report (*Globe and Mail*, 13 October 2023).

In Manitoba, thousands gathered in Winnipeg for two separate rallies on Canada Day, but instead of celebrating dressed in red and white, they remembered in orange. A rally called *No Pride in Genocide* started at noon at the Canadian Museum for Human Rights to honor the children who never came home after being taken to residential schools, and to call on the federal government to take action.

"It's a day of reflection, in many ways a day of protest. Canada can't be at peace with itself, unless it comes to peace and harmony with Indigenous governments, as was intended with the signing of the treaties," said Dennis Meeches, the Chief of Long Plain First Nation and spokesperson for Treaty One Nation (*CBC News*, 1 July 2021).

The final report of the Commission, issued in 2015, detailed many of the horrors that just now are commanding the attention of Canadians, but among Indigenous people, the tragedies of residential schools have been well known and passed down through the generations. Thus, as Gabrielle Victoria Fayant, co-founder of a youth organization called the Assembly of Seven Generations, asserts, "Most Canadians don't actually know the true history of Canada."

In light of the residential school abuses, several communities across Canada have canceled local Canada Day celebrations; an action based on the sentiment that a celebration praising Canadian history at these times does not seem appropriate. "Take this day and really think about what Canada means, how Indigenous people have been treated by the state of Canada," Fayant said (*CBC News*, 27 March 2019).

The reason that John Cooper Yesno brought his son Johnny to the Pelican Lake Residential School in 1943 will never be known for sure. By some accounts, he wished that his son would do better in life if he had a solid education. In the 1930s, Fort Hope did not even have a school at the time when Johnny grew up.

The first school on the reserve was not opened until 1955 at Old Home Point, which was named the John C. Yesno School, officially opened in September 1967. It was a year after the Residential School system ended. The only careers at the time when Johnny Yesno was growing up were those of trappers and fishermen.

The first school at Fort Hope, initially called the Fort Hope Day School which was constructed in 1965–66, opened in September 1967. One of the main reasons for the construction of this new school was that in the 1960s there was an influx of band members who were relocating onto the reserve from their traditional hunting and trapping territories.

Barbara, Bishop Clark, Gramma (Barbara) Goose, Mother (Jane Okeese), Athlee and Johnny Yesno

Source: Photo Courtesy of Caroline Yesno

An additional factor was that the Indian Act required Indigenous children (those with *Indian status* under the terms of the Indian Act) to regularly attend school. The original school building which consisted of four classrooms quickly outgrew the student population which required portable classrooms to be constructed.

Finally, Indian Affairs built an extension to the school for children from kindergarten to Grade 10 in 1989–90 which is still in use today. However, the school already had four portable classrooms in order to accommodate the growing size of the elementary grades which has doubled in size. As such, when John Cooper Yesno brought his son to the Pelican Lake Residential School in about 1943, he had no formal schooling or education.

As outlined in the Eabametoong First Nation website (*https://teachfor Canada.ca*), John C. Yesno, Johnny Yesno's father:

"Worked alongside the fur traders, the missionaries, and the government. John was self-taught and learned from his contacts to be able to speak, read, and write some of the English language. A Catholic priest taught him English and French and in exchange, John taught him the Ojibway language."

John C. Yesno was also an entrepreneur and operated a store in Fort Hope in competition with the Hudson's Bay Company post. He was also a tourist operator and commercial fisherman who foresaw that the old way of life of the Anishinaabe people who live off the land would someday be diminished, and the people would need modern tools to survive in the Euro-Canadian world. Thus, John Yesno saw education as a useful tool for coping with the modern way of life. Today the John C. Yesno Education Center stands as a tribute to his vision of a better way of life for the Eabametoong people.

The vision was that Eabametoong children would be educated initially in their home community from Kindergarten to Junior Secondary school, while living with their parents before moving south to complete their secondary and post-secondary education.

However, when Johnny Yesno was just a child in the early 1940s, as described in a *Windspeaker* report:

"In stepped the government to civilize the savages, and off went Johnny to the Pelican Residential School, just outside Sioux Lookout. He was only five and he was terrified. Packed with other children on a noisy train, Johnny had an identification tag hung around his neck. and, as he was often heard to say, he had no idea how he survived those awful years. His school memories are hazy, but the sharp edges emerging from that merciful cloud revealed images of physical and sexual abuse" (Meili 2010).

A Hypothesis Concerning the Growth of Residential Schools

It may all be a matter of chance, or there may be verifiable historical facts involved, but there would appear to be coincidental trends suggesting that Fort Hope's population growth is one of the reasons underlying the exodus of young people to residential schools.

Of course, at this point, the suggestion is hypothetical and deserves further research into both *push* and *pull* factors. As an example, the *push* factors may relate to a growing population in which the residents of Fort Hope were having difficulty finding enough resources to sustain a growing population of young people. On the other hand, the *pull* factors could be related to new opportunities, probably economic ones, that tended to draw people away from their home community. The answer probably lies in a combination of these two factors.

To initiate this investigation, I present data on the population growth of Fort Hope, collected during a research study conducted from 1974 to 1984. This study focused on the rail-line community of Collins, located in northwestern Ontario along the CNR rail-line, which became a new home for many families that had previously resided in Fort Hope. This research was essentially the basis of two studies, *The Ogoki River Guides* (Hedican 1986), and *Up in Nipigon Country* (Hedican 2001)

The historical record indicates that the completion of the Canadian National Railway (CNR) in 1911 signaled the start of new beginnings for the people of northern Ontario. A multitude of new trading posts emerged almost overnight along the rail-line; offering the Hudson's Bay Company its first real competition in the area since the demise of the Nor'westers a hundred years earlier.

Railroad construction, Innis (1970: 363) notes, "led to a marked increase in competition where former servants of the company deserted to join the ranks of the competitors." Independent fur traders on the railway had the advantage of inexpensive transportation costs, at least compared to transporting goods from England which was the case with the Hudson's Bay Company. This advantage meant that they could offer high fur prices coupled with low-cost food and trade goods.

To give an example, customers were charged $2.55 for 24 pounds of flour and six pounds of rolled oats at the Collins store in 1955. The same goods at the HBC post at Fort Hope cost $6.12 (Baldwin 1957: 79–83). It was through economic incentives such as these that much of the Albany River trade was diverted to the rail-line.

The early success of line stores was also due to another important factor— escalating population growth in the Fort Hope area coincident with the establishment of the railroad (Figure 1). As the population increased, trappers were pushed to the peripheral and less utilized areas of the band's territory. This process tended to isolate northern trappers from HBC influence and to increase gravitation toward independent traders on the railway.

Records available from the Indian Affairs Branch indicate that between 1909 and 1945, the population of Fort Hope increased by a startling 54%. Even more dramatic, half of this increase occurred in just a 10-year period prior to 1945. After this date, there is a sharp decline in Fort Hope's resident population, indicating substantial movement of persons away from their home community.

If we examine the records in more detail, we find an increasingly large number of Fort Hope families residing in new locations by the early 1940s; first at the larger centers of Sioux Lookout and Pickle Lake, and later at the rail-line villages of Collins and Ombabika (Table 1).

Within a decade, 34 Fort Hope families were not only trading at a rail-line location, but trapping there as well (Table 2). Only a few families, about 15% of the Fort Hope population, were still trapping in the vicinity of the reserve by the mid-1950s. In other words, there were now more Fort Hope families trapping and trading close to the railroad than in their home area, and Collins became a major focus of this demographic shift.

The suggestion, then, as far as further research is concerned, is to gather data on the population dynamics among the Northern Ontario Indigenous communities, and then correlate this data with corresponding figures in the growth of residential schools in the area.

A preliminary hypothesis could be also that population growth among the Northern Ontario Indigenous populations was a contributing factor to the growth of residential schools. One might begin with an examination of the number of students enrolled in the Pelican Lake residential school at Sioux Lookout which began operation in 1929. Then examine Fort Hope's population growth in Figure 1 below. It was in 1929, that Fort Hope's population growth began a dramatic upward trajectory, steadily increasing until 1945; afterward beginning a decline in the population curve.

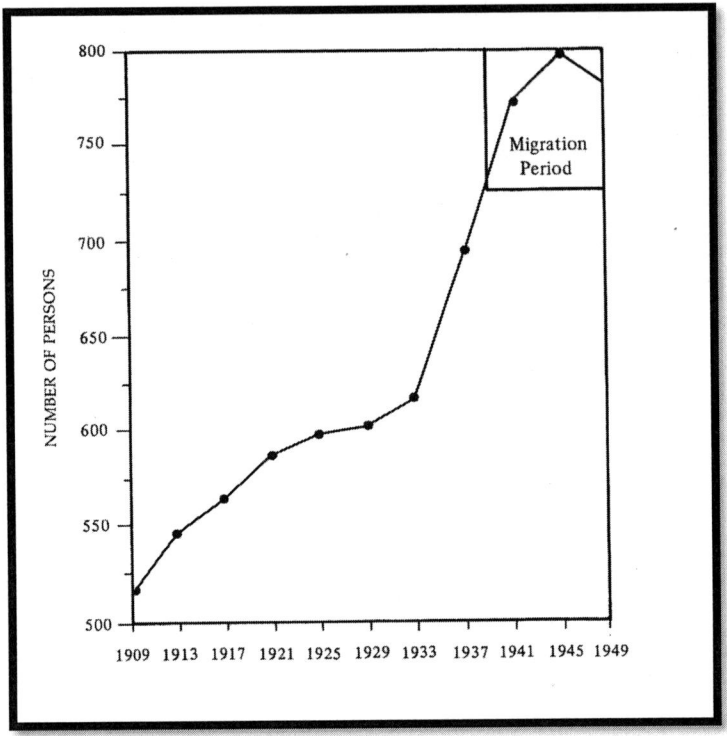

Figure 1: Population Change for the Fort Hope Band, 1909–49

Source: Hedican, *The Ogoki River Guides* (1986: 22)

Table 1: Locations of Fort Hope Families Receiving Treaty Payments, 1941–45

Locations of Fort Hope Families Receiving Treaty Payments, 1941-45					
	1941	1942	1943	1944	1945
Fort Hope	94	96	63	63	88
Lansdowne	58	45	65	64	63
Trout Lake	4	6	1	1	—
Ogoki	2	3	—	—	—
Osnaburgh	2	—	3	4	4
Pickle Lake	—	1	16	33	5
Sioux Lookout	—	2	13	24	2
Ombabika	—	1	—	—	18
Collins	—	—	—	—	13
Other[a]	1	2	4	4	4

[a] Lac Seul, Attiwapiskat and Frenchman's Head.
Source: Indian Affairs Branch records of treaty payments, 1941-45.

Source: Hedican, *The Ogoki River Guides* (1986: 23)

Table 2: Trapline Areas for Three Ojibwa Bands, 1954–55.

Trapline Areas for Three Ojibwa Bands, 1954-55			
Trapline Area	Fort Hope	White Sand	Nipigon House
Ombabika	9	3	—
Armstrong	—	12	—
Collins	26	3	3
Savant Lake	—	1	2
Fort Hope	29	—	—
Lansdowne	117	—	—
Pickle Lake	34	—	—

Source: Indian Affairs Branch records (1954-55), and Baldwin (1957).

Source: Hedican, *The Ogoki River Guides* (1986: 23)

The hypothesis, then, that one might formulate regarding the advent of the residential school system in northern Ontario is that a major contributing factor pertains to the population growth in the reserve communities in this area. As such, the residential schools could have been seen locally as a means of lessening the population pressure on the local reserve communities and thereby reducing pressure on the consumption of local resources.

Another related factor could be that sending young people to residential schools would reduce the need to construct elementary schools in the local communities. Therefore, the suggestion here is that these ideas, i.e., that there exists a correlation between local population growth and the establishment of residential schools, are worth investigating on a wider, regional basis.

Pelican Lake

The Pelican Lake Indian Residential School, also known as the Sioux Lookout Indian Residential School, or the Pelican Falls Indian Residential School was in operation from 1929 to 1969. During this time period, the school enrolled First Nation (Ojibwa or Anishinaabe and Cree) students from both the Treaty Three and Treaty Nine territories of the northwestern Ontario and eastern Manitoba region.

This region comprised a relatively large population base which by the late 1940s caused the school's capacity to be increased to about one hundred and 50 students.

Source: Anglican General Synod Archives, Toronto, Ontario

The Pelican Lake School was established in 1926, however the official opening did not occur until three years later. This residential school was one of nearly 40 schools operated by the Anglican Church in Canada. At its initial opening, the school housed a total of 125 students, which included both boys and girls. However, by the late 1940s the enrollment had increased to about 150 residents.

As with most residential schools, there was only a very limited interaction between the male and female students. As a general rule, students were brought to the school after being removed from their families when they were about six years of age, and remained in residence until they were about 12 years old.

The residential school system in Canada was more about inculcating or indoctrinating European-based Christian values into the members of Indigenous societies than it was solely about providing a sound educational system that would be comparable to other schools in the country.

As indicated in one assessment, "The function and intent behind the residential school system cohered with the assimilation objectives of the *Indian Act* (1876), the legislative framework that structures, even now, the state's relationship to Indigenous people in Canada. The residential school system was founded on the assumption that Western European ways of living and knowing were superior to Indigenous lifestyles. And, in order for colonization to work, Indigenous peoples' attachment to their land and culture had to be broken down and replaced with European values, beliefs, and practices" (Te Hiwi and Forsyth 2017: 83).

Thus, there was a direct connection between the sports that were played by the Indigenous students in residential schools and the assimilative agenda pursued by those holding power in the wider Euro-Canadian society. This connection between sport and colonization was clearly indicated in the final report of the Truth and Reconciliation Commission of Canada.

An important conclusion, then, is that "Sport is never about sport alone; rather, it is a visible expression of the unequal power relations that structures the relationships between different groups of people. Within the context of the Indian residential school system, sport became the vehicle through which those unequal relations were reinforced" (Ibid: 83). Thus, the residential school system was instituted as an important component of the colonization process, with the intent of accelerating the assimilation of Indigenous peoples, soon after the Canadian Confederation in 1867.

Political leaders in government, collaborated with church leaders and federal policy-makers by instituting a program of integration. The program focused on Indigenous youth by separating them from their families and thereby circumventing the transmission of cultural and social practices in the children's home communities.

However, this abrupt separation caused increased trauma for the Indigenous children, especially in light of the abusive treatment of the children. In turn, Indigenous students often resisted this abusive behavior by fleeing the residential schools, or otherwise, pushing back on the abuse and regimentation that they were forced to suffer through.

Further, compliance with the rules of behavior at residential schools was reinforced through physical education involving calisthenics, gymnastics, and forms of military drills which were designed to instill respect for the authority figures at the residential schools. However, sports teams such as the Black Hawks at the Pelican Lake School were still relatively uncommon until the 1950s.

By this time, an institutional change was taking place in terms of governmental policies toward Indigenous communities in that the focus began to shift from assimilation (instilling Euro-Canadian social and cultural practices in Indigenous communities) to integration (drawing Indigenous people into the realm of Canadian citizenship). In this regard, sports programs became one of the vehicles by which policy-makers attempted to encourage citizenship training for Indigenous Canadians (see Forsyth and Heine 2008).

As early as 1945, Indian Agent Gifford Swartman complained about the lack of recreational facilities at the Pelican Lake School. He promoted the idea that Indigenous boys had a natural preference for sporting activities, and on this basis, increased recreational activities should be encouraged.

It was not long after that a skating rink was constructed at Pelican Lake and a number of skate blades were purchased. However, finding funding for suitable boots to which the skate blades could be attached was an issue. At the Pelican Lake School, one of the administrators even got himself in trouble with the authorities in Ottawa because he unofficially loaned the school a trailer for carrying canoes and tried to obtain a replacement for it later.

"Bureaucratic rigidities," Miller (1996: 274–275) explained, "bull-headedness and downright stupidity on the part of Indian Affairs frequently frustrated administrators who tried to provide their school's children with amenities."

In terms of the main activities at the school, when Pelican Lake first opened, the students would only spend the first half of the day actually learning their lessons in the classroom. Then, in the latter half of the day, engaging in general labor about the school grounds. In these activities, there was a certain division of labor based on gender with the boys engaging in such tasks as carpentry, and the girls engaged in such domestic tasks as laundry and cooking.

As Miller (1996: 172) explains, "In exceptional circumstances, residential school children did not even spend half a day in the classroom. The boy who had the distinction of holding the number 1 at Pelican Lake Anglican School near Sioux Lookout, Ontario, recalled that he was only in the class during the first two of his eight years of attendance. After that, he claimed, 'I didn't do school at all'. He was an unpaid, full-time worker around the school for six years. It was not uncommon for principals desperate for help that would keep the school running to retain older students longer than necessary simply for the work they could do."

It was not until the beginning of 1947, that the school began a transition to a full-time educational agenda. As far as the conditions of the school were concerned, even the Anglican Church admitted that they were poor by most standards. As with many residential schools, Pelican Lake suffered from various deficiencies, such as underfunding, low staff retention, and overcrowding.

It appears also that, at the administrative level, the school suffered from poor coordination of policy directives as there were no less than five school principals from the years 1945 to 1951. Included in this group were a combination of Anglican Church ministers and non-sectarian principals.

They suggest that there could be conflicts in the school's policies on a year-to-year basis, as religious and non-religious directives jostled back and forth on a yearly basis. In 1948, as an example, an inspection of the Pelican Lake School noted that the buildings were in a deplorable state of untidiness. In addition, livestock apparently were free to roam freely about the school grounds which resulted in the existence of manure all over the place. As far as student behavior was concerned, the boys especially were described as terribly out of hand.

73

Even at meal time, stragglers frequently entered the dining hall late and several students were seen wearing their caps. The responsibility for these disciplinary deficiencies was squarely placed on the shoulders of the principal, John Evens, who was accused of definitely not exercising proper control over the children, as well as some of the staff.

Eventually, Evans was replaced with an Anglican Church minister, Reverend Wickenden, who apparently also had little success in promoting discipline among the school students. All of this was blamed on the lack of sufficient resources that were provided by the Indian Affairs administration; rather than see the poor affairs at the Pelican Lake School as part of a wider trend in the Anglican school system.

However, it was evident that such schools were operated in a manner that was hardly a credit to the Anglican Church. In fact, there were calls for the Pelican Lake School to be disbanded or scrapped altogether. Yet, as one Anglican Bishop argued, such an approach was ill-advised because the, "consequences of closing such a school [as Pelican Lake] or withdrawing from the existing partnership would deprive many of our Indian children of an opportunity for education under church auspices and open the door for uncontrollable influences over a wide region" (Te Hiwi and Forsyth 2017: 91).

Clearly, Anglican Church officials were struggling to maintain control over the residential school system. However, rather than attempting to improve standards of care and education for the school children at Pelican Lake, instead, church officials adhered to the argument that the culprit for the disturbing lower standards of clothing and feeding of children at the residential school was solely the fault of the Indian Affairs administration because of their "penny-pinching" policies (ibid).

It is difficult at this point in time to attribute the poor state of the Pelican School only to the financial policies of Indian Affairs. As far as the administrators of the Anglican church were concerned, the one area of fault that they would admit to was the decision made by the school's principals who were replaced almost on an annual basis. Of course, such a turnover at the top of the school's administration would certainly cause turmoil within the school itself because there would be a lack of consistency in school policies when each new principal took the helm of the school's administrative structure.

During certain time periods, an emphasis on regular routines of menial work took precedence over academic pursuits as the school struggled to maintain its activities operational. As an example, the boys were often involved in various forms of outdoor work such as farming activities and general repairs about the school while the girls engaged in kitchen work, such as cooking meals for the students, laundry, and general cleaning. Of course, the school itself was not the only building needing attention and maintenance as there were barns to house the livestock and various other sheds and associated structures.

Given that the school finances often did not allow for many outside adult workers, school children were forced into supplying the needed physical labor requirements, even though this time requirement probably detracted from the time the students spent engaging in educational instruction.

From the school administrators' perspective, the sorts of menial labor that the children provided and upon which the school depended was rationalized as providing a basis for the life skills that the students would require when they engaged in adult occupations later in life. In addition, prayers and religious education were also consistent features of school life which, as with the menial labor tasks, drew students away from the pursuit of educational objectives.

Meal times were also another problematic and contentious issue. "Anglican staff at the Pelican Lake School...responded viciously when a number of their students complained to their parents about feeling hungry after meals" (Miller 1996: 294).

When the parents took the students' complaints to the Indian Affairs office in Sioux Lookout, the matter was then passed on to the school authorities, who no doubt resented the criticism. Soon, after the school principal came to the girls' common room and asked all who said they were hungry to put their hands up, which most girls did.

The kitchen staff then wheeled a large cart into the room which was filled with bread. The students who had raised their hands were then required to consume the bread without any beverages. Then, another trolley filled with bread which was coated with jam, honey, and peanut butter was also wheeled into the room for the minority of the girls who had not complained to consume in front of the others. One student recalled that, such incidences "hurt very much, and that sure cured to not complain about being hungry" (ibid: 294). "Such sadistic measures," Miller (1996: 295) asserted, "might silence student objections, but they could not still hunger pangs in young people's stomachs."

Apparently, such mistreatment of Pelican Lake students was a common occurrence which on occasion led to abused students running away from the school. As an example, in the late 1940s, a runaway girl was later apprehended. Here, the punishment was one hundred blows with the strap. She also had her hair cut off with garden shears by the principal. Then her head was subsequently shaved (ibid: 324).

It was also later reported that some female students at the school were sexually and physically abused by other girls. "The girls' dormitory had effectively been run by a ring of bigger girls who followed the instructions of one particularly brutal female" (ibid: 336).

In this regard, the introduction of sporting activities provided a welcome diversion from the abuse that some students were experiencing at the school. As time went on, attention to the physical education of the students began to take precedence over the simple labor tasks; an emphasis that coincided with the disciplinary nature of residential schooling.

In general, there was little room for self-expression as far as the various drills and calisthenics were concerned which also tended to reinforce an emphasis on obedience to authority figures as instructors shouted out the appropriate commands for the exercises involved. In turn, the students moved in unison during these drills, much like the movements in military maneuvers.

Thus, an emphasis on sports, such as hockey, tended to reinforce the regimented and discipline-based lifestyle among the various students involved. Although teams such as the Black Hawks at the Pelican Lake School were a relative rarity during the early 1950s it was nonetheless an example of the federal government's efforts to expand Indigenous sport and recreation in Canada.

As such, the federal government, via the Indian Affairs Department, "sought to develop a more organized system of physical education by directly supporting school administrators and broadening the range of physical activities they offered to include play, games, and sport that, up to this point in time, were provided in an ad hoc fashion, usually out of interest by someone working at the school. The rapid expansion of residential school sports teams across the country became a critical extension of the new policy emphasis on integration" (Te Hiwi and Forsyth 2017: 85).

The renewed focus on physical education in residential schools was a strategic initiative by the Anglican Church and the federal government, aimed at advancing their civilizing agenda. This effort sought to systematically eradicate Indigenous cultures and social systems while simultaneously instilling Euro-Canadian religious and social values in the next generation of residential school students.

All in all, it would be fair to say that the term "submissive obedience" was an accurate characterization of both the Anglican Church and the federal government's use of sports and physical education to promote their wider agenda of social integration and "fitting into" Canadian society.

In a further attempt to improve the conditions of the Pelican Lake School, in 1946, the General Synod of the Anglican Church set up a special task force to investigate the situation, termed the Indian Work Investigation Commission in an effort to both review and hopefully raise the poor conditions in its schools. Later, after a three-year investigation, it was recommended that the Pelican Lake School be closed because the task force arrived at the conclusion that the school was operating under substandard conditions.

A cynical mind would suggest that the authorities of the Anglican Church never intended to conduct any meaningful ameliorative measures to improve the school conditions. But only used the Investigative Commission as a stop-gap measure to blunt the criticisms and divert attention away from the dreadful plight of the Indigenous children.

To the detriment of the students attending the school at the time, the Anglican Bishop successfully petitioned to keep the school going in full operation. It took another 40 years, however, for the Pelican Lake residential school to close in 1969 largely because of the substandard educational and living conditions that the Indigenous children had to endure. Also, another reason for the school closure was because of the mounting criticism leveled at the Anglican Church because of the charges of pervasive sexual and physical abuse that was largely ignored by the Anglican authorities at the time.

Eventually, there were lawsuits resulting from these reports of abuse. A number of former Pelican Lake students described the physical, psychological, and sexual abuse that they suffered at the school at the hands of the teachers and religious authorities in charge of the school at the time. According to an investigation into the conditions of the Pelican Lake School published in the *Canadian Journal of History* (Te Hiwi and Forsyth 2017), the physical abuse took the form of poor living conditions and corporal punishment when a student spoke their traditional language.

There were also times when students were prevented from attending classes at the school and instead were forced to engage in physical labor about the grounds. There were also instances of psychological abuse that first started when Indigenous children were taken away from their families and communities of origin.

Within the school, the abuse continued when children suffered public humiliation for wetting their beds, in addition to the sexual abuse inflicted upon them. All in all, over a dozen students reported that as a result of the actions of the Pelican Lake teachers, religious authorities, and other school staff they were the victims of sexual assault while they attended the school.

In reference to these reports of abuse at the Pelican Lake School, it has been indicated that "Discipline and regimentation in the pursuit of cultural change was a key feature of residential school life, so much so, that the strictness and severity of the discipline imposed by staff became abusive in many schools. [There were incidences] where the principal would lock up disobedient children, sometimes for days on end. Public humiliation, such as requiring students who wet their beds to wear their soiled sheets around at school, was another common method of exacting compliance. Such methods speak to a cruel indifference toward an already vulnerable population" (Te Hiwi and Forsyth 2017: 84).

Eventually, in 1996, an Anglican priest named Leonard Hands was charged with 19 counts of indecent assault resulting from his employment at the school during the 1960s. Hands was sentenced to four years in prison as a result of these charges which were initiated by Garnet Angeconeb, who was invested in the Order of Canada (see *Windspeaker* 2016). Thus far, Hands was the only person held criminally responsible for the abuse at the Pelican Lake School.

Sioux Black Hawks Hockey Team

1. Mr. Wilson 2. Frank Wesley 3. George Carpenter 4. Kelly Bull 5. Johnny
Yesno 6. Bishop Jefferson
Location: Ottawa 1951

Source: Anglican General Synod, Archives of Ontario, Toronto

Johnny Yesno (#5 in the accompanying photo) played for the Black Hawks
hockey team in 1951 when the members toured Ottawa, Toronto, and several
other Ontario locations. The goal of the hockey program was to facilitate
assimilating Indigenous students into the larger society. Thus, serving to
eliminate as much as possible the student's cultural background and familial
ties.

The hockey program was initiated by Gifford Swartman, the Indian
Agency's Superintendent. An outdoor rink was constructed. Local businesses
provided hockey equipment for the players. And after several years of practice
against teams in the Sioux Lookout and District Bantam League, the Black
Hawks team began to win their games.

As a result of their winning ways in the local competitions, in the spring of 1951, the Department of Indian Affairs financed a tour of Southern Ontario for the team. As an article in the *Toronto Star* (17 April 1951) by Gordon Campell indicated, the tour was "better than five years in school" according to the team's coach.

During the trip, team members met with the Premier of Ontario and the Governor General of Canada. Aside from using sports as a means of achieving discipline, "government officials and church administrators leveraged the team's success and growing media coverage as a useful public relations tool to promote the success of residential schooling to the Canadian public" (Te Hiwi and Forsyth 2017: 80).

A remarkable aspect of the Black Hawks hockey team was that none of the players on the team knew how to skate when the team was formed. Despite this setback, one of the fellows on the team, named Chris Cromarty said, "We were sneaking down at four in the morning…just to skate around the rink and play hockey" (Te Hiwi 2021: 99).

Tryouts for the Black Hawks hockey team began on the new school rink in December of 1948. None of the boys had sticks or skates which were, eventually, supplied by a grant from Indian Affairs and donations from local citizens. Even though none of the team members knew how to skate when they joined the team, their coach reported that within a few days, a dozen boys could skate the length of the rink without falling down.

By January 1949, a mere two months after the team was formed, their first game was scheduled to take place at the Sioux Lookout Memorial rink. Their coach was Peter Seymour, an Indigenous school staff member. Coach Seymour, himself, was a graduate of St. Mary's Indian Residential School. So he had a first-hand knowledge of the trials and tribulations suffered by the boys as a result of life at a residential school.

The Black Hawks were initially entered as a bantam-aged team in the Sioux Lookout and District Hockey League. During the first competitive year of 1948–49, the players improved steadily, although they did not stand out as a team in this first year of competition. However, by the second year (1949–50) of play it was obvious that the players had sharpened their hockey skills considerably.

The Black Hawks began their second year playing an exhibition game against the older midget team from Sioux Lookout winning 3-1. In fact, during this second season, the Black Hawks team only allowed 14 goals in 13 games which was an auspicious start for things to come. On their way to winning the Sioux Lookout and District Championship that year, they lost only one game.

This was a remarkable feat, considering that just a mere one year earlier few of the players could skate the length of a rink without falling down. It cannot be ascertained with any degree of certainty when Johnny Yesno began playing for the Black Hawks, however, the photo taken in 1951 would mean that during that year he would have been 12 or 13 years old depending upon the month that the picture was taken.

However, in March of 1950, an article appeared in the local Sioux Lookout newspaper, *The Daily Bulletin*, describing the success and style of play of the Black Hawks which accounted for their winning ways:

"Monday night at the local arena the Indian Residential School Black Hawks played a brand of hockey never before seen by local fans so far this season. The Hawks thoroughly shellacked an oversized Hudson team by a 6-1 score. The arena was really packed at last night's encounter and there was never a dull moment during the fast, hard-hitting game put on by both clubs.

The last time these two teams met the Hawks were edged out by Hudson 3-2, but there was no doubt in anyone's mind as to who played a superior brand of hockey last night and the Hawks really deserve credit for their fine win" (quoted in Te Hiwi and Forsyth 2017: 94).

After winning the Sioux Lookout Championship, the Black Hawks then traveled across northern Ontario to play the highly rated Geraldton bantam team for the Thunder Bay District Championship. The Black Hawks were victorious in this series beating the Geraldton team in three straight games.

The Black Hawks's success, however, exposed a controversy between the Indian Affair Department which tended to take credit for the hockey team's achievements; to the neglect of the Anglican Church principals and staff. It was later revealed that Indian Agent Swartman and Anglican Principal Wilson did not cooperate very well. As an example, the 1949–50 Black Hawks team photo included Indian Affairs personnel but not Wilson.

However, it is only fair to indicate that the 1951 Black Hawks team photo taken in Ottawa in which Johnny Yesno appeared included both a smiling Rev. Wilson and Anglican Bishop Jefferson. Eventually, these difficulties were resolved in an amicable manner with credit for the Black Hawk's success given to both parties.

In April of 1951, a tour was arranged for the Black Hawks team with two games to be played in Ottawa and one in Toronto. The team now had a new coach named Johnny McDonald who was a former NHL player, a move which, of course, brought further prestige to the team.

In what is now Thunder Bay, the Fort William [Thunder Bay] *Daily Times Journal* (19 February 1951) reported on the Black Hawk players' superior hockey skills, "reaction to the famous All-Indian team was unanimously favorable. [The players] showed unusual skating, stick-handling, and shooting ability and were even more conspicuous for their fine positional play."

In another Thunder Bay newspaper account, the Port Arthur [Thunder Bay] *News Chronicle* (21 February 1951) sports editor named Dick Elliot reported that the Black Hawks played a brand of hockey reminiscent of a bygone era:

"The old timers who ask, what is wrong with hockey today, undoubtedly would have taken heart had they watched the bewitching All-Indian bantams from Sioux Lookout. To our way of thinking, those brown-skinned young artists from the north could do more for the prestige of Canada's national game than any meticulously selected bunch of adults you could name, professional or amateur. Sure, why not send such a team on a world cruise?

They'd set Britain and the continent agog with their fine interpretation of a game that for years now has been moving steadily toward the same classification as professional wrestling. And the kids proved, moreover, that there is nothing wrong with hockey today that can't be cured, that two of the fundamentals of the game—playing the puck and position—still are profitable as well as pleasant to the eye."

The Black Hawks's remarkable style of play was a regular feature of the Ontario press by the early 1950s. As an example, a journalist for the Fort William *Daily Times Journal* (19 February 1951) reported that "the crowd's reaction to the famous All-Indian team was unanimously favorable," and went on to note that, "the team showed unusual skating, stick-handling and shooting ability and even more conspicuous for the fine positional play."

Another reporter, in the same article, noted that "the team players were noted for sticking to their positions at all times," and that "the Hawks drew repeated applause from delighted spectators with their accurate passing plays, particularly when breaking up gang attacks by the opposition."

It was becoming obvious that the Black Hawks hockey team was attracting attention across the hockey world with their basic brand of playing the puck and positional play. According to Dick Elliot, it was more reminiscent of hockey played years ago rather than today's style which appeared more like professional wrestling. Thus, the Black Hawk players were receiving praise from far and wide for their remarkable style of play and were considered a credit to the success of Indigenous sports, rather than a magnet for racist tropes common at the time.

In fact, one letter to the editor extolled the prestige of the Black Hawks team, noting, "You don't see any of the white kids playing like that. Honestly, there was more hockey played in that kid game than you would see in Junior or Senior games…It was amazing to see such tots holding up their heads while stick-handling to make sure of their passing and to see where their opponents were. It's hard to realize they have such stick-handling and skating ability after a couple of seasons of play" (Te Hiwi and Forsyth 2017:99).

The Southern Ontario tour included trips to Toronto and Ottawa. The tour consisted of three games, one game each against the East Browns and Combines of Ottawa and one game against Shopsy's of Toronto. It is hard to imagine a less likely transition for the Black Hawk players, from their seasonal rinks constructed of salvaged lumber situated in the back woods of northern Ontario, to Ottawa's Auditorium, and Toronto Maple Leaf Gardens. In addition, one of the referees for the games was hockey great Lionel Conacher (who was voted Canada's top athlete in the first half of the 20th-century).

The Black Hawks split their series with Ottawa, as reported in the *Hockey News* (28 April 1951), "Twelve Little Indians Take Ottawa by Storm During Peaceful Foray."

Media coverage of the games even reached as far as the Prairies in which an article in the *Saskatoon Star-Phoenix* (April 1951) commented on the gentlemanly conduct of the Black Hawks players, noting that "there was no rough-house or angry words. Just clean play, goodwill all around, and smiles…the Black Hawks went about their chores in a business-like manner even if they did pin defeat on the Browns. They made it painless by presenting their opponents with lacrosse sticks as a token of friendship between the second and third periods."

The Ottawa *Evening Citizen* (17 April 1951) commented on the viewer enjoyment provided by the Black Hawk's style of play, as "hockey fans who passed up the show missed a fast, clean match that thrilled the spectators from start to finish." After the Ottawa series, the Black Hawks teams traveled to Toronto to play at the celebrated Maple Leaf Gardens. Although they lost the one game played to the Shopsy's team, media coverage in the Toronto news media commented on the more gentlemanly play of the Black Hawk players in contrast to the competitively driven Toronto team members.

However, in an article in the *Toronto Telegram* (4 July 1951), it would appear that the Black Hawk team players lent a more "civil approach" to the home team as well. As noted in the Toronto newspaper, "Players for the Shopsy's team tended to play without their normal aggressive edge; the Toronto team was not playing as rough as they or any local minor club can. Normally an aggressive outfit. They played this one clean on the sportsmanlike instruction of Coach Oscar Brooks and Manager Jack Humphreys. Even at that, they absorbed all six penalities."

"Even though they were still on the losing end of the score, they never lost even part of their determination. Though four goals behind in the period's dying moments, they were still playing with everything in their command. Still, they weren't rough. In fact, they were given no penalties, compared to five issued to the Toronto team."

Indian Affairs was another winner, since, from a publicity point of view, the press coverage of the Black Hawks' sportsmanlike play tended to validate the department's efforts to use sport to develop good character among residential school students. As such, what happened off the ice, from a publicity point of view, was an equally if not more important aspect of the Black Hawks' hockey tour of Southern Ontario.

Nonetheless, there were still unfortunate racist overtones expressed in the press coverage of the hockey tour, as this headline in the *Toronto Telegram* (4 July 1951) indicated, "All-Indian Team on Ice Warpath: Bantams from Sioux Lookout on Lookout for Scalps." Yet, no matter how well the Black Hawks played, or however much they played according to prevailing standards of gentlemanly conduct, Te Hiwi and Forsyth (2017: 101) concluded, "They could not escape the racist undertones that permeated newspaper reports."

Johnny Yesno's Experience

One can only speculate on Johnny Yesno's experience with the Black Hawks hockey team's success. Certainly, there would be very few if any of the Black Hawk players from the most isolated regions of northern Ontario who would have experienced the positive accolades that his hockey team brought to the Pelican Lake Residential School.

Nor would any of the hockey players have met such famous hockey players as Montreal Canadian superstar Maurice "Rocket" Richard who mingled with the boys, signed autographs, and even refereed one of their games. Later, at Toronto's Maple Leaf Gardens, the players met hockey great Lionel Conacher; a member of Hockey's Hall of Fame and member of parliament who refereed one of the Black Hawk's games.

Then there was the wide array of important political leaders who took a shine to the team, such as the Kenora Member of Parliament who led the boys on a guided tour of the House of Commons. Other dignitaries who took an interest in the Black Hawk players also included Governor General Alexander. In Toronto, the Black Hawks were taken on a guided tour of Queen's Park where they met the Premier of Ontario, Leslie Frost.

When the tour was over, the Black Hawks players returned to their daily routine of religious instruction, morning and nightly prayers, and hard physical work at the residential school. The school authorities took pleasure in suggesting that the hockey program resulted in more cheerful and respectful students.

As indicated in a report by Fred Matters, Regional Supervisor of Indian Affairs, "Generally speaking, the condition of the [Pelican Lake] school has further improved since my last visit…Part of this can be credited to the work of the principal and the staff, also in large measure to the spirit that has been developed through sports, mainly hockey" (Te Hiwi and Forsyth 2017:104).

If there was one issue that stood out regarding the success of the Black Hawks hockey team, it was that this achievement tended to be regarded by the Indian Affairs and religious authorities as demonstrating the goals of the residential school system in general, which is to say, the important goals of assimilation.

As Te Hiwi and Forsyth (2017: 83) suggest, "Within the context of the Indian residential school system, sport became the vehicle through which those unequal relations were reinforced." In other words, "Sport is never about sport alone; rather, it is a visible expression of the unequal relations between different groups of people" (ibid).

The residential school system itself was in tune with the assimilationist objectives of the *Indian Act* (1876) itself. In turn, the assimilationist objectives of both the residential school system and the *Indian Act* were founded on the assumption that Western European societies were superior to Indigenous lifestyles.

Thus, in order for colonization to be an effective strategy, the attachment that Indigenous people had to their land and culture had to be terminated and replaced with European values and beliefs. We can only presume, then, that students such as Johnny Yesno, while no doubt enjoying the notoriety of his hockey team's success were likely to rebel against the regimentation; the strictness and severity of the discipline imposed by the school staff, and wider colonial objectives of residential school life.

Add to this also the public humiliation imposed on recalcitrant students and other methods of exacting compliance. One can understand the desire to rebel and escape from such repressive conditions, leading to the unfortunate fate of students such as Charlie Wenjack. Johnny Yesno would no doubt know his story all too well.

Shingwauk Residential School

Shingwauk Indian Residential School of Sault Ste. Marie Ontario was operated between 1873 and 1970 by the Anglican Church of Canada and the Canadian Government. The school had its origins in the 1830s when Chief Shingwauk petitioned Governor John Colborne to help provide resources for a so-called "Teaching Wigwam" in his home community of nearby Garden River.

Initially, in 1833, an Anglican missionary named William McMurray arrived in the Garden River First Nation with the result that a day mission was constructed in Sault Ste. Marie. Later, in 1873, the Shingwauk Industrial Home was built but was destroyed by fire after only six days of operation. Over the years, various other constructions followed, and by the 1880s, accommodations were provided for female students as well (Miller 1996).

In 1935, a new residential school was opened on the Shingwauk site. This new building was designed to house 140 students and contained such modern (for the time) conveniences as running water and electricity which the previous buildings did not have. In 1970, the Shingwauk school was closed by the Department of Indian Affairs.

Today, Shingwauk Hall forms the central building of Algoma University. A controversial aspect of Shingwauk's history is the Shingwauk Memorial Cemetery, which contains the graves of over 120 students and staff. It also contains many unmarked graves, which resulted from the use of wooden crosses before the use of stone headstones. Another controversial aspect of the cemetery is that an adjoining farm contains the graves of Shingwauk students, but their exact number is unknown.

As with many other residential schools in Canada, Indigenous students only attended classes for part of the day and were forced to engage in manual labor around the school for the other half of the day. As a general rule, the living conditions of the residential students have been determined to be poor and the quality of the education that the students received was seen as below that of other schools. There were also many cases later reported of neglect and abuse as well as the detrimental effects of the impacts of the forced assimilation process (for further information see Miller 1996; *CBC News* 9 July 2021).

Johnny's father, John Cooper Yesno, upon hearing that the headmaster at the Pelican Lake School had ordered that Johnny's head would be shaved stepped in and transferred his son to the Shingwauk Residential School in Sault Ste. Marie. A reporter for the *Windspeaker* (1 September 2010) magazine, Dianne Meili, suggested that "The transfer was good for the young boy because institution staff treated students better than those at the Pelican Residential School. At Shingwauk, the individuals really tried to help and support the students make their transition into the fast-changing white world. Johnny outdid himself in his new placement and proved to doubters that he could be academically successful." As an example, in grade 12, he was awarded an academic scholarship which allowed Johnny to enroll in the engineering department at the University of Waterloo.

Residential School Update

The Indigenous people of northern Ontario certainly have not forgotten the horrific abuses brought on them by the residential school system, but just retribution has been slow to emerge. However, Molly Hayes, a reporter for the Toronto *Globe and Mail* (12 October 2023) has written an article entitled "97-year-old nun charged with historical sexual assaults at residential schools," which details various criminal acts inflicted upon Indigenous students in the 1960–1970 period.

St. Anne's Indian Residential School was located in Fort Albany, Ontario, and operated from 1902 to 1976. It took Indigenous students primarily from the Fort Albany First Nation and the surrounding area. Many students reported physical, psychological, and sexual abuse, and 156 settled a lawsuit against the federal government in 2004.

Conclusion

The most significant point that could be made concerning Johnny Yesno's early life is that when he was removed from his community of origin at Fort Hope, and brought to the residential school at Pelican Lake in Sioux Lookout, he was put under significant assimilative pressure from this experience. He was also invariably removed from the culture, social patterns, and language that he was initially born into which provided a supportive lifestyle for his existence.

Not only was he removed from the cultural setting of his home community at an early age, but the residential schools were repressive institutions in which the teachers and other personnel worked to suppress a student's Indigenous background. This situation, in which young Indigenous persons were cut off from the supportive institutions of their home communities, and subsequently forced to adhere to the norms and values of an alien European-based social and cultural system; would no doubt have created a sense of confusion in the minds of the residential school students.

In sociology and cultural studies, the term "cultural dissonance" is used to describe situations in which a person experiences a sense of confusion over their place in society. "Cultural dissonance" describes a person's sense of discord, disharmony, confusion, or conflict, which is experienced by people in the midst of change in their social and cultural environment in which new norms and values are expected.

Research topics which focus on cultural dissonance tend to be interdisciplinary in nature, drawing from a wide range of disciplines and applying the findings to equally diverse fields and industries. As an example, studies into cultural dissonance take on a wide socio-cultural scope of analysis that delves into a wide range of topics such as economics, politics, values, learning styles, and cultural factors, such as language, tradition, ethnicity, cultural heritage, and especially educational formats and content.

An illustrative example cited in the social science literature involves Navajo police officers who are forced to implement European-based laws that could be in conflict with those practiced in the Navajo communities themselves (Gould 2002). In these cases, the Indigenous police officer could be seen as an agent for the outside, larger Euro-American society, and this situation could cause mixed expectations in the officer's role performance. A similar example of cultural dissonance could refer to the elected officials on Canadian reserves in which the role performance of these officials might be seen to conflict with traditional leaders and their values (Hedican 1991).

In the field of psychology, cognitive dissonance is described as the mental discomfort people feel when their beliefs and actions are inconsistent and contradictory, ultimately encouraging some change (often either in their beliefs or actions) to align better and reduce this dissonance (Harmon-Jones 2019). Relevant items of information include peoples' actions, feelings, ideas, beliefs, values, and things in the environment. Cognitive dissonance is typically experienced as psychological stress when persons participate in an action that goes against one or more of those things.

According to this theory, when an action or idea is psychologically inconsistent with the other, people will do all in their power to change either, so that they become consistent. The distress is triggered by the person's beliefs clashing with new information perceived, wherein the individual tries to find a way to resolve the contradiction in order to reduce their stress and mental discomfort.

Perhaps, the only mitigating factor in Johnny Yesno's residential school experience was the unexpected success of the Pelican Lake School hockey team. Given that most of the boys started their hockey experience without even knowing how to skate, their accomplishments were quite praiseworthy, to say the least. No doubt the hockey team's success on the rink was a welcome distraction for the school officials and diverted a focus on the otherwise scornful treatment of the non-hockey students.

As Hiwi and Forsyth so aptly remarked, "Of importance beyond the school, government officials and church administrators leveraged the team's success and glowing media coverage as a useful public relations tool to promote the success of residential schooling to the Canadian public" (2017: 80).

Remember, also, that Johnny Yesno did attempt an escape from the Pelican Lake School, so he was probably not entirely enamored with his overall experience there. Later, this escape attempt was made into a film called *Cold Journey*, which illustrated the impact of the residential school experience on his life, whereas he never made a film about his residential school hockey career.

Chapter Four
Social Change-Oriented Media

When Johnny Yesno began his film career in the mid-1960s, he already had a number of notable Indigenous actors, such as Jay Silverheels, Gordon Tootoosis, and Chief Dan George, whom he could use as role models. The 1960s, was also a time when significant changes were occurring in the film industry which was to transform the industry in later years. One of these programs, *Challenge for Change*, is the principal subject of this chapter.

One of the most significant developments in the Indigenous film industry was that the goal of many movies was less about entertaining the viewer. It was more about illustrating certain themes that affected Indigenous people at the time, such as buttressing colonial pressures, pointing to the negative aspects of residential schools, forced assimilation into Euro-Canadian society, and challenging Hollywood stereotypes. In other words, there was a certain "hidden agenda" at work in the Indigenous film industry, that was designed to enlighten those in the general public about the negative aspects of the Native experience in North American society.

Challenge for Change

Challenge for Change was a participatory film and video project created by the National Film Board of Canada in 1967, the Canadian Centennial. Active until 1980, *Challenge for Change* used film and video production to illuminate the social concerns of various communities within Canada, with funding from eight different departments of the Canadian government.

The impetus for the program was the belief that film and video were useful tools for initiating social change and eliminating poverty (Schugurensky 2005). As Druik says, "The new program, which was developed in tandem with the new social policies, was based on the argument that participation in media projects could empower disenfranchised groups and that media representation might effectively bring about improved political representation" (2010: 140). Furthermore, Stewart asserts that "the Challenge for Change films would convey messages from *the people* (particularly disadvantaged groups) to the government, directly or through the Canadian public" (2007: 49; see also Jones 1981).

The *Challenge for Change* program was designed to give voice to the *voiceless*. A key aspect of *Challenge for Change* was the transfer of control over the filmmaking process from professional filmmakers to community members, so that, ordinary Canadians in underrepresented communities could tell their own stories on-screen. Community dialogue and government responses to the issues were crucial to the program and took precedence over the quality of the films produced. In total, the program would lead to the creation of over 200 films and videos. Approximately 145 works in English and more than 60 in French (Waugh et. al. 2010; Watson 1977).

The activist documentary program *Challenge for Change*, which ran from 1967 to 1980, stands out as a particularly influential and original part of the National Film Board of Canada's critically acclaimed body of work. The films produced by this program were among the first to add portable video to the tested arsenal of 16 mm. It also challenged audiences, subjects, and filmmakers to confront sexism, poverty, and marginalization in the hope of developing community as well as political awareness and empowerment.

Pioneering participatory, social change-oriented media, the program had a national and international impact on documentary filmmaking. The first comprehensive history and analysis of its work was the publication of T. Waugh, M.B. Baker, and E. Winton's *Challenge for Change: Activist Documentary at the National Film Board of Canada* (2010).

The volume's contributors studied dozens of films produced by the program, their themes, aesthetics, and politics. It also evaluated their legacy and the program's place in Canadian, Québécois, and world cinema. An informative and nuanced look at a cinematic movement; *Challenge for Change* reemphasizes not just the importance of the NFB and its programs, but also, the role documentaries can play in improving the world.

Indigenous Film Making in Canada

The National Film Board of Canada (NFB) has been producing works about Indigenous lives and experiences since the early 1940s, but for the first three decades of the NFB's existence Indigenous people were restricted to being subjects in films by non-Indigenous directors.

It was not until the late 1960s when *Challenge for Change* ushered in a radical new participatory approach to production, that Indigenous people began putting their own stories on film. Since that time, the NFB has produced over 280 works by First Nations, Métis, and Inuit directors. At various times, there have been more than 20 projects by Indigenous directors that are underway at the NFB's studios across Canada.

Recently, Indigenous production has represented 9.5% of overall production spending at the NFB. These gains, however, were hard-won. The struggle of Indigenous people within the NFB mirrors broader social, and political struggles to confront Canada's legacy of internal colonialism and the long, repressive shadow cast by the 1876 Indian Act.

Indigenous media challenges the power of the state erodes communication monopolies and highlights government threats to Indigenous cultural, social, economic, and political sovereignty. Its effectiveness in these areas, however, is hampered by government control of broadcast frequencies, licensing, and legal limitations over content and ownership.

One of the most significant of these works, *Indigenous Screen Cultures in Canada* (Hafsteinsson and Bredin 2010), explores key questions surrounding the power and suppression of Indigenous narratives and representation in contemporary Indigenous media. Focusing primarily on the Aboriginal Peoples Television Network (APTN), the authors also examine Indigenous language broadcasting in radio, television, and film.

This publication also focuses on Aboriginal journalism practices, audience creation within and beyond Indigenous communities, the roles of program scheduling and content acquisition policies in the decolonization process, the roles of digital video technologies and co-production agreements in Indigenous filmmaking; and the emergence of Aboriginal cyber-communities.

As Bruyere (2010) indicates in *Choice Magazine*, "This is one of the first books to deal specifically with contemporary programming practices and content emerging from Aboriginal Canadian media organizations, primarily the Aboriginal Peoples Television Network (APTN)." This article continues its' assessment that "the book's key contribution is to present specific cases that show how mass media permit local instances of increased cultural and social agency among Indigenous groups and how Aboriginal media producers conceive of traditional knowledge, languages, and practices as vehicles of modern culture within a global mediascape."

Another important work that provides a critical overview of the portrayal of Indigenous people in Canada's film and television industry concerns Mary Jane Miller's (2008) *Outside Looking In: Viewing First Nations People in Canadian Dramatic Television Series* which was published by McGill-Queen's Indigenous and Northern series. In her introduction to the topic, Miller explains:

"The way they are framed [portrayals of Indigenous people in the media] change over time; the context provided by financial arrangements, by other programs, and by reviewers in magazines and newspapers shapes both the programs and viewers' perceptions of the programs" (2008: 4).

In another related publication, Hilger's (1995) *From Savage to Nobleman*, focuses on Native American characters and gives a unique perspective for understanding stereotypes and the interplay of racism, sympathy, and empathy in the historical periods of narrative film. In this study, Hilger traces the portrayal of Native Americans, from the silents and early sound films through films of each decade which provides a useful overview over various time periods. Each of the historical chapters begins with detailed interpretations of representative films such as *The Vanishing American, They Died with Their Boots On, Cheyenne Autumn,* and *Dances with Wolves.*

Another relevant publication is Rollins and O'Connor's (2003) *Hollywood's Indian: The Portrayal of Native Americans in Film.* As the authors explain in their introduction:

"The image of the American Indian, more than that of any other ethnic group, has been shaped by films. Why? Because the characteristics that define the American Indian are dramatically conveyed by this powerful 20th-century medium. All American ethnic groups, of course, are defined—stereotyped if you will—by Hollywood. But no other provides the opportunity to convey that image in a narrative form in terms of rapid physical movement, exotic appearance, violent confrontation, and a spirituality rooted in the natural environment" (2003: ix).

The Ballad of Crowfoot (1969)

The Ballad of Crowfoot was the first Indigenous-directed film to be made at the NFB. Released in 1969, this short documentary was one of the most influential and widely distributed productions made by the Indian Film Crew (IFC), the first all-Indigenous unit at the NFB. *Crowfoot* was directed by Willie Dunn, a Mi'kmaq/Scottish folk singer and activist who was part of the historic Indian Film Crew. It was the first all-Indigenous production unit at the NFB.

The film is a powerful look at colonial betrayals, told through a striking montage of archival images and a ballad composed by Dunn himself about the legendary 19th-century Siksika (Blackfoot) chief who negotiated Treaty 7 on behalf of the Blackfoot Confederacy.

The Ballad of Crowfoot is among the most popular and most widely screened films from the IFC program. Filmed entirely by members of the Indian Film Crew, the First Nations unit was founded by the NFB's National Indian Training Program in cooperation with the Company for Young Canadians. *The Ballad of Crowfoot* asserted Aboriginal rights and placed the media in the targeted community's hands.

The skillful compilation of archival photographs in combination with the stirring use of director Willie Dunn's original song create a space in which deference and tribute are paid to the legendary Blackfoot leader while the stakes for contemporary First Nations struggles are laid bare. A rousing finale of contemporary newspaper headlines cataloging a series of injustices against the First Nations people through Canada's history establishes an informative bridge to the actions and issues captured in CFC films (Dunn 1969, *https://pluto.tv/ca/on-demand/on*, accessed 29 May 2024).

Atanarjuat: The Fast Runner (2001)

Atanarjuat: The Fast Runner is a 2001 Canadian epic film directed by Inuit filmmaker Zacharias Kunuk and produced by his company Igloolik Isuma Productions. It was the first feature film ever to be written, directed, and acted entirely in the Inuktitut language. Set in the ancient past, the film retells an Inuit legend passed down through centuries of oral tradition. It revolves around the title character, whose marriage with his two wives earns him the animosity of the son of the band leader, who kills Atanarjuat's brother and forces Atanarjuat to flee on foot.

The film premiered at the 54th Cannes Film Festival in May 2001 and was released in Canada on 12 April 2002. A major critical success, *Atanarjuat* won the Caméra d'Or (Golden Camera) at Cannes, and six Genie Awards, including Best Motion Picture. *Atanarjuat* was also a commercial success, becoming Canada's top-grossing release of 2002, outperforming the mainstream comedy *Men with Brooms*. It grossed more than US$5 million worldwide. In 2015, a poll of filmmakers and critics at the Toronto International Film Festival named it the greatest Canadian film of all time. It also topped the CBC's 2023 list of the 50 Greatest Films Directed by Canadians (*CBC News*, 1 July 2023).

The plot for *Atanarjuat* begins at Igloolik (*Place of Houses*) in the Eastern Arctic wilderness at the dawn of the first millennium, Qulitalik bids goodbye to his sister Panikpak, wife of Kumaglak, promising to come if she calls for help in her heart. She gives him her husband's rabbit's foot for spiritual power. In a flashback, the community is visited by the strange shaman Tungajuaq.

During a spiritual duel with the visitor, the camp leader Kumaglak dies. The visitor removes the walrus-tooth necklace from Kumaglak's body and puts the necklace around the neck of Kumaglak's son Sauri, who thus becomes camp leader. Much later, the shaman's magic has poisoned the community with hatred. Tulimaq, the laughing stock of the camp, is having bad luck hunting and can barely feed his family, but Panikpak brings meat for Tulimaq's children, while Atanarjuat and Amaqjuaq hope that one day they will make things right.

Atanarjuat grows up to be a fast runner, Amaqjuaq is strong, and they are rivals with Sauri and his son Oki. During a game of *wolf tag*, Atanarjuat pursues the beautiful Atuat, provoking jealousy in Oki. Oki's sister, Puja, also shows interest in Atanarjuat. In a punching duel with Oki, Atanarjuat wins the right to marry Atuat. Later, Atanarjuat leaves his wife Atuat at a camp to hunt caribou, but he stops at Sauri's camp, where he is persuaded to take Puja on the hunt. Camping by a lake, Atanarjuat and Puja sing, flirt, and have sex.

Atanarjuat is in an unhappy marriage with Atuat and Puja. He catches his brother having sex with Puja and strikes Puja. She runs to Sauri's camp and tells them that Atanarjuat tried to kill her, so Sauri and Oki decide to kill Atanarjuat. Panikpak, however, remains skeptical of Puja's accusations. Puja returns to Atanarjuat's camp apologizing and is accepted back.

One day the women decide to go find eggs, but first Puja places a boot outside the tent where the men are resting. Oki and two henchmen sneak up and plunge their spears through the tent wall. Amaqjuaq is killed, but Oki is startled by a vision of his grandfather Kumaglak. Atanarjuat, naked and barefoot, bursts out of the tent and runs for miles across the ice, pursued by Oki's gang. Atanarjuat escapes by following a vision of Qulitalik and jumping into a wide-open crack in the ice. Eventually, he collapses in exhaustion with bloody feet. He is rescued by Qulitalik and his family, who conceal him when Oki arrives in pursuit.

Back at Igloolik, Sauri refuses to let Oki have Atuat, but Oki rapes Atuat, who is comforted by Panikpak. During a hunt, Oki stabs Sauri while claiming it was an accident, and takes over as camp leader. In her heart, Panikpak summons her brother Qulitalik to come, as they agreed years ago. Qulitalik feels her call and makes magic with the rabbit foot. At Igloolik Oki catches a rabbit with his bare hands, eats it, and falls under a spell that makes him forget his grievances.

Qulitalik and the family make the long sled journey back to Igloolik with Atanarjuat, who has healed. Atanarjuat is joyfully reunited with Atuat but rejects Puja. The spell-happy Oki just wants to have a feast but Atanarjuat prepares an ice floor in an igloo and invites Oki and his brothers inside. He slips antlers on his feet to grip the ice and subdues them, declaring that the killing is over.

It is now time to confront the evil that has plagued the community for so long. With everyone gathered together, Qulitalik calls forth the spirits, and the evil shaman Tungajuaq appears, grunting like a polar bear. Qulitalik confronts the shaman with the powerful spirit of the walrus and magic soil. Panikpak shakes the walrus-tooth necklace, and the shaman is destroyed and vanishes. Panikpak tells the group it is time for forgiveness: Oki, Puja, and their friends are forgiven for their evil deeds but are exiled from Igloolik forever (Angilirq 2002).

The film is set in the Eastern Arctic wilderness at the dawn of the first millennium (Isuma Igloolik Productions, 2007). The names of Atanarjuat and his brother first appeared in writing in the journals of the explorer Captain George Lyon, who took part in a British expedition to search for the Northwest Passage in 1821–23 (Eber 2008). The Inuit believe the story of Atanarjuat to be more than five centuries old.

This agrees with geomorphological estimates that Qikiqtaarjuk (Herschel Island), Inuktitut for little island and now a peninsula of Igloolik Island, on which much of the action occurs, became a peninsula about 500 years ago due to isostatic rebound. The main elements of the original story are that two brothers are betrayed by their wives and help set up a sneak attack.

Rivals plunge their spears through the walls of the brothers' tent, but the fast runner makes an escape across the ice, naked and barefoot. After being rescued and healed, the fast runner sets up his own ambush and succeeds in killing his rivals. It was the first Inuktitut-language screenplay, and the project became the first feature film in Inuktitut (Evans 2010).

Writer Paul Apak Angilirq, director Zacharias Kunuk, and many others on the production team had heard about the Atanarjuat legend when they were young. Over the course of five years, Angilirq interviewed seven Elders for their versions of the story and combined them into one treatment. The final script was developed by the team of Angilirq, Norman Cohn (producer and cinematographer), Kunuk, Herve Paniaq (tribal elder), and Pauloosie Qulitalik. Angilirq died due to cancer during film production in 1998 (Angilirq 2002; Kunk 2002).

Despite the emphasis on accuracy, the film takes liberties with the original Inuit myth: "At the film's core is a crucial lie," which is that the original legend ended in a revenge killing, whereas in the film Atanarjuat stops short of shedding blood (*CBC News*, 1 July 2023). Kunuk (2002) felt this was "A message more fitting for our times," and agreed that it probably reflected the influence of Christianity and its concept of forgiveness on contemporary Inuit.

After Igloolik Isuma Productions applied to Telefilm Canada in the spring of 1998 for financial support, plans were made to begin filming in Igloolik, Nunavut in April. The month was important because April is typically the only time of year in northern Canada when camera equipment can film winter scenes without malfunctioning due to cold. Kunuk found there was a lack of funding available from Telefilm and the Canadian government, which prioritized English and French-language productions over the languages of Aboriginal Peoples in Canada and would not provide more than $100,000 for a film in an Aboriginal language, which would make Atanarjuat impossible.

Due to difficulty with funding, Isuma instead successfully appealed for support of the National Film Board of Canada. Although the NFB had abandoned fiction, Isuma argued that in documenting Inuit mythology, Atanarjuat was similar to a documentary film. The budget was then approved at $1.96 million.

Achieving historical accuracy was paramount to the production. According to anthropologist Bernard Saladin d'Anglure the biggest challenge was resurrecting the beliefs and practice of shamanism, "the major frame of reference for Inuit life" (d'Anglure 2002). Research into historical sources—often the journals of European explorers—provided the basis for the reconstruction of clothes and customs. Elders were also consulted. In an interview, Paul Apak Angilirq said:

"We go to the Elders and ask for information about the old ways, about religion, about things that a lot of people have no remembrance of now...They are helping us write down what people would have said and acted in the past, and what the dialogue would have been like...We speak *baby talk* compared to the Elders. But for Atanarjuat, we want people speaking real Inuktitut. When we are writing the script, they might jump in and say, 'Oh, we wouldn't say such a word to our in-law! We wouldn't say anything to our brother's wives! It was against the law!'" (*Igloolik Isuma Productions*, 9 May 2008).

The filming crew was 90% Inuit. Filming began in 1999, stretching from 3 p.m. to 3 a.m., given the sun was always up. Cohn used natural light in shooting with his Sony DVW 700 digital camera, avoiding switches from the automatic camera settings. The film production pumped more than $1.5 million into the local economy of Igloolik and employed about 60 people. Given the small population, everyone in Igloolik knew at least one crew member. The film premiered at the Cannes Film Festival in May 2001. It was also screened at the Toronto International Film Festival in September 2001 (Adilman 2002).

Its' commercial release in Canada came on 12 April 2002, with the only bidder for distribution rights being Alliance Atlantis and its affiliate, Odeon Films. It had already been playing in France for seven weeks and was on 83 screens. The film opened in New York City on 7 June 2002 (Fox 2002).

Atanarjuat: The Fast Runner was praised by critics (Adilman 2002). On Rotten Tomatoes, the film has a positive 93% rating based on 133 reviews, with an average rating of 8.1/10. The site's consensus reads, "Compelling human drama and stunning cinematography make *The Fast Runner* an absorbing experience." On Metacritic, the film has a score of 91 out of 100 based on 29 critics. Brian D. Johnson (2002) of *Maclean's Magazine* hailed it as a masterpiece and a landmark in international film, writing, "This movie doesn't just transport you to another world; it creates its own sense of time and space."

In the *Toronto Star*, Peter Howell (2002b) wrote "the film overcame the stereotypes of the 1922 film *Nanook of the North* and defines an epic in every way." A. O. Scott (2002) from *The New York Times* praised the film, stating, "Mr. Kunuk has accomplished the remarkable feat of endowing characters from an old folk tale with complicated psychological motives and responses. The combination of dramatic realism and archaic grandeur is irresistibly powerful." Critics and filmmakers in the Toronto International Film Festival named the film fifth in the Top 10 Canadian Films of All Time (see *CBC News*, 8 February 2002; Howell 2002a; Melnyk 2007).

Tautuktavuk: What We See (2023)

Indigenous filmmakers continue to make strides in Canada, building industry capacity on their own terms and telling stories that both honor their communities and reach out to global audiences. Toronto's 2023 slate offers audiences and buyers vital, provocative, and world-premiering works from established creators and up-and-comers.

Tautuktavuk (What We See) is the latest from Isuma Productions, the collective of Inuit-owned media companies best-known for Camera d'Or-winning *Atanarjuat: The Fast Runner* (2001). *Tautuktavuk* is written and directed by film veterans Carol Kunnuk and Lucy Tulugarjuk, who also play sisters helping each other heal from past and present trauma (Schneller 2023).

With pandemic radio updates in the background, the sisters video chat about their daily lives and experiences of domestic abuse. The healing power of community is shown in scenes—hunting and distributing of community food, traditional songs sung in Inuktitut, and drum-dancing—that blend reality and fiction.

"When I was a child, it was rare to see drum-dancing because it was banned [by colonial entities], but my father kept the tradition, thank goodness," Tulugarjuk says. 'If we are bringing our identity and strength into this film, there have to be drum-dancing and songs' (Howell 2023). *Tautuktavuk* (What We See) draws from its filmmakers' lives to tell a powerful story of siblings doing their best to connect during the pandemic. Co-directed by Carol Kunnuk and Lucy Tulugarjuk, *Tautuktavuk* (What We See) presents a relationship between two sisters—one in Montreal and the other in Nunavut—who each deal with trauma in their own way.

Set during the beginning of the global COVID-19 outbreak, the film is told almost entirely through video chats, revealing how isolating the lockdowns are for the sisters—also played by Kunnuk and Tulugarjuk, blurring fact and fiction—especially, with the significant physical distance between them. As *Tautuktavuk* (What We See) unfolds, the contrast between the sisters' experiences begins to narrow. At first, we see extremely familiar scenes of each person speaking to their device's camera, alone from their home, but this begins to open up to communal settings. The elder sister Saqpinak (Kunnuk) is often surrounded by grandchildren and hosts a live TV event with Elders performing ajaajaa songs.

The younger sister Uyarak (Tulugarjuk) is with her beautiful daughters in her Montreal apartment and gets a traditional hand-poked tattoo. This connection between the sisters and their culture is also the impetus for opening up hard discussions about domestic and childhood sexual abuse. Uyarak has a lot of questions about an experience of childhood sexual abuse that has recently bubbled to the surface for her. Saqpinak, however, waits until they're finally reunited in Igloolik to share her own story (Howell 2023; Schneller 2023).

Bones of Crows (2022)

Bones of Crows is a multigenerational epic film that shares the tragic history and reality of the Indian Residential School System in Canada. Written, produced, and directed by Marie Clements, Métis/Dene, the independent film opened in theaters across Canada on Saturday, 3 June, after making its world premiere at the 2022 Toronto International Film Festival.

"I believe if you've had a parent or parents or family members that have gone through the residential school experience, this is a story that resides in all of us to some extent," Clements told ICT before the film premiered at TIFFI. I found myself thinking about wanting to really look at this experience, not just as a singular event that happened way back when, as people want to sometimes place it, but have it as a living, breathing thing, that we could see in our parents or seeing, in my case, as my mother and my aunties and uncles.

The film is an account of the life of Cree matriarch Aline Spears and a powerful indictment of the abuse of Indigenous people, as well as a stirring story of resilience and resistance. As Bhandari suggests in a *Globe and Mail*

(31 May 2023) article, "Marie Clements won't let Canada forget its painful past with sweeping epic *Bones of Crows*."

The film is carried by the lead performance of Grace Dove, Shuswap, of *The Revenant*, who plays Spears, a boarding school survivor who becomes a code talker for the Canadian Air Force during World War II. Like the recently lauded film by Martin Scorsese, *Killers of the Flower Moon*, the film tells of the acts of Indigenous genocide that became the foundations of the nation and that live on in Indigenous people today. The lens in this case is held by an Indigenous woman who lives with this reality.

"That experience also had domino effects on my brothers' and sisters' generation and my generation," Clements said. "It was a real opportunity to look at it in a multigenerational way and at the same time be really affected by current events, what's happening with bodies of our children being found. These things were happening as we were shooting" (Hughs 2023, accessed 1 June 2024).

Canada has shocked the world with its recent discoveries of remains as it faces the most painful part of reconciliation with its past. On May 23, 2021, the Tk'emlups Te Secwepemc First Nation announced that the remains of 215 children had been found in unmarked graves around the Kamloops Indian Residential School. In the months and years since, numerous First Nations have been doing similar searches around former schools and are discovering graves or anomalies in the grounds that could be the remains of long-ago students.

"We shot at the Kamloops Residential School while there was a memorial outside and while hundreds of people were gathering there to pay respect," Clements recalled. "So, it was very synchronous in a way to have to be so inside a story that involves a lot of our stories around this experience, but also to see it played out in real-time, and how history has a way of unearthing things that we didn't know and hopefully for a deeper understanding, but also for some kind of resolution" (Morrisseau 2023, accessed 1 June 2024).

In a time, when theater screens are blotted with superhero, fantasy, and horror escape films, it is rare for an independent film to find space. *Bones of Crows* can be found at Cineplex and Landmark Cinemas across Canada.

Challenging Hollywood Stereotypes

For over a century, North Americans have viewed various Hollywood movies that have served to shape the public's perceptions of Indigenous people, such as the Indian Princess (*Pocahontas*), the loyal sidekick (Tonto), or the wise elder (*Little Big Man*).

While there have been more recent exceptions, such as roles played by Canadian Dan George, for many years Indigenous people were portrayed by members of the white-settler population themselves in red face. The list of white people playing noble savages is quite lengthy, such as Burt Lancaster, Anthony Quinn, and Elvis Presley for example. They are usually in over-exaggerated feathered headdresses, war paint, and other stereotypes based on Hollywood's interpretation of Plain Indians.

In fact, even by the 1920s, Indigenous people began a protest movement against the use of these white actors in Western films. The *War Paint Club*, founded in the early 1920 was organized in Los Angeles with the sole objective of protecting Indigenous peoples' employment in the film industry. It is difficult, however, to ascertain if the members of this club saw such employment as an economic or a cultural issue (see La Potin 1987: 164; Hedican 1988: 384–385).

John Ford's iconic 1939 Western, *Stagecoach*, starring a host of well-known movie stars such as John Wayne, Andy Devine, and others was deemed in 1995 to be "culturally significant," and as such the Library of Congress placed it for preservation in the National Film Registry, a sort of cinematic hall of fame. Others are not so generous in their appraisals, as many see this portrayal of the Apache, specifically, and Indigenous people in general, as bloodthirsty savages, as "wagon burners," or as another obstacle that white people have to overcome in their quest for civilized society.

In the 2009 documentary *Reel Injun*, Anishinaabe writer and arts advocate Jesse Wente called *Stagecoach* "one of the most damaging movies for Native people in history":

"Stagecoach is the iconic Western. It's the Western that all others were really modeled after and it's one of the most damaging movies for Native people in history. You have white society inside a stagecoach and they are besieged on all sides by Native people, by the wild of America.

Those who are stopping progress, those who are backward, those who are vicious and bloodthirsty. Stagecoach summed up and gave the opinion of

Native people for decades, to the populace in the U.S. That's how they thought of us and it is because of John Ford that they thought of us like that and that Native people may have even thought that themselves" (accessed 2 June 2024; see also Wente 2021).

In addition, in a *Washington Post* article (22 November 2017), Kevin Gover, a member of the Pawnee First Nation of Oklahoma and Director of the Smithsonian's National Museum of the American Indian, comments that "movies and television perpetuated old stereotypes or created new ones, particularly, ones that cast Indigenous people as obstacles to, rather than actors in, the creating of the modern world." In other words, television shows and Hollywood movies have a tendency to condition North American viewers to conceptualize Indigenous American people as relics of the past who are no longer relevant participants in today's world.

This perception feeds into another myth about Native Americans, that they are a "dying race," or what used to be called "the vanishing Red Men." But, in fact, census material in both Canada and the United States clearly shows that Indigenous people in both countries are increasing in numbers. In some cases, the population increases of Indigenous peoples are well beyond that of their Euro-American counterparts. In Canada, for example, from 2006 to 2011 the First Nations population increased by 23% (Canada, 2012).

From the 1970s onwards, there was a more (apparently) sympathetic portrayal of Indigenous people. Chief Dan George turned in an Oscar-nominated performance in *Little Big Man* and brought some humor to the big screen with his role as an old Cherokee in Clint Eastwood's *The Outlaw Jose Wales*. In the 1990s, *Dances with Wolves* included an Oscar-nominated performance by Graham Green (Six Nations Oneida) for his role of Kicking Bird.

The film, though, had its critics, such as Russell Means' complaint about the depiction of his Lakota people; the only armed force to defeat the US military on US soil, and the charge that this is really only a film "about a white guy." Then there was the obvious step backward with Johnny Depp's portrayal of Tonto in the *Lone Ranger* remake. Depp's portrayal of Tonto is an excellent example of what Rayna Green (1984: 30–55) has called the *Tribe called Wannabee*, or "playing Indian" by Euro-Americans (see also Deloria 1998: 189–190; R. Green 1992).

Ward Churchill, well-known Native American activist and author of the controversial *Pacifism as Pathology* (2007), who was at one time fired, then reinstated, by the University of Colorado for his political views, argues that the myths and stereotypes built up around the Native American were no accident. He maintains that they served to explain in positive terms the decimation of Native tribes and their ways of life by so-called "advanced cultures in the name of progress," thereby making it necessary to erase the achievements and very humanity of conquered peoples.

"Dehumanization, obliteration or appropriation of identity, political subordination, and material colonization are all elements of a common process of imperialism," Churchill says. "The meaning of Hollywood's stereotyping of American Indian can be truly comprehended only against this backdrop" (in Media Smarts: *Common Portrayals of Aboriginal people*, accessed 15 April 2020; see also Bataille and Silet 1981; Berkhofer 1978; Churchill 2001; O'Connor 2003; and Singer 2001).

As these cultural stereotypes, both positive and negative, begin to become promoted and established in movies and other media, such as television, radio, and the internet, they also in time could become seen as "truthful narratives," and in the process become more firmly embedded into the group consciousness. It is also possible that Indigenous people themselves begin to believe in these tropes. Also, in these figurative or metaphorical expressions that colonial settlers use as a storytelling device in their attempts to convey Indigenous people in any number of ways, they begin to be instilled in a national consciousness, such as HBC Governor George Simpson's description of Indigenous people as "child-like" or their cultures as "repugnant."

Such characterizations can be seen by some Indigenous peoples as containing a certain truth value and so they may become ashamed of their Indigenous language, people, or cultural traits. For this reason, many Indigenous people think that the major source of oppression results from the Eurocentric attitudes of those in the dominant society that occur in colonial relationships.

As an example, Maureen Schwarz in her study entitled *Fighting Colonialism* (2013) suggests that the popular images of Indigenous peoples are an important aspect of the colonial process that subjugates such people because these images portray and promote negative stereotypes of Native North Americans.

"Images meant to depict Native North Americans," Schwarz (2013: 1) argues, "have traditionally stood as signs or fetishes for such contradictory concepts as primitiveness, nature, spirituality, unbridled sexuality, violence, nobility, or heathenness, depending on the particular time and agenda of the presenters and the code or codes understood by the various audiences." Such negative stereotypes have their origins historically in the attitudes expressed by people in power, such as George Simpson and others in the Hudson's Bay Company.

It is for this reason, Schwarz (2013: 2) contends, that the "colonized classically begin to believe the stereotypes promulgated by the colonizers." Furthermore, as Antonio Gramsci points out in utilizing his concept of *cultural hegemony*, "when ensconced within a full range of institutionalized and governmental structures and activities," such a representational regime often results in a "marked sense of fatalism and passivity" on the part of the oppressed who come to accept their own exploitation.

In addition to noting the oppressive effect hegemonic culture can render, Gramsci (1971) articulates that hegemony has little meaning unless paired with the notion of domination, which in the case of Native Americans became instituted in governmental policies and practices. As such, this process reveals the integral relationship between hegemonic culture and force (as quoted in Boggs 1976: 39–40). However, "Contemporary American Indians demonstrate power and agency through the production and consumption of these age-old images to battle colonialism at home" (Schwartz 2013: 12). The sorts of "age-old images" that she is referring to include such metaphorical symbols as the Indian Princess (Pocahontas), Mother Earth, and the Ecological Indian.

Wagon Burner Imagery

Those who were alive during the decades between 1950 and 1970, would probably be well aware of the huge popularity of Western movies and television shows. Almost every night after supper families were bonded to their television sets watching *The Rifleman*, *Bonanza*, *Gunsmoke*, or *Have Gun Will Travel*, among a host of other screen adventures.

One of the most popular of these shows was *Wagon Train* (1957–1965) which for a while held the number one spot in the Neilson Ratings. The show usually began with the wagon train leader, played by Ward Bond, bellowing out his iconic "Wagons Ho!" Even in my own family when we were starting out on a journey someone would inevitably shout the familiar "Wagons Ho."

To liven up the production and stimulate fan interest, various well-known stars made their arrival, such as Ronald Reagan in one of his last screen appearances (see also Daniel Francis 1993, for Canadian examples). So off went the long snake-like wagon train, set in the post-civil war period, traveling on its weekly jaunt traversing a vast and forbidding territory from Missouri to California populated by hostile tribes of Sioux Indians.

Before long the awaited attack would begin, the wagons would form a prescribed defensive circle, with the raging savages, made to look horrific in their painted faces, often played by Italians or dark-faced eastern Europeans, began the expected assault. The white male settlers sought refuge behind wagon wheels taking potshots at the encircling warriors, while their women folk and children huddled together in the wagons above attempting to endure a dreadful fright. Each episode varied in its intensity; sometimes the warriors were driven off until another show or the Sioux were victorious.

If the latter occurred, the warriors' booty was the screaming white-settler women and girls, dragged off by their hair to await their ignominious fate. Sometimes the dead white men were scalped against a piteous backdrop of whoops and war cries. So, off the warriors would go with their captives slung over their horses' backs, the distraught and disheveled women apparently resigned to the rape and murder that would surely follow (Aleiss 2005).

In chronological terms, these Western movies and television shows are a further extension of the Wild West shows of previous generations which depicted Indigenous people in stereotypical terms and conveyed these images to an ever-larger audience. These shows were promoted by such Western heroes as Buffalo Bill Cody whose everyday life on the Great Plains added a measure of historical authenticity.

However, in these shows, Native Americans in particular were often portrayed in a sensationalistic and exploitative manner. Buffalo Bill's Wild West shows which ran from 1883 to 1915 tended to romanticize the American Frontier and usually consisted of re-enactments of historical events combined with displays of showmanship. Indian war battle re-enactments were an important centerpiece of these shows such as depictions of the Battle of Little Big Horn.

For example, Buffalo Bill, the hero, rides into the battle scene in an attempt to save General Custer; however, Custer has already been killed so Buffalo Bill attempts to avenge his death by killing and scalping a Sioux chief called Yellowhead (Moses 1996). Native performers were also a critical part of the Wild West shows. These "show Indians" were largely derived from the Plains Nations, such as the Lakota Sioux, and were used to depict historic battles especially those appearing in attack scenes of white settlers. These shows, one reviewer suggests, "generally presented Native people as exotic savages, prone to bizarre rites and cruel violence" (Stanley 2014: 24).

In addition, Native women were often dressed in "exploitive," non-traditional clothing combined with immodest attire such as leather shorts, none of which would have ever been worn in reality. Another interesting aspect of these shows is that Chief Sitting Bull was a star attraction along with other familiar Native American names who performed in the show, such as Chief Joseph and Geronimo. These personages were presented as friends of Buffalo Bill and were introduced to President Grover Cleveland.

In a book on the relationship between Sitting Bull and Buffalo Bill entitled *Blood Brothers*, Deanne Stillman suggested that "this relationship was a sign that America has embarked on the painful and necessary journey of healing our original sin; the betrayal of the Native American" (2017: xvi-xvii).

However, this would hardly seem to be the case since Native Americans continue to be the victims of racist attitudes, policies, and institutions. It is also possible to interpret the friendship between Sitting Bull and Buffalo Bill in terms of the "noble savage imagery" in that Sitting Bull has now atoned for his struggles, and has now come as "pure" in his intentions.

In other words, Sitting Bull has largely seen the errors of his ways in resisting the assimilative power of American civilization. Ironically perhaps, Sitting Bull was killed on 15 December 1890, at the hands of the Indian Agency police on the Standing Rock Indian Reservation during an attempt to arrest him when authorities feared that he might be joining the Ghost Dance movement (see Adams 1973; Utley 1993).

Wagon Train and all those other Westerns, now seem so long ago, as if in a dream. Yet, we are left to wonder what this was all about; the murderous Sioux, the beleaguered settlers, and the horrendous indignities that were inflicted upon these poor innocent travelers? Well, in hindsight, and with the benefit of 50 years of reflection in history's rearview mirror, we can begin to put Ward Bond, his other intrepid travelers, and his Indigenous foes in perspective. One rather obvious aspect is that the negative stereotyping of Indigenous peoples served a political purpose for the white-settler population.

When Indigenous peoples are seen by the general Euro-American population as violent, savage, and an uncontrollable threat to the settlers themselves, then it would seem appropriate to develop policies to enclose this violence. One method is to institute a reservation system as a method of containment.

Another method is to remove Indigenous populations from areas of major white settlement centers as in the so-called *Trail of Tears*. Further suppressive methods could also be applied using the full force of the American army such as the quelling of the *Sioux Uprising* at Wounded Knee and the imprisonment of its' recalcitrant leaders (Churchill, Hill, and Hill 1978).

The Pocahontas Story

The Pocahontas story, which President Trump often referred to in his campaign rallies concerning Democratic rival Elizabeth Warren during his election speeches, is probably just a popular myth and has no basis in known facts. Certainly, Trump's use of the Pocahontas imagery is used in a demeaning manner, to subjugate the position of Indigenous women in society, and as a divisive tool against his female political opponent.

"The imagery is so ingrained in the North American consciousness," Anderson suggests, "that even Native people have, in dark times, internalized these beliefs about their grandmothers, their aunties, their daughters, and themselves" (2000: 99). Native American women are also frequently sexually objectified and are often portrayed in a stereotypical manner as being promiscuous. Such misconceptions lead to murder, rape, and violence against Native American women and girls by non-Native men.

In *Killing the Indian Maiden*, Marubbio explains that Native Americans, when seen at all, are still viewed as one-dimensional forms:

"They are America's racial other and alter ego, rejected to justify the violent treatment of them as part of progress and civilization, yet also desired for the freedom, land, and innocent state they represent" (2006: 4; see also Marubbio and Buffalohead 2018).

In her article, *The Pocahontas Perplex*, Cherokee scholar Rayna Green describes the manner in which Europeans first portrayed an image of Native women that mirrored Western attitudes toward the earth:

"Draped in leaves, feathers, and animal skins, as well as in heavy jewelry, she appeared aggressive, militant, and armed with spears and arrows….She was the familiar mother-goddess figure full-bodied, powerful, nurturing but dangerous; embodying the wealth and danger of the New World" (1984: 19, see also Green 1992).

As the white settlers became more familiar with the land, the Native American queen imagery was reduced. She became less powerful, more like a sexualized girl, and the *Indian Princess* imagery became more prevalent such that she could then be "used for the colonizer's pleasure and profit" (Cook-Lynn 1996: 145). In turn, the American movie industry attempted to capitalize on the archetypical Native girl in a voluptuous yet innocent-looking image. Thus, some of America's most revered institutions have demonstrated that they are capable of racist tendencies.

As an example, one can examine Walt Disney's production of *Pocahontas* (1995). This film appears to honor or pay tribute to Indigenous women; however, it does little more than exploit them for commercial gain. The heroine absurdly sings with forest animals, evidencing a far too common "one-with-nature" trope, and wears provocative costumes that Pocahontas would never have worn in real life. As for the fate of Pocahontas's people is concerned, within 20 years after the period depicted in the movie, the Powhatan Confederacy was practically exterminated at the hands of the surrounding colonists (see Mihesuah 2009: 14).

Then there is another Disney favorite, *Peter Pan*, the beloved children's classic, with its descriptions of redskins carrying tomahawks and knives, their naked bodies glistening with oil strung around them are scalps, of boys as well as pirates (McLaurin 2019: 2). These are powerful images that impress the minds of growing children which are probably not forgotten in adulthood. As Emma LaRocque (1997: 75–96) indicates, Disney's *Pocahontas* combines many of the typical stereotypes of Indigenous people; part noble savage, part princess, part loose squaw.

It would have been possible to portray Pocahontas as a strong Native leader, but instead, her character becomes a sort of sleazy, promiscuous urchin who is easy, available, and willing (Kidwell 1992: 97–107, see also Kidwell 1978). Thus, the "good" Native woman who is willing to make herself available to the white male settler is elevated to princess status (Green 1984: 20). In a similar vein, Carol Sparks has traced this squaw to princess transition in accounts of the Navajo.

In the 19th-century, the princess image of Native women was found in the adventurous accounts of explorer's records, but this image eventually was downgraded. In this new personification of the diminished princess imagery, "Not only could the squaw be pitied, but her very existence justified American intrusion into her land and society" (Sparks 1995: 135).

In a similar manner, Sarah Carter (1997) demonstrates how both the Canadian state and the national press deliberately promoted dirty squaw imagery in the later 1800s; such images seemed to justify the repressive measures used against Indigenous people at the time. She noted for example that:

"One inspector of the [reserve] agencies noted in 1891 that the women did not have soap, towels, wash basins, or wash pails, nor did they have any means of acquiring them." Similarly, it was frequently noted that the women were short of basic clothing and had no textiles or yarn to work with. Yet in official public statements, the tendency was to ascribe blame to the women rather than drawing attention to conditions that would injure the reputation of government administration (Carter 1997: 162).

Similar rationales were used to depict Native women as poor parents, a justification was therefore used to remove their children from their homes and place them in residential schools or foster homes. The sorts of negative images of Indigenous women became ingrained in the Canadian consciousness. Janice Acoose described how these negative images affected her own feelings of self-worth when she was attending school:

"I shamefully turned away from my history and cultural roots, becoming to a certain extent, what was encouraged by the ideological collusiveness of textbooks, and the ignorant comments and peer pressure from non-Indigenous students" (1995: 29).

Aboriginal author Kim Anderson sums up the effects of racial stereotypes on Indigenous people, especially women, "who fostered destructive and hateful attitudes toward themselves. This self-hatred is rooted in internalized racism that comes from the negative self-concepts of racist stereotypes, internalized racism spreads like a disease through Native communities. This results in self-destructive behaviors, including addictions and involvement in violent relationships" (2000:106).

When one internalizes a negative stereotype of oneself the consequences can be destructive of the individual and the community relationships which are the very fabric of Indigenous society. (See the results of the 2019 final report of Canada's National Inquiry into Missing and Murdered Indigenous Women and Girls, *http://www.mmiwg-ffada.ca*/ accessed 30 August 2020).

"From the moment they encountered Indigenous people in the Western hemisphere," Krech (2010: online) explains, "Europeans classified them in order to make them sensible. They made the exotic comprehensible with familiar categories. In the process, they reduced men and women to stereotypes, to caricatures, noble or ignoble, benign or malignant, rational or irrational, human or cannibal; savages all."

European settlers engaged in demeaning narratives of the Indigenous people they encountered, and since these people were characterized in a negative manner, an opportunity was afforded the Europeans to disenfranchise them and, in the process, divest them of their lands and heritage. Thus, cultural encounters involve attempts by members of different societies to understand people not known to each other previously. Understanding the cultural behavior of the members quite different from our own is a challenging task, especially when there are few clues or guidelines that can be utilized to aide in this task.

All of this previous discussion is meant to understand the context and role of Johnny Yesno's role in his films, most of which he had no control over. There are many myths about Native Americans that stem from peoples' acceptance of stereotypical depictions derived from the news media, Hollywood movies, and television shows. Many white North Americans have probably never met or even talked to a Native American in person, so they lack first-hand knowledge on which to base their opinions. This lack of information leaves white Americans susceptible to believing in all sorts of faulty information that is just not factual.

For this reason, Fleming 2006: 213) suggests, "Stereotyping is a poor substitute for getting to know individuals at a more intimate, meaningful level. By relying on stereotypes to describe Native Americans, whites come to believe that Indians are drunks, get free money from the government, and are made wealthy from casino revenue. Or [on the other hand] they may believe that Indians are one with nature, deeply religious, and wise in the ways of spirituality."

Either way, a belief in stereotypes whether positive or negative is a poor basis on which to base one's attitudes toward other people. The use of negative stereotypes can also be understood to play a significant role in the colonial process because these stereotypes serve to justify the paternalistic attitudes that have historically informed and articulated the interaction between Indigenous peoples and Euro-Americans.

One might conclude, then, that portrayals of Aboriginal peoples in the wider society have historically allowed for the exercise of symbolic power over the oppressed members of society. In this light, Susan Hegeman suggests that "most of the pervasive stereotypes of Indians (as savages, noble or otherwise; as *vanishing* relics of a past era; as sidekicks and squaws, and so on) present Indians as distinctly different from, and distinctly like what Euromericans see, or wish themselves, to be" (1989: 145).

However, Indigenous people have been known to push back at such negative stereotypes of themselves. For example, Indigenous authors Bonita Lawrence and Enakshi Dua have employed the term "decolonizing colonialism" in an attempt to "challenge the ongoing colonization of Aboriginal peoples" (Lawrence and Dua 2011: 20). From their perspective Canada, for example, should be regarded as a colonist state, or as they term it, a "settler society". "Settler states," in their view, "are founded on, and maintained through, policies of direct extermination, displacement, and assimilation" (2011:20).

Conclusion

One might conclude from the preceding discussion that, from an Indigenous point of view, the people of First Nations ancestry are apt to comprehend the history of North America quite differently than the history presented in the textbooks written by members of the colonial society and taught in the school rooms of North America.

Unfortunately, as far as the role of the history of the fur trade in America is concerned, the British and later Canadian historians have largely ignored any pretenses of an Indigenous perspective. They preferred instead to promulgate visions of heroic adventure, honorable companies of businessmen, and so forth which are ultimately forged into a false narrative of North American colonial history. In North America, there is a long history of using such language to subjugate Indigenous populations (Hedican 2013: 165–169; 207–12).

Indigenous actors and actresses are well aware of the negative stereotyping that has been promulgated in the media and, as such, many attempt to push back on this racial typecasting in their own roles in movies and films.

The changes that have occurred in Indigenous filmmaking have been used as an example of "social change-oriented media". In Canada, the *Challenge for Change* program, initiated by the National Film Board in 1967, was designed to give voice to the "voiceless" and to place more control of filmmaking in the hands of those in the local communities. *The Ballad of Crowfoot* (1969), for example, was the first Indigenous-directed film to be made under the auspices of the National Film Board, which was directed by Mi'kmaq activist and songwriter Willie Dunn.

Atanarjuat: The Fast Runner (2001) was the first film influenced by the *Challenge for Change* program to have an international impact. Directed by Inuit filmmaker Zacharias Kunak and produced by Igloolik Isuma Productions, *Atanarjuat* won six Genie Awards including Best Motion Picture. A film critic of the Toronto International Film Festival called *Atanarjuat* "the greatest Canadian film of all time."

A subsequent film review in *The New York Times* praised *Atanarjuat*, suggesting that "the combination of dramatic realism and archaic grandeur is irresistibly powerful" (Fox 2002). Later, in 2023, another Isuma Production, *Tautuktavik* (What We See) which was set during the global COVID-19 outbreak also received critical acclaim as one reviewer commented that "the film brings our [Inuit] identity and strength in film" (Howell 2023).

Bones of Crows (2022) is another important Indigenous film, directed and produced by Métis Marie Clement, which is focused historically on the tragedy of the Canadian Indian Residential School system. In a review published in the *Globe and* Mail (31 May 2022), the film has been called "a powerful indictment of the abuse of Indian people in Canada." And, as director, Clements commented, *Bones of Crows*, "was a real opportunity to look at it [the residential school system] in a multigenerational way and at the same time be really affected by current events; what's happening with bodies of our children being found. These things were happening as we were shooting" (Hughs 2023).

Recent Indigenous films are part of an important trend toward challenging the prevalent stereotypes in the movie industry. In previous decades, Indigenous peoples have been portrayed as "bloodthirsty savages" or "wagon burners" in the *Stagecoach* mode.

In many films, Indigenous women have been sexually objectified or as promiscuous seductresses. Commenting on the Disney movie *Pocahontas*, Emma LaRoque (1997: 75) suggests that "the prevailing negative tropes of Indigenous women are unfortunate because they are powerful images that impress the minds of growing children which are not forgotten in adulthood." On the other hand, current Indigenous films serve to "push back" on such negative Hollywood stereotypes as part of a buttressing of the colonial process in an attempt to challenge the ongoing colonization of Aboriginal peoples (Lawrence and Dua 2011: 20).

Chapter Five
Indigenous Canadian Movie Stars

As a form of introduction, it would be useful to place Johnny Yesno's life in the context of other Indigenous personalities in Canada, especially those who lived in the movie and political arena. Johnny Yesno did not grow up in a social or political vacuum and he was probably affected as many Indigenous people are by the negative stereotypes of Indigenous life in Canada.

He also would have no doubt been influenced by actors in the film industry whether or not these influences were in positive or negative mode. For these various reasons, this chapter reviews the career in film of a number of Indigenous Canadian actors. This review is not based on any predetermined, selective process but is created rather on the availability of literature on each of the individuals described herein. As such, no claim is made for example of any proper sampling techniques in the selection process, but is used more as a heuristic device as much as anything else.

Jay Silverheels (1912–1980)

Source: https://commons.wikimedia.org/wiki/File:Jay-silverheels-01.png

Jay Silverheels (born Harold Jay Smith, 1912–1980) was well known for his role as Tonto in the television series *The Lone Ranger*. Silverheels was born on the Six Nations of the Grand River Reserve, near Hagersville, Ontario, and was the grandson of Mohawk Chief A. G. Smith. His father, Captain Alexander Smith, was wounded and decorated, for his service at the Battle of the Somme and Ypres during World War I. Jay Silverheels, one of 11 children, was an excellent athlete, especially in lacrosse, and was inducted into the Canadian Lacrosse Hall of Fame in 1997. In 1938, he placed second in the middleweight class of the Golden Gloves tournament.

Harry J. Smith was born into a prominent Mohawk-Seneca family at Six Nations of the Grand River, Ont., 75 miles west of Buffalo. The Six Nations lands have been reserved for the Haudenosaunee people since 1784, originally granted by King George III in return for their service to the Crown in the American Revolution. All the peoples of the Iroquois Confederacy live there— Mohawk, Cayuga, Oneida, Onondaga, Seneca, and Tuscarora; it has always been a place proud of its culture and heritage (*The Canadian Encyclopedia* 2013).

Part of that heritage is lacrosse—*tewaaraton*, the Creator's Game. Harry Smith and his brother and cousins, like so many young men at Six Nations, excelled at the sport. Harry had no idea at the time, but lacrosse would turn out to be his springboard to fame and fortune. In 1931, the owners of the Toronto Maple Leafs and Montreal Canadiens wanted to fill their empty hockey arenas during the summer months. So, they moved lacrosse, an outdoor game for eons, to indoors and started a professional league. It was at just the right time for Harry Smith, 19, and his brother and cousins George (*Chubby*), Russell (*Beef*), and Sid (*Porky*).

The Smith boys turned pro with Toronto Tecumseh, a club named after the great Shawnee chief who fought for Indian autonomy in the War of 1812. Next, they suited up for the Buffalo Bowmans, who played at the Broadway Auditorium (today a Public Works Department garage known as the Broadway Barns). They also played in other leagues for Rochester, Albany, Geneva, and even Hornell.

In Atlantic City, they formed a barnstorming team that went to Los Angeles to demonstrate lacrosse at the 1932 Olympics. For much of that decade, Harry lived in Buffalo. He had a couple of children. He entered the 1937 Golden Gloves boxing tournament, won the middleweight division, and got all the way to the Atlantic States title bout at Madison Square Garden in New York City. Late in the 30s, Harry went back to L.A. to play lacrosse, and there, handsome and athletic, he was "discovered". Hired to do extra and stunt work in a string of films, he was always either credited as Harry Smith or, more often, went uncredited altogether. He resettled in Los Angeles, kept working, and finally earned his first role as Jay Silverheels, his old lacrosse nickname, in 1946.

Two years later, he broke through with a part in the Humphrey Bogart film *Key Largo*, and a year after that, he entered the new medium of television as Tonto in *The Lone Ranger*. Silverheels, perhaps, the first Native actor to portray an Indigenous person in a leading role in Hollywood, always played Tonto with dignity. But he was bothered by Tonto's subservience to the Lone Ranger, and by the pidgin English Tonto was always forced to speak.

Silverheels was a celebrity when he returned to Six Nations for an official visit in 1957, but when asked what he thought of the role he played he answered, "Tonto is stupid." Silverheels went on to become a strong advocate for Indigenous people in film and television; he founded and ran the Indian Actors Workshop in Los Angeles in the 1960s. In the end, perhaps, his most important role was the vital part he played in curtailing the screen industry's long habit of casting whites, rather than Native actors, as Indians.

Indeed, Jay Silverheels turned out to be just as boldly effective in Hollywood, on-screen and off, as he was back in Buffalo when he was the fastest man on the floor of the old Broadway Auditorium (Klein 2013, 2016). In 1937, while playing on a lacrosse team in Los Angeles, Silverheels impressed a film director with his athleticism and was subsequently signed as a stuntman in various westerns and serials.

As Brantford, Ontario author and historian, Zig Misiak (2013), explains, "Silverheels had the attributes, athletic, loved horses, and so crossing the border again is where things opened up for him from lacrosse." Misiak wrote what he believes to be the first, and possibly the only biography of Jay Silverheels, titled *Tonto, The Man in Front of the Mask*. He had the help of Silverheels's nephew, Steve Smith, in chronicling Harry Smith's upbringing and struggles with being stereotyped as he climbed from model to stuntman, to extra, to speaking roles.

Misiak takes the reader back to when Silverheels came home in 1957 and was the Grand marshal of a parade through Brantford. It was also a parade that Misiak attended and even got an autograph from Jay's mother. Another memory from his childhood was going to the Capitol Theater in Brantford to see the early Lone Ranger movies. Seeing as there was no cinema on the Six Nations, he says many from the territory would also attend. "When they saw this, they'd say, 'Uncle Jay was up there and he was saying something in the language,'" Misiak said.

The Indigenous members of the audience were then treated to the show within the show. As Tonto spoke his native tongue on-screen, Misiak recalls he was actually speaking gibberish sentences in Mohawk. "The beaver was turned upside down and ran into a tree. You know, you're looking at a guy and thinking he's saying the bad guys are just over the hill. You know, and they'd be laughing. And they'd be the only ones laughing," Misiak said.

He used the name Silverheels as his screen name because this was his nickname given to him as a lacrosse player because of his running speed. He began playing in major films by the 1940s. He acted alongside major Hollywood stars such as Humphrey Bogart and Edward G. Robinson (*Key Largo*, 1948), James Stewart and Maureen O'Hara (*Broken Arrow*, 1950), Audie Murphy, and Anne Bancroft (*Walk the Proud Land*, 1956), Glenn Ford (*Santee*, 1973), and was awarded a star on the Hollywood Walk of Fame.

His greatest fame, though, was his role as Tonto on *The Lone Ranger* (1949–1957). In this fictional plot line, a group of Texas Rangers were killed, with only one *lone* survivor. The Lone Ranger and Tonto subsequently ride throughout the West challenging lawbreakers and attempting to restore justice.

When the series ended, Silverheels continued to be typecast as a Native American in a number of movies and television episodes. On 6 January 1960, he portrayed a Native American fireman trying to extinguish a forest fire in the episode *Leap of Life* in the syndicated series, *Rescue 8*, starring Jim Davis and fellow Canadian Lang Jeffries.

Silverheels also appeared in an episode of the TV series *Love, American Style*. The segment, *Love and the Test of Manhood*, first aired on 11 February 1972. Eventually, he went to work as a salesman to supplement his acting income. He also began to publish poetry inspired by his youth on the Six Nations Reserve and recited his work on television. In 1966, he guest-starred as John Tallgrass in the short-lived ABC comedy/Western series *The Rounders*.

After Silverheels's stint on the *Lone Ranger* series, he still found himself typecast as the "stoic Indian". Playing the "Indian warrior or squaw", was the sort of limited role, all Indigenous actors faced. Silverheels decided to do something about it. With fellow actor Will Sampson, he founded the Indian Actors' Workshop in 1966. His goal was to see Indigenous actors get decent parts in films, and he set up free nightly classes in an L.A. church basement, teaching everything from stunt work to elocution, audition etiquette, and proper nutrition. Silverheels became an outspoken activist for Indian rights and a respected teacher within the Indigenous acting community.

He appeared on talk and variety shows performing his own poetry. In later years, he began a second career as a harness racer. Silverheels also had a brief boxing career, which saw him compete as a middleweight in a Golden Gloves bout in New York City's Madison Square Garden.

As Petten (2017) writes in a *Windspeaker* article, "Silverheels' character was little more than a cultural stereotype, with Tonto speaking broken English and always subservient to the Lone Ranger. But as the first Native American actor to play a Native American on television, he broke new ground for Native actors; something he would dedicate much time and effort to throughout the rest of his life."

As the author also explains, in 1966, Silverheels, wanting to do something to help other Native actors break into the business, started up the Indian Actors' Workshop in Los Angeles, offering training and advice gleaned from his own personal experience. Through the workshop, by serving as an example and, later in his career when his fame gave him some clout in the business, he fought for more and better roles for Native actors.

Silverheels helped train the next generation of crews and actors but was partially paralyzed in 1975 by a series of strokes that would eventually kill him in 1980. It was an especially unjust illness, hitting just as Silverheels was finally beginning to get large parts in films like *Santee* that allowed the public, and Silverheels himself, to see what a fine actor he truly was.

Silverheels left behind a legacy that is still being felt and fought for, by a new generation of Indigenous actors. Tina Keeper, Michael Horse, Peter Kelly Gaudreault, and Tom Jackson speak about how Silverheels inspired them and helped forge a path that is still being followed and improved upon, by Indigenous actors, writers, and directors today (*Spokesman Review*, 6 March 1980).

Despite the typecasting, Silverheels in later years often poked fun at his character. In 1969, he appeared on Johnny Carson's *The Tonight Show*, stating

"My name is Tonto, I hail from Toronto, and I speak Esperanto." Silverheels was also an early founder, along with Will Sampson, of the Indian Actors Workshop in Echo Park, Los Angeles. In his spare time, he also bred and raced Standardbred horses. In 1993, Silverheels was inducted into the Hall of Great Western Performers in Oklahoma City and has a star on the Hollywood Walk of Fame (Klein 1980; Misiak 2013; *Washington Post* 1980; Klein 2013, 2016).

Chief Dan George (1899–1981)

Source: https://creativecommons.org/licenses/by/2.0/

Chief Dan George was a Tsleil-Waututh actor, poet, and public speaker who was born on 24 July 1899, on the Burrard Indian Reserve in British Columbia and died on 23 September 1981, in North Vancouver. Through his film roles and personal appearances, Dan George helped improve the popular image of Indigenous people, which was often represented in stereotypical ways.

Born Geswanouth Slahoot, he received his English name, Dan George, at St. Paul's residential school. He was sent there when he was five years old. Before he started acting at the age of 60, George had worked as a longshoreman, construction worker, school bus driver, logger, and itinerant

121

musician. He was also chief of the Tsleil-Waututh Nation (Coast Salish people) from 1951 to 1963 (Armstrong 2005: 14).

Dan George's acting talent was discovered in 1960, after which he performed in a succession of roles as a gentle Indigenous elder on Canadian television and stage. His role as Ol' Antoine in the CBC's *Cariboo Country* (1960) was well-received, as was his role as Rita Joe's father in the original production of George Ryga's *The Ecstasy of Rita Joe* (1967, published 1970). Ryga expanded George's initially minor role in the play after seeing him perform. George appeared in many television series including *Bonanza, The Littlest Hobo, Kung Fu, The Beachcombers,* and *Marcus Welby, M.D.*

Chief Dan George was formerly the chief, from 1951 to 1963, of the Burrard Inlet Band of North Vancouver, British Columbia (also known today as the Tsleil-Waututh Squamish First Nation). After his term ended, he retained the honorary title of chief.

Among his many movie roles, Chief Dan George appeared in *Little Big Man* (as Old Lodge Skins, 1970), *The Outlaw Josey Wales* (Lone Watie, 1970), *Harry and Tonto* (Sam Two Feathers, 1974), and *Shadow of the Hawk* (Old Man Hawk 1976). His various television roles included *The Beachcombers* (Chief Moses Charlie, 1972–1981), *Spirit of the Wind* (Moses, 1979), and *McCloud* (Chief Stillwater). Seen by many as a role model for Indigenous peoples, George refused to play roles or appear in films that in some way demeaned Indigenous peoples and culture. Despite his Hollywood success, Dan George never forgot his roots; George's main residence remained his home on his reserve.

George was also well known for his poetic writing style. In 1974, George wrote *My Heart Soars* followed by *My Spirit Soars* in 1983, both published by Hancock House Publishers. The two books were later combined to form *The Best of Chief Dan George* which went on to become a best seller and continues to sell well today (Chief Dan George and Helmut Hirnschall 2004). One of his better-known pieces of poetry, *A Lament for Confederation,* has become one of his most widely known works (*The Canadian Encyclopedia* 2007).

During his acting career, he worked to promote better understanding by non-Aboriginals of the First Nations people. His soliloquy, *A Lament for Confederation*, is an indictment of the appropriation of Native territory by European colonialism. It is a prose poem about the oppression and resurgence of Indigenous peoples in Canada was performed at the City of Vancouver's celebration of the Canadian centennial in 1967.

This speech is credited with escalating Native political activism in Canada and touching off widespread pro-Native sentiment among non-Natives (AMMSA: The Aboriginal Multi-Media Society 2008). George called for the empowerment of Indigenous peoples in settler society—a message that still held resonance 50 years later, during the celebrations for Canada's 150th anniversary. As his great-grandson, Sid Bobb, has said about Canada since George's powerful performance, "Much has changed and much remains the same." Indigenous peoples in Canada continue to advocate for recognition of their treatment in the past and for means of moving forward (Yoggy 1998: 138).

Chief Dan George's *A Lament for Confederation* remains as powerful as ever. On 1 July 1967, he delivered the following speech to 32,000 people celebrating Canada's 100th birthday at Empire Stadium in Vancouver. The crowd expected a celebratory event, but instead, Chief Dan George's powerful performance called into question the meaning of Confederation and the impact of colonization on Indigenous people.

At first, the audience was silent, but later gave Chief Dan George a standing ovation. The speech made national headlines the following day (*CBC News*, 10 October 2017). Here is the text below of his complete soliloquy:

"How long have I known you, Oh Canada? A hundred years? Yes, a hundred years. And many, many seelanum more. And today, when you celebrate your hundred years, Oh Canada, I am sad for all the Indian people throughout the land. For I have known you when your forests were mine; when they gave me my meat and my clothing. I have known you in your streams and rivers where your fish flashed and danced in the sun, where the waters said, 'Come, come and eat of my abundance'. I have known you in the freedom of the winds. And my spirit, like the winds, once roamed your good lands.

But in the long hundred years since the white man came, I have seen my freedom disappear like the salmon going mysteriously out to sea. The white man's strange customs, which I could not understand, pressed down upon me until I could no longer breathe. When I fought to protect my land and my home, I was called a savage. When I neither understood nor welcomed his way of life, I was called lazy.

When I tried to rule my people, I was stripped of my authority. My nation was ignored in your history textbooks—they were little more important in the history of Canada than the buffalo that ranged the plains. I was ridiculed in your plays and motion pictures, and when I drank your fire water, I got drunk—very, very drunk. And I forgot.

Oh Canada, how can I celebrate with you this centenary, these hundred years?

Shall I thank you for the reserves that are left to me of my beautiful forests? For the canned fish of my rivers? For the loss of my pride and authority, even among my own people? For the lack of my will to fight back? No! I must forget what's past and gone. Oh God in heaven! Give me back the courage of the olden chiefs. Let me wrestle with my surroundings. Let me again, as in the days of old, dominate my environment. Let me humbly accept this new culture and through it rise up and go on.

Oh God! Like the thunderbird of old, I shall rise again out of the sea; I shall grab the instruments of the white man's success—his education, his skills, and with these new tools I shall build my race into the proudest segment of your society. Before I follow the great chiefs, who have gone before us, Oh Canada, I shall see these things come to pass.

I shall see our young braves and our chiefs sitting in the houses of law and government, ruling and being ruled by the knowledge and freedoms of our great land. So shall we shatter the barriers of our isolation. So shall the next hundred years be the greatest in the proud history of our tribes and nations" (Chief Dan George and Helmut Hirnschall 2004:12–13; also found in *https://monova.ca/chief-dan-georges-lament-for-confederation*; accessed 12 June 2024).

Chief Dan George is remembered as a talented actor and Indigenous spokesperson. In 2008, Canada Post commemorated his legacy with a special stamp. A school in Toronto and another in Abbotsford, British Columbia, as well as a theater in Victoria, British Columbia, also bear his name—a testament to the ongoing influence that his works have had on various communities.

In 1971, George was made an officer of the Order of Canada. In addition, he was included on the Golden Rule Poster under *Native Spirituality* with the quote: "We are as much alive as we keep the earth alive" (Teesdale 2004: xviii).

His success, and the celebrity that came with it, made George's life busier, but there were few outward signs that he had become a Hollywood star. He continued to live on the reserve in the same little house he had built for his wife and six children. Throughout his acting career, George was always aware that in addition to being seen as a talented actor, he was also seen by many as a representative of Indigenous people.

He wanted to succeed, not so much for himself, but for the Indian people who would have their own self-confidence boosted by his success, and who would look at what he had accomplished and believe they too could accomplish more. That was a responsibility he took very seriously, worried that any failure he had in his career would mean he was failing the Indian people. And, throughout his career, he refused any role he felt was demeaning to Native people (AMMSA: The Aboriginal Multi-Media Society 2008).

Chief Dan George was a spokesperson for Indigenous people. He believed in the humanity within and wanted to bring everyone together, creating an understanding between humans and closing the gap. This was achieved by talking about similarities and not differences. He wanted truth and reconciliation before the same words took on a different meaning after 2015. He redefined the Indian image and erased stereotypes (*The New York Times*, 24 September 1981).

Tantoo Cardinal (1950-)

Tantoo Cardinal at the 2025 Sundance Film Festival

Source: *https://creativecommons.org/licenses/by-sa/4.0/*

Rose Marie *Tantoo* Cardinal is a film and television actress of Cree and Métis descent who was born in 1950 and raised in the hamlet of Anzac, Alberta. Rose Marie *Tantoo* Cardinal was born the youngest of three children to Julia Cardinal, a woman of Cree and Métis descent. The lack of electricity inspired her to use her imagination while playing in the bush.

Her grandmother nicknamed her *Tantoo* after the insect repellent they used while picking blueberries together. She taught Cardinal the Cree language, the traditional ways of their culture, and the difficulties she would face growing up Métis in Canada. Cardinal has said that it was walking behind her grandmother where she first learned to act.

Tantoo Cardinal gave her first performance in Grade 7 with the title role in Anzac's Christmas concert play *The Wise Old Man*. She left Anzac at age 15 to attend Bonnie Doon High School in Edmonton on a bursary. Upon moving to Edmonton, Cardinal frequently encountered racist taunts. She discovered the negative stereotypes of Indigenous people, which contrasted sharply with the people and communities she knew. This experience inspired her to pursue acting and create positive representations of Indigenous communities. She joined a Native Youth Group to help create support networks for Indigenous families.

Cardinal's early acting work included a mix of radio, theater, and industrial films. The introduction of Canadian content regulations in the early 1970s created a new (but still modest) demand for Indigenous actors in Canadian stories. Cardinal landed her first professional role in a 1971 CBC docudrama about Catholic missionary Father Albert Lacombe. She was discovered while petitioning for the construction of more schools on Alberta reserves (*Canadian Encyclopedia*, 1 May 2023).

Cardinal starred in her first feature film, the romantic historical drama *Marie-Anne* (1978), filmed in Edmonton. Anthony Hall of Cinema Canada cited her *dynamic performance* as one of the film's few highlights. After small roles in the action movie *Death Hunt* (1981: about *Mad Trapper* Albert Johnson) and the sports drama *Running Brave* (1983), Cardinal had a breakthrough playing Rosanne Ladouceur in Anne Wheeler's *Loyalties* (1986).

The film drew positive reviews for its accurate portrayal of Indigenous life and for Cardinal's powerful performance. Cardinal was nominated for a Genie Award for Best Actress. She also received best actress awards from the Alberta Motion Picture Industry, the American Indian Film Festival, and several international film festivals.

After moving to Los Angeles in 1986, she appeared in the films *Candy Mountain* (1987) and *War Party* (1988); as well as the TV movies *Gunsmoke: Return to Dodge* (1987) and *Divided Loyalties* (1990). As a Canadian actress, Cardinal has played significant roles in various notable films and television series, including *Dances with Wolves* (1990)*, Black Robe* (1991), *Unforgiven* (1992), *Legends of the Fall* (1994), and *Through Black Spruce* (2018). "She is likely the most recognizable Indigenous actress in North America," according to film commentator Brian Johnson (2019).

In four of the movies that she appeared in 2018, her disparate roles have required her to speak half a dozen First Nations languages. As an example, she acted in Cree, Apache, Paiute, Cherokee, Ojibwe (Anishinaabe), and Gwich'in. Cardinal has played a role in developing Indigenous characters with an eye to authenticity. A notable example pertains to her role in Kevin

Costner's 1990 classic *Dances with Wolves* which is regarded as a milestone, in which Sioux actors speak subtitled Lakota. In this film, she was the wife of a medicine man played by fellow Canadian and Oscar winner Graham Greene.

Cardinal gained international recognition playing Black Shawl in the Oscar-winning *Dances with Wolves* (1990), opposite Kevin Costner and Graham Greene. The story of a civil war soldier and his friendship with a Sioux band, *Dances with Wolves* attempted to correct Hollywood's negative portrayal of Indigenous characters; it features the Lakota language and Indigenous actors in the ensemble.

Cardinal impressed Costner and casting director Elizabeth Leustig by translating her role into Cree for the audition and by conveying the experience she brought to the role. As Elisabeth Leustig, the film's casting director, told *Entertainment Weekly* in 1991, "There's a certain hardship in her face that's very appealing. You can tell that her life has not been an easy one."

Leustig then continues with her rationale for choosing Tantoo for a *Dances with Wolves* role: "It wasn't a big role she's only on-screen for a few minutes— but Tantoo Cardinal wanted to play Black Shawl, Kicking Bird's sweetly sardonic wife, more than any role of her career." "The minute I read the script, I knew this was something special," the 40-year-old Alberta-born Métis Indian explains. The minute that casting director Leustig saw Cardinal's face, she wanted her, too. Cardinal's career, in fact, hasn't been easy. She struggled for years playing bit parts in fire-prevention spots and race-relations documentaries. It wasn't until recent years that things started taking off. In 1986, she starred in *Loyalties*, a hit Canadian movie, which was followed by *The Black Robe*, an Australian-Canadian production set in the 1600s (Svetkey 1991).

Dances with Wolves was a blockbuster and one of the defining films of the 1990s. It grossed more than $424 million worldwide and won seven Academy Awards, including Best Picture. The film was widely praised for giving Indigenous actors dynamic, multidimensional speaking parts, although it still received some criticism for recounting history from a settler perspective. The film has nonetheless remained a source of pride for Cardinal.

"I think the power of *Dances with Wolves* is that it brought some positive images forward that we were really, really needing and that was extremely important," she told the *First Nations Drum* newspaper in 2002. "For some, it touched a place of spirit and belief, and it made people feel good". She then explained her motivation for her Indigenous advocacy work further when she indicated that:

"Occasionally, you feel that burden; that additional responsibility to your community, but without this vision of work that has to be done I wouldn't be here; things have to change, the truth has to be told, the misrepresentations have to be eliminated. So, we have a responsibility to act because it is what we can do that might make a difference. Today I don't feel like it's a responsibility, it's just a place to be. It's my life and it's a gift to have that purpose" (Cardinal 2002, 28 December *wwwfirstnationsdrum.com*).

Cardinal followed *Dances with Wolves* with the acclaimed *Black Robe* (1991). The film tells the story of a Jesuit priest on a mission to convert the Huron to Catholicism in the early 1600s. *Black Robe* was generally praised for its sense of authenticity and its sensitive depiction of Indigenous characters. Cardinal twice declined the film because the story drew upon church records and a colonial gaze. She and co-star August Schellenberg suggested script changes and improvised on set to improve the representation of the Indigenous characters. Eventually *Black Robe* won six Genie Awards, including Best Picture, and was a box office success.

In 1994, Cardinal performed in three films, including Edward Zwick's Oscar-winning historical epic *Legends of the Fall* with Brad Pitt and Anthony Hopkins. In *Silent Tongue*, written and directed by Sam Shepard, she played the title role. For her part as Bangor, the strong-willed companion of a logging baron in *Where the Rivers Flow North*, Cardinal received the best actress award at the American Indian Film Festival.

Reflecting on Cardinal's career in 2015, Tony Wong wrote in the *Toronto Star* (20 February), "She is at her finest when she plays a woman named Bangor with the kind of blunt, raw and outspoken humanity that shreds the meek, sexualized, and ultimately Disneyfied image of the Indian female as Pocahontas." Cardinal has called Bangor her favorite character. "She was from a world of women that nobody writes about or sees, and she was a combination of many women I had known with a survivalist kind of background" Wong writes.

Cardinal also appeared as Turtle Mother in *Tecumseh: The Last Warrior* (1995). Later, she also played a major role alongside Adam Beach in Chris Eyre's *Smoke Signals* (1998); it was marketed as "the first feature film written, directed, and produced by Native Americans." *Smoke Signals* was a hit on the

129

festival circuit, winning both the Filmmakers' Trophy and the Audience Award at the Sundance Film Festival.

In 2009, Tantoo Cardinal was made a member of the *Order of Canada* "for her contributions to the growth and development of Aboriginal performing arts in Canada, as a screen and stage actress, and as a founding member of the Saskatchewan Native Theater Company" (Office of the Secretary to the Governor General, 30 December 2009). Later, in 2017, she was named the winner of the Academy of Canadian Cinema and Television's Earle Grey Award for Lifetime Achievement. Cardinal has also been involved with various social issues, such as on 23 August 2011, when she and dozens of others were arrested while protesting the proposed extension of the Keystone Pipeline.

At times, her film roles have an activist component as well, such as her role in the 2018 film *The Grizzlies*. She played a high school principal who is skeptical that a first-time teacher is capable of addressing the social issues, prevalent in the Nunavut community of Kugluktuk. This role illustrated Tantoo Cardinal's legacy as a combination of acting and advocacy. Her career broke down barriers for Indigenous actors. She has used the power of positive representation to challenge negative images and stereotypes and to honor the history of Indigenous people in Canada.

"I always felt that as an actor we have to have the courage to go into the territory of hard experiences and tell the truth of what's happened to us as human beings," Cardinal said in 2010. "That's where you find understanding. You don't come through generations and generations of genocide and holocaust to be wimps, to be portrayed as monotoned and one-sided characters".

Cardinal is also an outspoken environmentalist. She drew upon her experience seeing the changes to Fort McMurray to advocate against the Alberta oil sands and the contamination of water for resource extraction. In 2011, she was arrested with fellow actor and activist Margot Kidder while protesting the Keystone XL pipeline outside the White House (*Canadian Encyclopedia*, 1 May 2023).

According to a *CBC News* report of the incident (23 August 2011):

"Just as dozens of others since Saturday, Kidder and Cardinal were charged with failing to obey an order governing protests on the sidewalk, police said. Both were expected to be released later Tuesday. Cardinal—who is from Fort

McMurray, Alta., the heart of oilsands country—said she believes oilsands development is destroying the environment and making people sick. It's progressively broken my heart over time to see the destruction that has gone on," she said. "Fort McMurray, the tar sands…it's a place that we can see really how sick Earth is and how sick we are as a people. I am here to be part of a voice to say, 'Wake up.'"

The $7-billion Keystone XL pipeline has approval from Canada but needs a final nod from the United States before it can go ahead. It would nearly double the amount of crude the U.S. imports from Alberta's oilsands, and travel through environmentally sensitive areas of the American heartland to Gulf Coast refineries.

Tantoo Cardinal says the one thing she has fought for in her more than four decades of working in film, television, and theater is to simply be relevant. "To be considered a human. Not an Indian in the roles I play." That has been a tough mission statement working in a media that has traditionally marginalized Aboriginals. Fortunately, Cardinal has played a lot of Indigenous roles over the years and, in so doing, has made an outsized impact on the perceptions of what mainstream culture thinks First Peoples should or shouldn't be.

"I think for so many years we have been in the back drawer. We weren't being included in the conversation. We didn't have our stories told; people don't even know we're there. Or that we have complexity and dimension," says the 64-year-old Cardinal in an interview with the *Toronto Star* in 2015. "In many ways, that's why I started acting. It was very much connected to trying to have a voice."

Such a voice would speak out about the violence against Aboriginal women which is once again in the headlines. And Cardinal says she can't understand why the federal government has rejected calls to have a national inquiry into missing and murdered Aboriginal women, most recently with the brutal attack on 16-year-old Winnipeg student Rinelle Harper in November.

"This is such a crucial issue. We should really be examining the attitudes and behaviors toward Aboriginals. We have been made to feel worthless. We have been abused for generations. Throughout history, they have been trying to snuff out [Indigenous] women. We really need to look at the roots of this" (Tony Wong, *Toronto Star*, 20 February 2015).

Tantoo Cardinal has joined other First Nations icons including Dan George and Greene who are "performers who were cast in classic westerns but could maintain a dignity and singularity," according to Jesse Wente, director of Canada's Indigenous Screen Office. "The fact that Tantoo has those Hollywood credits and that her celebration comes when she's in the antithesis of those movies that are Indigenous-led, shows the remarkable breadth of her career" (Johnson 2019).

For her significant contribution to the growth and development of Indigenous performing arts and her advocacy for Indigenous people and for the environment, The University of Winnipeg proudly bestowed an Honorary Doctor of Letters on her.

In recognition of her career's work in film and advocacy work, Tantoo Cardinal also received the Governor General's Performing Arts Award for 2021:

"In a career spanning 50 years and more than 120 film, television, and theater roles, Métis actor Tantoo Cardinal has helped transform the face of film and television when it comes to portraying Indigenous people and stories. One of the most widely recognized First Nations actors of her generation, she has portrayed complex and diverse characters and challenged negative stereotypes of Indigenous culture and communities. As a performer, mentor, and cultural and environmental activist, she has blazed a trail with her talent, widening and improving the path for others to follow."

In receiving this award, Cardinal further explains that:

"I have chosen my path from where I hope to be able to make some change," she says. "It's tied into what I completely believe in: the stream of life force and salvaging enough of our stories and ceremonies to start building again. I see it as a responsibility' (*https://ggpaa.ca/award recipients— Governor General's Performing Arts Awards, GGPAA*, accessed 10 June 2024).

According to *Tibute.ca* Cardinal is:

Considered to be the "most widely recognized Native Actress of her generation," Tantoo has been honored for her many accomplishments and contributions to the Native artistic community, with a lifetime contribution Eagle Spirit Award from the Native Indian Film Festival in 1990. In 1998, she received a National Aboriginal Achievement Award to recognize her work in theater, television, and film (*https://www.tribute.ca/people/biography/tantoo-cardinal/*) accessed 10 June 2024.

In addition, when she became a member of the *Order of Canada*, it was noted that Cardinal is:

"An accomplished and celebrated actress, Tantoo Cardinal has advanced Aboriginal performing arts in Canada. Known for her authenticity, she has brought to life complex and diverse Aboriginal characters and has worked to dispel stereotypes.

Her performances in both film and television, including *Dances with Wolves*, *Legends of the Fall*, and *North of 60*, have helped to blaze a trail in an industry where few roles for Aboriginal women previously existed. A founding member of the Saskatchewan Native Theater Company, she serves as an inspirational role model to aspiring youth, nurturing talent in those wishing to pursue a similar path (*https://www.gg.ca/en/honours/recipients/*).

This tribute is certainly a fitting summary of a lifetime exemplified by praiseworthy achievements in so many fields of endeavor.

Graham Greene (1952-)

Graham Greene 1998

Source: https://creativecommons.org/licenses/by-sa/3.0/

Graham Greene is an Oneida First Nations actor who was born in Ohsweken, on the Six Nations Reserve in Ontario in 1952. He is probably best known for his nomination for an Academy Award for Best Supporting Actor for his performance in *Dances with* Wolves (1990).

Other notable film roles were in *Thunderheart* (1992), *Maverick* (1994), *Die Hard with a Vengeance* (1995), *The Green Mile* (1999), *Skins* (2002), *Transamerica* (2005), *Casino Jack* (2010), *Winter's Tale* (2014), *The Shack* (2017), *Wind River* (2017), and *Shadow Wolves* (2019). He has also hosted the reality crime documentary show *Exhibit A: A Secret of Forensic Science* (Shea 2017).

Graham Greene (b. 1952) began his acting career when he graduated from Toronto's Center for Indigenous Theater program in 1974. In addition to his Best Supporting Actor nomination for the role of Kicking Bird in *Dances with Wolves*, Greene has also won two Gemini Awards for Best Performance in *The Adventures of Dudley the Dragon* and *North of 60*. In recognition of his film career and support for Indigenous actors, he was awarded an Honorary Doctor of Law degree from Wilfrid Laurier University in 2008. In 2016, he received the Outstanding Supporting Actor award for the film *Longmire* by the RNCI Red Nation Awards (Bonomolo 2022).

For over a decade, Greene was a busy actor on Canadian television, and in supporting roles in small features, until 1990's *Dances with Wolves* made him not just a familiar face, but a star. He earned an Oscar nomination for playing Kicking Bird, a performance in an English-language film, but not in English.

"It took three months to learn the dialogue. I had no idea what I was saying," Greene recalls, "and I had to learn it phonetically. I'd be running 10 miles a day with my headphones on, listening to the translations, mumbling away in Lakota, and people were looking at me funny. But I got it down" (Parke 2021).

It was a tremendous undertaking for first-time director Kevin Costner. "He did fine," Greene says. "We stayed out of his way and let him make his decisions. I only questioned him once, [when Kicking Bird] was going nuts looking for a peace pipe. I said, 'He's a medicine person. He would never lose a peace pipe. Why do you want me to do that?'" He said, "Because it looks good." I said, "Good enough" (Parke 2021).

Two years later, Greene starred with Val Kilmer and Sam Shepherd in the groundbreaking *Thunderheart*, which defined the feel of contemporary Res' (reservation) westerns like *Longmire, Yellowstone,* and the Tony Hillerman/Joe Leaphorn films. It wasn't hard to convince Greene to do it. "I love *The Badlands*" Greene said.

My agent said, "I got a film for you. It's in South Dakota. And you have to ride a motorcycle."

I said, "I'm in."

"Want to read it?"

"Don't have to."

"Val was a strange fellow to work with. I just couldn't get into his head, what he was thinking, what he was doing. He was very to himself" (Shea 2017).

While he's done several period westerns, Greene has done many more contemporary roles. "I like working in modern times. Doing period films is a lot of work. It's hard on the crew, the cast, everybody. I guess my favorite one was doing *Molly's Game*, playing the judge. Aaron [Sorkin], the director, was looking at me sitting behind the bench. I had a puzzled look on my face."

He said, "Are you all right?"

I said, "Yeah. I've just never seen the bench from this side before."

After a long career of playing good guys, he got to go to the dark side, playing the evil Malachi on *Longmire.*

"Yeah, I had fun playing that. They wrote that because Lou Diamond [Phillips] kept bugging them. 'You've got to get Graham Greene on the show'. So, they wrote the part of Malachi. I read it and went, 'Oh boy, that's perfect'."

"After the second season, they let me just go and do what I wanted because I knew the character so well. Like when I did *Goliath*, playing a nasty casino owner," opposite Billy Bob Thornton. "It was fun. It said I turned into a crow at night and watched people. I adapted these gestures; tilted my head looking at people and making a clucking noise. Playing villains is fun. Being nice all the time; it's boring" (Shea 2017)

Another of Greene's favorite roles was in the series *Defiance*, in which he and director Michael Nankin talked in a sort of shorthand, he says, "Because we knew all these old films the kids had never seen."

"Do you want me to do a Bogart in this?"

"Yeah, that would be great". And they go, "What's a Bogart?"

"When you slowly turn around, look at somebody, and snarl at them."

135

"One of the things that I really want to do, now that I am getting older and fading fast, is teach kids what to do in front of the camera. Because a lot of them don't know. They'll stare at the ground and mumble."

I said, "No, the camera's going to be over my left shoulder, look at my left eye; talk to me, not the ground."

"I advise them to spend two- or three-years doing theater, because you've got to learn discipline, or you won't last very long."

They ask, "How did you last this long, Mr. Greene, 40-some years?"

And I say, "I've got a thick skin and a hard head" (Parke 2021).

Greene's Academy Award-nominated role as Kicking Bird in the 1990 film *Dances with Wolves* showcased his talents to audiences beyond his native Canada. In an interview with *Cine Movie*, Greene recounts a story of being tossed from a horse during production.

When director Costner asked if he wanted a break, the actor retorted that he was more interested in finding the horse for payback. He stated that it was difficult for him to learn how to speak the Lakota language properly. Having not grown up speaking a native language, he said, "I couldn't figure out how they ordered their language. Its structure is totally foreign to English or French" (Haas 2021).

Greene was featured as Arlen Bitterbuck who was convicted of murder, awaiting execution on death row in the Oscar-nominated *The Green Mile* (1999). The character was an elder of the Washita Tribe and a member of a Cherokee Council, his nickname was *The Chief*. The character's execution is the first witnessed in the movie and is depicted from start to finish.

As it is the first depiction of an execution in the movie, Greene's death is noted as being a fairly accurate portrayal of the procedure. In 2005, he played the potential love interest of the female lead in *Transamerica*. A review of the movie praises Greene's performance as having "charming earthiness". But also notes that his character is allowed to find the transgender character attractive as "he's allowed to be open-minded because he's a Navajo. In other words, a spiritually open-minded outsider, as opposed to your typical Middle American" (Odden 2012).

In June 2008, he was awarded an honorary doctor of law degree from the Brantford campus of Wilfrid Laurier University. He was appointed a member of the *Order of Canada* in the 2015 Canadian honors (Dixon 2004; *The*

Chronicle-Herald, 1 July 2015; Governor General of Canada, accessed 8 June 2024).

Alanis Obomsawin (1932-)

Source: *https://creativecommons.org/licenses/by/2.0/*

Alanis Obomsawin is a filmmaker, singer, artist, and activist primarily known for her documentary films. She has written and directed many National Film Board of Canada documentaries on First Nations issues. Obomsawin relates that "the basic purpose [of her films] is for our people to have a voice […] no matter what we're talking about whether it has to do with having our existence recognized, or whether it has to do with speaking about our values, our survival, our beliefs, that we belong to something beautiful, that it's okay to be an Indian, to be a native person in this country" (Pick 1999: 78).

Her best-known documentary is *Kanehsatake: 270 Years of Resistance*, regarding the 1990 Oka Crisis in Quebec. Obomsawin's first film came to the attention of the National Film Board (NFB) in the mid-1960s when she held fundraising concerts to pay for the construction of a swimming pool in Odanak.

Children in her community were no longer able to swim in the Saint Francis River but were not allowed to use a pool in a neighboring community, which was for white residents only.

Obomsawin's success in raising funds for the construction of a pool for Odanak children was through an interview about her film in a report by the CBC-TV's Telescope series, which was seen by NFB producers Joe Koenig and Bob Verrall. "It was from there the National Film Board (NFB) saw it and I was invited by some producers to talk to some of the filmmakers there," said Obomsawin. "I discovered that they had a studio that only catered to [the] classroom, with educational film strips" (Taylor 2015).

They invited the singer-storyteller to their film board to work as an advisor on a film about Aboriginal people. She went on to direct films of her own while continuing to perform and fight for justice for her people. Obomsawin directed her first documentary for the NFB, *Christmas at Moose Factory*, in 1971. As of August 2017, she has directed 50 films with the NFB, with her documentary film *Our People Will Be Healed*, about the Helen Betty Osborne Ininiw Education Resource Center in Norway House Cree Nation, premiering in the masters-program of the 2017 Toronto International Film Festival (Brownstein 2016).

Obomsawin's next films include: *Incident at Restigouche* (1984), a powerful depiction of the Quebec police raid of a Micmac reserve; *Richard Cardinal: Cry from a Diary of a Métis Child* (1986), the disturbing examination of an adolescent suicide; *No Address* (1988), a look at Montreal's homeless; as well as *Mother of Many Children* (1977).

She filmed an entire series of films about the 1990 Oka crisis. The first, as mentioned previously, *Kanehsatake: 270 Years of Resistance* (1993), was a feature-length film documenting the 1990 Kanien'kehá:ka uprising in Kanehsatake and Oka. It has won 18 international awards.

It was followed by *My Name is Kahentiiosta* (1995), a film about a young Kahnawake woman who was arrested after the 78-day armed standoff, and *Spudwrench—Kahnawake Man* (1997), profiling Randy Horne, a high-steel worker from the Mohawk community of Kahnawake. The 2000 NFB release *Rocks at Whiskey Trench* was Obomsawin's fourth film in her series about the 1990 Oka crisis (Voyageur, Beavon, and Newhouse 2011).

Her credits include *Gene Boy Came Home*, about Aboriginal Vietnam War veteran Eugene Benedict. The *Mi'gmaq of Esgenoopetitj* (Burnt Church), New

Brunswick were the subject of her 2002 documentary, *Is the Crown at War with Us?* exploring a conflict with the Department of Fisheries and non-native fishers over fishing rights.

Her 2003 NFB documentary *Our Nationhood*, chronicles the determination and tenacity of the Listuguj Mi'gmaq First Nation to use and manage the natural resources of their traditional lands. In 2005, Ms. Obomsawin completed her short drama *Sigwan*, following a young girl who is aided by the animals of the forest. In 2006, she completed *WABAN-AKI: People from Where the Sun Rises* which is a look at the people and stories from her home reserve of Odanak (Robb 2015).

In 2009, she finished the documentary *Professor Norman Cornett*: Since When Do We Divorce the right answer from an honest answer? Looking at the dismissal of unorthodox McGill University religious studies lecturer Norman Cornett, which was destined for its world premiere at the Hot Docs film festival. In 2010, Obomsawin completed a short drama, *When All the Leaves Are Gone*, about her experiences attending public school in Quebec.

Her 2012 documentary *The People of the Kattawapiskak River* on the Attawapiskat Housing Crisis was conceived when Obomsawin was present in the community in 2011, working on another film for the NFB (Dunley 2012). Obomsawin's 2013 documentary *Hi-Ho Mistahey!*, about Shannen Koostachin, a First Nations education activist, premiered at the 2013 Toronto International Film Festival.

Obomsawin's 2014 documentary 'Trick or Treaty?' was the first film by an Indigenous filmmaker to screen in the masters-program at the Toronto International Film Festival. Obomsawin began conceptualizing the film in 2010 when she was invited by Stan Louttit, Grand Chief of the Mushkegowuk Council, to film a conference the band was hosting regarding Treaty No. 9.

Her 2016 documentary *We Can't Make the Same Mistake Twice*, explored a human rights complaint filed against the Canadian government over discrimination against First Nation children, which had its world premiere on 13 September at the 2016 Toronto International Film Festival.

At the 2021 Toronto International Film Festival, a special retrospective program of Obomsawsin's films was presented. Obomsawin was named as that year's recipient of TIFF's Jeff Skoll Award in Impact Media. Obomsawin also taught at the Summer Institute of Film and Television in Ottawa. A retrospective of her work was held from 14 to 26 May of 2008 at the Museum of Modern Art in New York City.

That same month, she was honored with the Governor General's Performing Arts Award for Lifetime Artistic Achievement, Canada's highest honor in the performing arts, at Rideau Hall in Ottawa. In the spring of 2009, Obomsawin was honored with a special retrospective at Hot Docs and received the festival's Hot Docs Outstanding Achievement Award. In 2010, she was named to the Playback Canadian Film & Television Hall of Fame.

Obomsawin was named an Honorary Fellow of the Royal Society of Canada for 2013. In January of that year, the Academy of Canadian Cinema & Television announced that Obomsawin would receive its Humanitarian Award for Exceptional Contributions to Community & Public Service, presented at the 2nd Canadian Screen Awards. At the 2013 Toronto International Film Festival, she was a recipient of a Birks Diamond Tribute to the Year's Women in Film.

In October 2015, she received a lifetime achievement award from Chile's Valdivia International Film Festival. In February 2015, the Montreal-based arts peace advocacy group Artistes pour la paix presented her with its lifetime achievement award. In March of that year, she was among the first 35 people named to the inaugural *Ordre des Arts et des lettres du Québec*. In November 2016, she received the Clyde Gilmour Award from the Toronto Film Critics Association, which called Obomsawin "a significant architect of Canadian cinema and culture." (*CBC News*, 24 November 2016).

Also in 2016, she received two of Quebec's highest honors when she received the Prix Albert-Tessier for contributions to the cinema of Quebec in November and was named a Grand Officer of the National Order of Quebec, in June of that year. In March 2017, she received the inaugural Prix Origine at Montreal's Bâtisseuses de la Cité Awards, for her work on Indigenous issues.

In June 2019, she was named a Companion of the *Order of Canada*. In May 2017, Obomsawin received an honorary doctorate from McGill University's School of Continuing Studies. That same month, she was named a commander in the newly created Order of Montreal, recognizing individuals who have contributed to the development of Montreal. Ryerson University awarded her an Honorary Doctor of Laws in June 2018 (Harewood 2006; Lewis 2006).

Gordon Tootoosis (1941–2011)

A Canadian actor of Cree and Stoney descent, Gordon Tootoosis made his film debut in the western film *Alien Thunder* (1974) with Donald Sutherland and Chief Dan George. Tootoosis also provided memorable performances in television and movies, including the role of *One Stab* in *Legends of the Fall* (1994), the role of *Growling Bear* in the Steven Spielberg produced miniseries *Into the West* (2005) and the role of *Chief Red Cloud* in the HBO film *Bury My Heart at Wounded Knee* (2007).

His television credits include guest appearances on *Friday the 13th: The Series* (1987), *MacGyver* (1985), *Northern Exposure* (1990), *The X-Files* (1993), *The Magnificent Seven* (1998) and *Smallville* (2001). Tootoosis provided the voice of *Kekata* in Disney's animated feature *Pocahontas* (1995) and Sheriff Gordy in *Open Season* (2006).

He was acclaimed for his commitment to preserving his culture and to telling his people's stories. He once said, "Leadership is about submission to duty, not elevation to power." He served as a founding member of the board of directors of the Saskatchewan Native Theater Company. Tootoosis offered encouragement, support, and training to aspiring Indigenous actors. He served as a leading Cree activist both as a social worker and as a band chief. Mr. Tootoosis was awarded membership in the *Order of Canada* on 29 October 2004.

The investiture ceremony took place on 9 September 2005. His citation recognizes him as an inspirational role model for Aboriginal youth. It notes that as a veteran actor, he portrayed memorable characters in movie and television productions in Canada and the United States.

Tootoosis was raised with his 13 siblings in the Plains Cree tradition until he was forced from his home; taking Indigenous children away from their communities and into residential schools was Canadian government policy at the time. Tootoosis was placed in a Catholic residential school, where he was treated harshly and forbidden to speak his own language. His father John Tootoosis was an activist for Aboriginal rights, which got young Gordon into trouble at school. After his traumatic school years, Tootoosis went into social work, specializing in work with children and young offenders.

His interest in his own cultural traditions led him to become an accomplished Native dancer and rodeo roper, and he toured with the Plains Intertribal Dance Troupe in the 1960s and 1970s throughout Canada, Europe, and South America, becoming one of North America's most popular pow-wow announcers.

His father was one of the founders of the National Indian Brotherhood and former head of the Federation of Saskatchewan Indian Nations (FSIN). Gordon himself served as the chief of his band and as a vice president of FSIN. Tootoosis married Irene Seseequasis in 1965. They had three daughters, Glynis, Alanna, and Disa, and three sons, Lee, Winston Bear, and Clint. After their daughter Glynnis died of cancer in 1997, they took the responsibility of raising her four children in Saskatoon (*CBC News* 2011; *Vancouver Sun* 2011a, 2011b).

Gordon Tootoosis was a prolific actor and a fierce advocate of Aboriginal rights and often combined both efforts with the roles he played. He overcame a troubled childhood and alcoholism to become an exceptional role model for his fellow Plains Cree and others across North America. He was also a co-founder of the Saskatchewan Native Theater Company, which changed its name to the Gordon Tootoosis Nīkānīwin Theater Company in 2015.

A descendant of Yellow Mud Blanket, who was a brother of the legendary Plains Cree leader Pîhtokahanapiwiyin (Poundmaker), Gordon Tootoosis, was raised with his 13 siblings in the Plains Cree tradition until he was taken from his home and placed in one of the infamous residential schools, where he said that he was treated harshly.

His father, John Tootoosis, was an activist for Aboriginal rights, which got the younger Tootoosis into trouble at school, including an expulsion when teachers caught him singing pow-wow with fellow students. John Tootoosis was the founding chief of the Federation of Saskatchewan Indian Nations (FSIN) and later became one of the founders of the Assembly of First Nations. Gordon later served as chief of his band and vice president of the FSIN.

After his traumatic school years, Gordon Tootoosis lived briefly in Whitehorse, where he worked as a mentor for youth. He then went into social work with the Saskatchewan Department of Welfare, specializing in work with children and young offenders. His interest in his own cultural traditions led him to become an accomplished pow-wow dancer and rodeo roper. He toured throughout Canada, Europe, and South America with the Plains InterTribal Dance Troupe in the 1960s and 1970s, becoming one of North America's most popular pow-wow announcers.

After breaking into acting with a recurring role in the Edmonton-shot TV series Stoney Plain, Tootoosis made his film debut as the Cree fugitive Almighty Voice in the Canadian feature *Alien Thunder* (1974, released on video as Dan Candy's Law). The film starred Donald Sutherland and Chief Dan George, apparently one of Tootoosis's idols.

Tootoosis then appeared in many theater, television, film, and radio productions, including the Genie Award-winning *Black Robe* (1991) and the Oscar-winning *Legends of the Fall* (1994), with Brad Pitt, Sir Anthony Hopkins and Tootoosis's close friend, Métis actor Tantoo Cardinal.

Tootoosis's character, One Stab, also the film's narrator, was changed from Cheyenne to Cree at Tootoosis's insistence, an example of how he helped shape Hollywood's sensitivity to Indigenous characters. Tootoosis regarded *Legends of the Fall* as the favorite film production of his career.

Tootoosis followed *Legends of the Fall* with another major Hollywood success, Disney's *Pocahontas* (1995), in which he voiced the character of Kekata, a Powhatan shaman. The film was one of the year's biggest hits. It won two Oscars and grossed nearly $150 million, although it generated some controversy for romanticizing the Pocahontas myth. That same year, Tootoosis played Chief Powhatan in the live-action Canadian co-production, *Pocahontas: The Legend*.

Other film credits include, *Leaving Normal* (1992), with Meg Tilly; *Lone Star* (1996), with Kris Kristofferson and Matthew McConaughey; *Alaska* (1996), with Charlton Heston; and the thriller *Reindeer Games* (2000), with Ben Affleck and Charlize Theron. Tootoosis also appeared in the Canadian films *Song of Hiawatha* (1997), alongside Graham Greene, Litefoot, Russell Means, and Irene Bedard. Hank Williams *First Nation* (2005), which was adapted into a short-lived TV series of the same name in which he reprised his role as Adelard Fox; and the gritty, low-budget gem *On the Corner* (2003), which earned Tootoosis the Best Supporting Actor Award at the American Indian Movie Awards.

Throughout his career, Tootoosis carefully selected roles that did not perpetuate negative stereotypes of Indigenous communities. In 1992, he spotlighted Aboriginal culture on Canadian television by appearing in *Peacemaker*, one of the first Heritage Minutes. Tootoosis played an elder who teaches his granddaughter about the Haudenosuanee (Iroquois) legend of the *Tree of Great Peace* and the origins of the Haudenosaunee Confederacy.

Conclusion

There can be no doubt that the various Indigenous movie stars whose lives are discussed in this chapter were deserving of widespread recognition in the history of the North American film industry. However, what many people have overlooked, or not been aware of, is the multifaceted dimensions of these film performers beyond their lives on the big screen. Jay Silverheels is a good example.

He was selected to be inducted into the Canadian Lacrosse Hall of Fame, was an accomplished boxer who placed second in the middle Weight Golden Gloves Tournament and was instrumental, along with Will Sampson, in founding the *Indian Actors Workshop* in Los Angeles in an effort to facilitate increased Indigenous roles in the film industry. Jay Silverheels was also an outspoken activist for Indigenous rights and in this role often appeared on various television talk shows such as Johnny Carson's *The Tonight Show*.

In a similar manner, Chief Dan George worked to improve the popular image of Indigenous people who were often presented in stereotypical ways in the movie industry—as *wagon burners*, or *promiscuous squaws*, for example. Chief George had a reputation for refusing to engage in film roles which in any way were demeaning to Indigenous people and their cultures.

In his controversial soliloquy, *A Lament for Confederation*, he attempted to express his contempt for the *settler mentality* which could be seen to deny the rights of Indigenous people. All in all, his statement could be interpreted as one reason for the escalation of Indigenous political activity in Canada during the 1960s and beyond.

Tantoo Cardinal was also well known throughout her film career for her advocacy role in promoting Indigenous rights which resulted in her nomination for the best actress for a Genie Award as well as a number of other best actress awards. She is especially known, along with fellow Canadian Graham Greene, for her role in *Dances with Wolves* (1990), which won seven Academy Awards including Best Picture. This film was largely seen as an attempt to correct Hollywood's negative portrayal of Indigenous characters, such as using the Lakota language.

As Tantoo Cardinal (2002) recounts in her article, "Voices from Native America," in the *First Nations Drum* newspaper, "the power of *Dances with Wolves* is that it brought some positive images forward that we really, really needed and that was extremely important." Furthermore, a *Toronto Star* article (Wong 2015) noted that "Tantoo Cardinal served to shred the meek, sexualized…[Disney] image of the Indian female as Pocahontas."

In addition, when Tantoo was awarded the *Order of Canada* it was noted that "Cardinal helped blaze a trail in an industry where few trails for Aboriginal women previously existed." It is certainly a fitting tribute to her tireless advocacy efforts to improve the position of Indigenous people in the North American film industry with positive imagery and to shred previous demeaning Hollywood portrayals of Aboriginal peoples which were so prevalent in past decades.

Indigenous actor Graham Greene also had a prominent part in *Dances with Wolves* in his role of Kicking Bird for which he was nominated as the Best Supporting Actor in the Academy Awards for 1990. While his advocacy role in support of Indigenous people is not as obvious as some other film stars, Grahame Greene was a graduate of Toronto's Indigenous Theater program in 1974, thus acting in support of Indigenous role models in the movie industry.

He also played significant parts in a variety of movies such as The *Green Mile* which lent support for Indigenous role models in films that were not overtly Indigenous in nature. His career also led to numerous awards and honorary university degrees, several Gemini Awards, and an *Order of Canada* all of which have made Graham Greene a significant role model for Indigenous performers in the arts.

The contributions to the film industry of Alanis Obomsawin are certainly multifaceted in nature, however, the role that she has played in the development of the documentary film industry which focused on Indigenous issues is certainly among her most important contributions, and perhaps, not as fully recognized as fully as it should be. As she stated, "The basic purpose [of her films] is for our people to have a voice" (Pick 1999: 78).

Overall, she directed over 50 films with the Nation Film Board of Canada which featured most significantly the plight of Métis children (Richard Cardinal) and the Quebec police raid on the Micmac reserve of Restigouche. In addition, her film *Kanehsatake* which focused on the 1990 Oka Crisis in Quebec brought attention to the significant conflicts of interest between Indigenous people, on the one hand, and the larger government structures of federal and provincial legal systems.

A 2008 retrospective of the film contributions of Alanis Obomsawin was held at the Museum of Modern Art in New York City, thus demonstrating the international accord by which she is held in the film industry. Her award of the *Order of Canada* in 2019 was a further recognition of her far-reaching contributions to "giving a voice" to Indigenous people.

The life of Gordon Tootoosis is another significant example of an Indigenous person combining an advocacy role and noteworthy contributions to the film industry. His film career can be summed up with his statement that "Leadership is about submission to duty." As an example of this commitment, Gordon Tootoosis played a significant role in encouraging and supporting Indigenous actors with the foundation of the Saskatchewan Native Theater Company of which he was a founding member. His award of the *Order of Canada* in 2014 served as another inspirational basis as a role model for Aboriginal youth.

He put his commitment to advocacy when he served as chief of his band and played a leading role in the Federation of Saskatchewan Indian Nations. It is an organization in which he served as vice president and of which his own father was a founding member.

In summary these overviews of notable Indigenous Canadian actors clearly demonstrate how their advocacy efforts in promoting positive role models for Aboriginal youth provide a crucial counterbalance to the regrettable stereotypes perpetuated by Hollywood regarding Indigenous peoples and their cultures.

Chapter Six
A Rising Star

Johnny Yesno made his international mark by winning the North American Indigenous Dancing Championship in 1963. According to his sister and co-author Caroline Yesno, his dance of choice was the *hoop dance*, which is a complex mix of maneuvers that resembles more of a series of gymnastic exercises than a dance per se. Nonetheless, the hoop dance is certainly unique in many ways. This dance was thought to be part of a healing ceremony which was designed to restore balance and harmony in the world. The hoop represents the never-ending circle of life. The hoop dance is performed by a solo dancer, who begins with a single hoop which represents the circle of life.

The Sacred Hoop Dance is a metaphor that gives a message of people creating unity. The four colors of the hoops are symbols of interdependence and unity, the four human races, the four seasons, and the four directions of the compass. As the hoops move, they speak of renewed creation for all living things (*https://discoverytheater.org/forms/guides/2019/nov/Hoop; Smithsonian Institution, 2019*; accessed 19 June 2024).

According to Indigenous writer Basil Johnston, in Anishinaabe culture a Manitou named Pukawiss, brother of Nanabozho, who was born to live among the people, created the hoop dance. Unlike the other boys, Pukawiss did not show an interest in running, swimming, or hunting. He only wanted to watch the animals. His fascination with things drove his father's interest away from him toward his other brother Maudjee-kawiss, therefore, leading to everyone calling him Pukawiss: the disowned or unwanted. Pukawiss learned so much about life in the movements of eagles, bears, and snakes that taking their life would have been wrong.

The animals had much to teach human beings about values and relationships like loyalty, kindness, and friendship. Pukawiss taught his village about the animals by spinning like an eagle in flight, hopping through grass like rabbits, or bouncing like a baby deer (Johnson 1995: 31; see also Heth 1993: 65–81).

Film footage of Johnny Yesno's dance championship is apparently not available, at least at the time of this writing. However, in the National Film Board Movie *Cold Journey*, Johnny Yesno performs the hoop dance at a pow-wow to the applause of the surrounding crowd of gatherers. As an article in *Sootoday* (5 December 2021) reiterates, "Another equally important accomplishment of young Yesno's life also came in his early adulthood. In 1963, Johnny competed against 92 contestants and won the North American Indigenous Dancing Championship."

It was about this time that Johnny was "bitten by the acting bug" as the saying goes. While working for an engineering firm in Toronto, he joined a dance group that was known to perform for tourists in the city. It was at just such a performance that Johnny Yesno's star quality shone and was observed by a CBC producer, landing Yesno a role in the premiere episode of the CBC's 1966 drama, *Wojeck*.

As the *Windspeaker* magazine also indicates, Johnny Yesno "found a creative outlet for himself with a dance group that performed at a city tourist spot. It was just a spare-time gig, but it gave Johnny his big break" (Meili, 7 April 2018). It was during a Toronto Indigenous dance festival that Johnny Yesno was first noticed for his talent which eventually led to a starring role in the Hollywood movie *King of the Grizzlies* a few years later. However, before this role, he appeared in several other acting opportunities that are discussed below.

Wojeck: The Last Man in the World (1966)

Wojeck is a Canadian dramatic television series, which aired on CBC Television from 1966 to 1968. It was arguably the first successful drama series on English Canadian television. The star of the show, John Vernon, had earlier played coroner Steve Wojeck in an episode of Bob Hope Presents for the *Chrysler Theater* titled *Tell Them the Streets Are Dancing* which was broadcast on 17 March 1966.

Steve Wojeck is a crusading big-city coroner who regularly fights moral injustices raised by the deaths he investigated. He often tackles tough and controversial issues. The first episode of the series examines the role of racism in the suicide of a young Anishinaabe man played by Johnny Yesno.

Although it was one of the highest-rated shows on Canadian television in its' time, only 20 episodes of the series were made, because Vernon was lured to Hollywood by the promise of more money than the CBC could offer. He only returned to the role once, for a TV movie *Wojeck: Out of the Fire* (1992). The first season (1966–67) was filmed in black and white, while season two (1967–68) and subsequent episodes were shot in color.

Wojeck is best remembered as the show that changed the face of Canadian television drama. Up until the time of the series, Canadian dramas had been rather sedate little affairs that rarely captured the interest of Canadian television viewers. However, when Wojeck appeared on CBC in 1966, Canadian television forever changed. *Wojeck* was based on the exploits of real-life Toronto coroner Dr. Morton Shulman and starred John Vernon as Dr. Steve Wojeck. Created by Phillip Hersch, the real-life cases of Dr. Shulman inspired each weekly episode.

Shulman, who was renowned as a health and safety crusader was well known in Toronto. Shulman extended the influence of his office through his inquiries into deaths caused by institutional and industrial negligence and forced issues of improved safety standards. Each week, over 3 million viewers tuned in as the title character addressed such issues as abortion, drug abuse, poor working conditions, police brutality, abuse of the elderly, Native rights, and auto safety issues.

Wojeck caused viewers to be gripped by their television sets. The barriers that the series broke down were thematic as much as stylistic or technical. Under the guidance of Executive Producer Ronald Weyman and Associate Producer David Peddie, the writers explored issues that had rarely been confronted so directly in television drama. In fact, the issue at their center can categorize many of the programs as much as by the actual story.

Part of the success of *Wojeck* was a result of its visual style. It was the first time the CBC had produced a filmed dramatic series for its national audience. Executive producer Ronald Weyman drew upon his experience at the National Film Board to deliver stories which had the look of authenticity. This was especially true in the first season when each episode was in black and white. Weyman and Director of Photography Grahame Woods shot the black-and-white film production on location with a lightweight camera. Cameras were hand-held and conventional production values were sacrificed for a down-and-dirty naturalism in the style of documentaries.

The program, and the series that ensued, tried to confront contemporary social issues through Wojeck's inquiries. The program's documentary style and the roots of the stories in the headlines of the day established standards and format that have filtered through CBC television drama ever since. John Vernon played Wojeck; stalwart, quiet, and understated. Wojeck was frustrated or driven to outrage by people, officials, and institutions that failed to provide answers or acknowledge responsibility. He regularly questioned the decisions he had to make and though he was in many senses of the word your typical hero, Wojeck was invested with a greater vulnerability and depth than most television heroes.

Wojeck was the first TV series to feature forensic pathology in the investigation of crime and has been the central theme of several other TV mystery-suspense dramas, beginning with the BBC's *The Expert* in 1968. Other programs include: *The Last Man in the World* in which Wojeck tries to find out who assisted the suicide of an Ojibwa man (Johnny Yesno) who was locked up in jail.

The episode has flashbacks that show the racism between First Nations people and white people. At the 19th Canadian Film Awards in 1967, Episode One, *The Last Man in the World*, tied for Best Film for TV. Cinematographer Grahame Woods won the award for best Black-and-White Cinematography and Ron Kelly won for Best Director. Indigenous actors in addition to Johnny Yesno as Joe Smith also include Gene Lahache as Charlie Keethiuk.

In the first program in the series, known as one of the finest, Johnny Yesno stars as a young Indigenous man who arrives in Toronto from Moosonee in northern Ontario. The complications of his new life in the city, the racial prejudice he encounters and the hooker he mistakes for a girlfriend, propel him to commit suicide in a jail cell.

Unfolding in flashback structure, the story is driven by Wojeck's search for the source of the belt in which Joe hung himself. Visually and aurally adventurous, the program was regarded as stretching the conventions of television drama to gain both immediacy and dramatic, emotional power. Twelve of the episodes were shown in the UK on BBC One. As such, the Wojeck series could be regarded as having an international audience. (26 June

151

1969 BBC One UK; accessed 20 May 2024, *https://ctva.biz/Canada/Wojeck.htm*).

Central Themes

The series debut episode, *The Last Man in the World* features Johnny Yesno in the role of Joe Smith, a Cree from Moosonee, who comes to the city in search of work and is driven to end his life in a jail cell. Steve Wojeck investigates and uncovers aspects of the alien society that led Joe to his death.

Wojeck gained both critical and commercial success. *The Last Man in the World* won the Wilderness Award as the CBC's best film production of the year, and an award at the Monte Carlo Film Festival. The series was sold to foreign markets in the U.K., Sweden, Holland, Belgium, Ireland, Finland, and Yugoslavia. The series' success, however, had as much to do with the subject, the script, and above all the acting. The writers for *Wojeck* created stories around a big-city coroner and his quest for justice. The character and setting were novel twists on the very popular 1960s American genre of workplace dramas that focused on the exploits of such professionals as lawyers, doctors, and even teachers or social workers.

Ultimately, *Wojeck* was a victim of its own success. The source for weekly topics soon dried up and writers began scrambling for headlines to base their stories around. The show failed to find a US network buyer; they felt the series was too controversial and featured too much bad language but they did like star Vernon and the show's creator, Phillip Hersch.

In addition, while Dr. Shulman initially approved of the program, allowing access to his files and offering his office for filming, he became disassociated himself when the series ran Chrysler commercials featured new faster cars which were death machines in the eye of the coroner. Surprisingly, the show was later relaunched a few years later in the U.S. as NBC's *Quincy*, M.E.

Wojeck did return in a 1992 TV movie called *Wojeck: Out of The Fire* where he returned to Toronto in search of a baby killer and sought to reconcile with his long-suffering wife who had dumped him in 1978. *Wojeck* had no real successors. Weyman and others did produce a number of forgettable dramas in the next few years, but none could match the appeal of the imports. Ironically the very success of Wojeck had spelled trouble for CBC's drama department.

John Vernon was lured away to Hollywood, where he came to specialize in playing villains. Indeed, Weyman later claimed that much of the talent that had contributed to the appeal of Wojeck was drawn away to the greener pastures in the United States. The memory of that brief, glorious moment was sufficient to justify replaying some of the episodes of Wojeck on the CBC network over 20 years later. (Published on 12 February 2019. Written by Bob Furnell (2004) for *Television Heaven* (*https://televisionheaven.co.uk/reviews/wojeck*).)

Wojeck found its inspiration in the impactful work of Dr. Morton Shulman, Toronto's chief coroner. Shulman's investigations into deaths due to institutional and industrial neglect, which emphasized the need for improved safety standards, influenced the series. *Wojeck* explored safety standards through naturalistic filmmaking. John Vernon's portrayals confronted many dilemmas and tackled societal and drug issues, like abortion and addiction.

The show bravely addressed topics like homosexuality and elderly neglect, gaining acclaim and international recognition. Back in the mid-1960s, Canadian-made drama series were a rare commodity. Then came *Wojeck*. Gritty and unapologetic, it was the first Canadian series that was popular both with critics and viewers.

From the start, *Wojeck* was a different kind of TV show. It starred stage and TV veteran John Vernon in the title role of Dr. Steve Wojeck; a crusading coroner who was called in to investigate contentious crime scenes (the character was alleged to be loosely based on former Toronto coroner Dr. Morton Shulman). Wojeck could be both bombastic and belligerent when confronted with mindless bureaucracy and red tape.

He would rather tackle matters head-on to uncover the truth. Like many great Canadian series, however, *Wojeck* burned brightly but briefly. Despite receiving several international TV awards, the show was canceled after its second season. Nearly a decade later, NBC would recreate the series and call it *Quincy*, starring Jack Klugman as a crusading coroner, but it just wasn't the same (*Globe and Mail* Toronto, 31 March 2001). As a concluding statement, Mary Miller in her study of Canadian television and film in *Outside Looking In*, states that "Yesno had done a brilliant job as the protagonist in the *Last Man in the World* on *Wojeck*" (2008: 430).

Racial Profiling

The show begins with Joe Smith (Johnny Yesno) engaged in a fistfight with a police officer. Joe knocks the officer down while a large crowd gathers around and cheers on the combatants. The officer stays down on the ground and is kicked by Joe who yells at the officer to get up and continue the fight. Soon, a patrol car arrives with the officers arresting Joe and taking him away.

Eventually, while stirring in jail, Joe comes to believe that his life in the larger Euro-Canadian society is a hopeless one; that he will never be able to evade the violence and criminal justice system which is oppressing him, and as a consequence, he takes his own life.

For many Indigenous people such a sight would be a common occurrence, especially those who live in urban environments. We are not told in this case what incident prompted the fist fight; all we see is the aggressive Indigenous man pummeling a white authority figure. Such incidents fill the pages of the academic literature under such rubrics as *racial oppression, systemic or institutional racism,* and *racial profiling,* among a host of other headings. As an example, in their study entitled *Racial Profiling in Canada,* which includes the subtitle *Challenging the Myth of a Few Bad Apples,* Tator and Henry (2006) draw links among the relationships between Canada's criminal justice system, policing, and racial and ethnic minorities. Their central argument is outlined as follows:

"The first crucial argument in racial profiling is its links to the practice of racialization; practices that can be seen to operate in virtually every sector of society. *Racialization* is part of the broader process that inferiorizes and excludes groups in the population…the discourses around criminal acts by particular minority groups depend on essentialized and stereotypical thinking. Moreover, racialization begins with ideology, which is then filtered through everyday micro-interactions and discourses of police, security officers, judges, journalists and editors, educators, politicians, and bureaucrats, among others (2006: 8–9)."

The contention that Tator and Henry make in their study is that Indigenous and colored persons are seen in the criminal justice system to be *problem people* or, using their term, *bad apples.* Such people in Canadian society are seen by the authorities in the criminal justice system as in need of special scrutiny by the police because there is an *a priori* expectation that such persons are seen as troublemakers.

There is a self-fulfilling prophecy involved in this sort of logic because of the fact that Indigenous and colored people are overrepresented among the prison population in comparison to the people in the larger society. As an example, according to statistics provided by Corrections Canada, Aboriginal adults are incarcerated over six times more often than anyone else in Canadian society. Even though Indigenous peoples form less than 5% of the total Canadian population, they nonetheless account for over 17% of all federal inmates in this country. Of course, such statistics are apt to vary by province, and percentages of Indigenous peoples in any given area, among other variables. In the province of Saskatchewan, as an example, it has been noted that Indigenous people are incarcerated at almost 10 times the overall provincial rate (Smith 2006:81).

Possibly one of the reasons for this higher-than-average incarceration rate is that Indigenous people are subjected to greater scrutiny than other citizens because of the expectation that they are "problem people." As such, they are charged criminally at a greater rate than other Canadians, which would be a factor that could go some distance as an explanation for these alarming statistics.

As such, these overall incarceration rates can then be used as a justification by authorities for continuing the profiling of Indigenous people, in a seemingly endless cycle of detentions, arrests, and incarcerations. From the perspective of an Indigenous person such as Joe Smith, such a cycle might seem like a hopeless situation without any expectation of finding a way out. Then, when those in the larger non-Indigenous society view these unfortunate statistics, they are apt to believe that Indigenous people are just prone to commit crimes and as a result, they form stereotypical negative images of Indigenous people.

What those in the larger society would not understand are the reasons underlying these statistics in the first place. Most of this has to do with certain economic factors such as the endemic poverty on many reserves or the racial oppression and profiling that inhibits their acceptance by those in the larger (Euro-Canadian) society. As an example of racial profiling and the resulting negative stereotypes of First Nations people, Ponting (1998: 279–82) has studied the negative stereotypes that form the basis of the public's opinion that have emerged from a myriad of sources especially as they have been portrayed historically in the film industry as evidenced by many Hollywood *cowboy* and *Indian* movies.

Such movies have tended to promote a negative stereotypical view of Indigenous peoples as uncivilized, bloodthirsty, and wagon-burning, wild savages. There is also the persistent stereotype of the *drunken Indian*, which is problematic in promoting a positive view of Aboriginal persons. As Ponting so forcefully articulates, "Even though stereotypes are often false or contain only a kernel of truth, where they persist, great harm is done to Native people, especially to their identity. Furthermore, even stereotypes that are no longer part of popular culture still exert a debilitating influence on subsequent generations of Native people" (1998: 279). Thus, it is difficult to escape the harmful representations of the past that were promulgated in the Western movies of previous generations.

It is a concern, then, that movies and other forms of popular culture such as television shows frequently perpetuate harmful depictions of minority groups. This is the essence of Tator and Henry's research in which they conclude that "racialized images and ideas embedded in popular culture and other social institutions fuel moral panic among the White dominant culture. Moral panic thus becomes the vehicle of the dominant ideology; as such, it marginalizes, inferiorizes, and stigmatizes [Indigenous] people" (2006: 54). In this regard, the media can become complicit in the subjugation of minority groups, especially in the context of policing.

Furthermore, as Martin argues, "A crisis in governance becomes a matter of public concern when a ruling or a judgment has considerable media interest, such as a ruling on a controversial subject. A minority of these cases generate a sufficient challenge to legitimacy that special responses evolve or are called upon, such as public inquiries, legislative changes, or reforms to modes of civilian review, often driven by community and media pressures" (2007: 258–259).

In other words, the media can become a powerful force not just in disseminating *news*, but in shaping the very social and political stories that they are covering. Thus, the news media is capable of playing a role in determining, in a partial sense at least, the outcome of events that the public retains of negative minority group images.

In terms of Indigenous-police relations, especially those concerning confrontations over land claims, resource issues, and other contentious matters, the police officers involved cannot be expected to have much familiarity or training in the legal, constitutional, or political aspects of such disputes. The role of the police officer is more specifically engaged in exercising the rule of law, rather than attempting to act as constitutional legal experts in the fiduciary aspects of Indigenous land claims.

"It would be extraordinarily difficult," Pue (2007: 132–133) suggests, "to mark precisely where one constitutional right; freedom of expression or Aboriginal entitlement, for example, must give way to another, the preservation of the peace, perhaps. Such boundaries demarcate the frontier between lawful and unlawful police conduct."

Ontario's Racist Attitudes

There is evidently, in such cases which are discussed above, a conspicuous lack of clarity in Indigenous-police relationships that hinders the execution of the proper role of the police when disputes arise in the context of demonstrations that involve inter-racial groups and relationships. Such was the case involving the Ipperwash protest in which an OPP officer shot and killed an Indigenous protester named Dudley George (Hedican 2008, 2012, 2013). As was reported in the *Report of the Ipperwash Inquiry* (2007: 66: 71) by the Hon. Sidney B. Linden:

"The occuplers saw the OPP dressed in riot gear, standing shoulder-to-shoulder in rows and stretched across the road...The police officers were equipped with bulletproof vests, shields, batons, helmets, and guns.

The Aboriginal people had no protective clothing and had simply stockpiled rocks, sticks, and stones on the inside border of the park fence...Acting Sergeant Deane discharged his semi-automatic gun. He fired three shots in rapid succession at Dudley George."

The issue that led to the unfortunate death of the unarmed protester named Dudley George was essentially a land claim protest over the ownership of Ipperwash Provincial Park. It is obvious in this case, as the Linden Inquiry aptly illustrates, that the OPP used excessive force when they engaged with the Indigenous protesters. There were numerous factors involved that led to the death of Dudley George. One important factor was the attitude that the protesters held by the Premier of Ontario, Mike Harris.

In the recorded testimony regarding a closed-door meeting with Premier Harris, Attorney General Harnick stated under oath that the Premier ordered in a loud voice, "I want the fucking Indians out of the park." Harnick testified before the Linden Inquiry that he was "stunned" by Premier Harris's insensitive and inappropriate remark (see Hedican 2013: 162).

Furthermore, as Commissioner Linden stated in his summary of the event, "In my view, Premier Harris's comments in the dining room [meeting], and generally the speed at which he wished to end the occupation of Ipperwash Park, created an atmosphere that unduly narrowed the scope of the government's response to the Aboriginal occupation. The Premier's determination to seek a quick resolution closed many options" (Linden 2007: 49).

Thus, one can conclude that the tragic events that led to the death of Dudley George were aggravated by the racist attitudes of the Premier of the Province himself. In fact, a taped conversation that involved conversations by OPP Inspector Ronald Fox (who attended the so-called *dining room* meeting at Queen's Park) and Inspector John Carson, who was the commander overseeing the standoff at Ipperwash Provincial Park, led to this recording:

"John, we're dealing with a real redneck government...[T]hey are fucking barrel suckers; they just are in love with guns...[T]here's no question they couldn't give a shit less about Indians" (Linden 2007: 50). In addition, another important contributing factor that led to the tragedy pertained to the racist and culturally intolerant attitudes of several OPP officers themselves which, in turn, were a reflection of Mike Harris's racist disposition.

As an example, the officer in charge of the OPP Emergency Response Team at Ipperwash, Sergeant Stan Korosec, was recorded as saying on the day before Dudley George was killed, "We want to amass a fucking army. A real fucking army and do this. Do these fuckers big-time" (Linden 2007: 27).

It would appear that such negative attitudes toward Indigenous people helped by Ontario's police officers are not unusual in the surrounding population of Ipperwash Park. On the morning of 6 September 1995, Mayor Fred Thomas of the town of Forest apparently approached Inspector Carson in an attempt to convey his concerns that his community felt "terrorized" by the events at Ipperwash Provincial Park. No reason was given by the mayor for this perceived heightened level of concern, aside from the information that Indigenous people were involved in the occupation, and perhaps, Mayor Thomas felt threatened by their presence during the protest.

Also visiting the command post that Wednesday was MPP Marcel Beaubien who conveyed to Inspector Carson that the "Premier is in constant touch [with him]. Good communication" (Linden 2007:33). In additional testimony presented during the Linden Inquiry, OPP commissioner O'Grady expressed his opinion that it was not appropriate that politicians such as MPP Beaubien and Mayor Thomas should attend at the police command post because they could possibly influence the decision-making taking place by the OPP officers.

Commissioner O'Grady also expressed his opinion that some topics of discussion between the Incident Commander and MPP Beaubien were "regrettable." This was especially the case with the references to Premiere Harris's personal views and wishes which probably did not reflect the attitudes toward Indigenous people generally held by the members of Ontario's government. What is also regrettable is the perception, founded in fact or not, that the white politicians in the area surrounding Ipperwash Park have an inside track on the flow of information of what occurred on 6 September 1995.

During the testimony also recorded by the Linden Inquiry was evidence provided by one of the Aboriginal witnesses that several police officers who were attending in a location near the park made racist comments during an altercation. During the incident, several Indigenous park occupiers began to move about a dozen picnic tables to the Ipperwash parking lot in an apparent attempt to control access to the area of the park entrance.

Not long afterward, officers in three OPP cruisers approached the parking lot and one of the cruisers smashed into the assembled picnic tables on which some of which Aboriginal protesters were sitting at the time, causing them to break up under the impact of the resulting collision. Aboriginal protesters then began to fling the broken pieces of the damaged tables onto the hood of several OPP cruisers amid much yelling and commotion.

Then, during the ensuing turmoil, several Aboriginal witnesses subsequently testified that a number of OPP officers began to make racist comments during the squabble, referring to the occupiers as "wagon burners" and "wahoos." According to the subsequent testimony, one of the OPP officers then pointed at Dudley George and said, "Come on out, Dudley. You're going to be the first." Next, an OPP officer pulled out a can of pepper spray and spayed it at some of the protesters, who in turn threw sand in the officer's face (Linden 2007: 27).

Racist Imagery

There were other disturbing incidents attributed to OPP officers that were revealed in the testimony held during the Linden Inquiry which could be described as contributing to the racist imagery toward Indigenous people. Aside from the aggressive and culturally insensitive remarks made by these officers during the Ipperwash Park protest, several police officers were apparently responsible for designing and distributing racist items even after the shooting death of Dudley George by OPP officer Kenneth Deane.

According to testimony recorded during the inquiry several OPP officers procured T-shirts and related "memorabilia" as mementos or souvenirs of the events of 6 September. Then, on the day of Dudley George's funeral, held on 11 September 1995, his sister, Pam George, discovered that mugs and T-shirts with the OPP insignia, mixed mockingly with Indigenous symbols, were being sold in convenience stores around the town of Forest, Ontario.

One of the items included a coffee mug with an OPP shoulder flash with an arrow through it, and on the other side, an OPP shoulder flash with the words *Team Ipperwash 95* written below. In addition, one of the T-shirts depicted a feather on its side below an OPP crest presumably representing the death of the local Indigenous culture, but of course, many interpretations of this imagery are possible. Curiously, the OPP officers who were responsible for all of these anti-Indigenous items went on to testify at the Linden Inquiry that they "believed these images and the objects themselves were benign and that it was not inappropriate to possess or sell them" (2007: 30).

It is certainly hard to believe that given the heightened sense of emotions in the area around Ipperwash Park with the death of Dudley George that the OPP officers who were responsible for the distribution of these disturbing items would not regard the T-shirts and coffee mugs as portraying racist imagery.

The Ipperwash inquiry also learned of a second T-shirt that was produced during the course of the inquiry hearings, almost 10 years after the shooting death of Dudley George, which depicted a TRU [Terrorist Response Unit] symbol (a sword breaking an arrow in half over an anvil) which represented the OPP Emergency Response Team [ERT] quelling the park protest. As reported in the Ipperwash Report, "The use of the broken arrow imagery targeted a distinct group of people by their race through the use of violent imagery. It is a negative, stereotypical symbol of the Aboriginal people in the context of the ERT teams exercising their power over the occupiers" (2007: 30).

What is especially evident from this discussion as far as the Ipperwash protest is concerned is that there have been racist attitudes expressed from the very top of Ontario's political structure, by the Premier himself and MPP Beaubien, and down through the authority structure of the OPP. One might argue that Ipperwash is a specific case and does not reflect historical trends in Ontario's political, legal, and authority structure.

However, a strong case can be made that this view is incorrect and that over the last 50 years or so there have been many altercations between Indigenous protesters and Canada's police forces that resulted in injury and even the death of Indigenous people. To name a few, one could include the following in such a list: the Anicinabe Park occupation, Kenora, Ontario (1974); the Teme-Augama Anishnabai Logging Blockade (1988); the Innu and the Goose Bay Air Base Occupation (1988); the Lubicon Lake Cree Confrontation (1988); the Mohawk Oka protest (1990); the Gustafsen Lake Standoff, British Columbia, (1995); the Burnt Church Fishing dispute, Nova Scotia (2002); Caledonia and Grand River Land Dispute (2006); Grassy Narrows Mercury Poisoning blockade, northern Ontario (2006); and Akwesasne Border Confrontation (2009). Many more incidents in which Canadian police forces used excessive force to "subdue" Indigenous protesters could be added to this list (see Hedican 2013: 97–141).

Unfortunately, very few people in the political community and police-legal structure have any detailed knowledge of the Indigenous communities whose members have engaged in such protests or for that matter the reasons why the protests have taken place at all. As an example, a social scientist familiar with Indigenous issues in Canada has provided this condemnation of Canadians' lack of knowledge regarding Indigenous issues, especially those who are in positions of author and decision-making in governmental bodies. As Professor Wayne Warry (2007: 19) relates:

"Sadly, the type of first-hand experience I have is all too often lacking in our politics and media. Too often commentators with little or no practical experience in Aboriginal communities are prepared to voice their opinions about Aboriginal issues. I have met career bureaucrats who have never ventured into a reserve or remote First Nation. Even today, it is common for columnists in Toronto, Vancouver, Edmonton, or Ottawa to write about solutions for Aboriginal peoples without ever experiencing Aboriginal life."

The most unfortunate aspect of this commentary is that these very columnists who have "little or no practical experience" concerning Indigenous communities are the very ones that many politicians and law enforcement officers have traditionally relied upon for their information regarding Indigenous issues. For the most part, what is particularly lacking among governmental decision-makers is the very contextual information that would be necessary to make informed decisions about Indigenous issues. This is the very point that law professor Gordon Christie (2007: 147) makes when he comments that, "contextual analysis is critical to making sense of the appropriate relation between the police and the Canadian government when these two bodies intersect with the interests of both Aboriginal nations and Aboriginal individuals within Canada."

It is also critically important when attention is turned to particular disputes, for no scenario played out in the arena of Canadian-Aboriginal relations can be adequately understood outside its place within the larger legal, constitutional, historical, and political landscape.

Thus, one can conclude that these "contextual variables" of history and politics are apt to make relationships between Aboriginal peoples and the state political-law enforcement agencies a particularly complex matter when it comes to policing acts of confrontation and resistance. Then, when one also factors in the virtual lack of first-hand knowledge of Aboriginal communities by politicians and law enforcement officers, conflicts are bound to occur.

Aboriginal Suicide in Canada

The inaugural season of *Wojeck* in 1966 that Johnny Yesno appeared in began with a violent confrontation between Joe Smith and a police officer which ended with the suicide of Joe Smith while in police custody. The issue of Aboriginal suicide in Canada is a particularly important one given the poverty and racial discrimination that exists in this country.

So, one may ask, what are the suicide rates for Indigenous people in Canada and how do these rates compare to those that exist for the larger population? Statistics on this topic are available from Canadian Census reports which demonstrate that suicide rates have consistently been shown to be higher among First Nations people, Métis, and Inuit in Canada than the rates that exist among those in non-Indigenous populations (Kumar and Tjepkema 2019; see also Eggertson 2015; Hallett et. al 2007; Mehl-Madrona 2016;).

This report indicates that the suicide rate among First Nations people (24.3 deaths per 100,000 persons) was three times higher than the rate among non-Indigenous people (8.0 deaths per 100,000 persons). Among First Nations people living on-reserve, the rate was about twice as high as that among those who are living off-reserve. However, suicide rates varied by First Nations band, with just over 60% of bands having a zero rate. Suicide rates and disparities were highest in youth and young adults (15–24 years) among First Nations males and Inuit males and females.

In more specific terms, regarding age distribution, the 15–19 age group accounts for the highest percent (10.12%), followed by 10–14 years (9.48%), then (9.16%). After 20–24 years of age (8.415%), the suicide rate for Indigenous people declines steadily as the age groups decrease except for the 45–49 age group at 7.04%. In terms of age-specific suicide rates (per 100,000), males generally have higher suicide rates than females. For example, in the 15 to 24-year age group, female suicide rates (52.9%) are considerably less than for their male (78.8%) counterparts.

Which factors, then, can be seen to account for the disparity in suicide rates between the Indigenous and non-Indigenous populations of Canada? The authors of this report provide background information that is seen to provide some of the important factors involved:

"The historical and ongoing impacts of colonization forced placement of Indigenous children in residential schools in the 19th and 20th centuries, removal of Indigenous children from their families and communities during the *Sixties scoop,* and the forced relocation of communities. These [factors] result in the breakdown of families, communities, political, and economic structures."

Also, additional factors include the loss of language, culture, and traditions; exposure to abuse; intergenerational transmission of trauma; and marginalization. These are suggested to be associated with the high rates of suicide (Kumar and Tjepkkema 2019, *Cohort profile: The Canadian Census Health and Environment Cohorts [CanCHECs]* statcan.gc.ca, accessed 20 May 2024). This report aimed to update the reasons seen to account for Indigenous suicide from the various historical factors itemized above to several socioeconomic factors, such as household income, labor force status, level of

163

education, marital status, and geographic factors such as living on or off a reserve.

Aside from various statistical analyses one wonders if a cognitive approach to Aboriginal suicide is apt to reveal the reasons behind suicide attempts. One may leave a suicide note which attempts to explain the rationale behind their suicide, but can the validity of this explanation be relied on? In all, what is obvious is the person who attempts suicide feels that life is no longer worth living, whatever the reason. Suicide affects all of the world's populations and is influenced by such factors as mental disorders, depression rates, and overall life satisfaction. This would suggest, then, that Indigenous people have a much deeper level of frustration, or desperation than the larger Canadian population since the death rate by suicide among Indigenous people is three times that of their non-Indigenous counterparts.

In addition, statistics demonstrate that unintentional injuries are the leading cause of death in Canadian Indigenous children and youth, occurring at rates three to four times the national average (Banerji 2012). In fact, it is thought that as many as 25% of all accidental deaths among Aboriginal youth may actually be unreported suicides (Chandler and Lalonde 2004: 111–123).

Unfortunately, there are few studies on Indigenous suicide that do not focus on broad-ranging generalities and statistical computations. One exception to this more general rule is the study by Alvin Evans which is entitled *Chee: A Study of Aboriginal Suicide*. Benjamin Chee lived with anger and frustration for more than 30 years before he took his own life.

An Ojibway artist who killed himself just as he was beginning to gain international recognition, Chee is one of the thousands of Aboriginal people in Canada who have committed suicide. Al Evans is a former RCMP officer who explored Chee's rough, yet creative life. It revealed how the clash between Indigenous and Euro-Canadian society has affected the suicide rate of young Native men and women, which as the previous statistics illustrate, are now among the highest in the world.

Using his in-depth understanding of Native self-destructive behavior and information from interviews with Chee's mother, close friends, and fellow artists, Evans shows that understanding Benjamin's suicide requires moving beyond psychological analysis to include the damage that contact with White society has caused Native culture, heritage, status, and meaning of life. Evans argues that White society needs to understand these dynamics to be involved in the healing process of Aboriginal peoples in Canada—or to at least avoid hindering their recovery. This study also suggests that knowledge of Indigenous suicide would benefit from studies of specific individuals and the lifestyles that contributed to such desperate acts of self-destruction.

Conclusion

This chapter has taken a specific incident of Indigenous suicide in the inaugural episode of the CBC television series, *Wojeck*, of the 1960s and placed it in a wider context in Canadian society for further analysis. In the incident depicted in this episode, Johnny Yesno portrays the acute frustration of Indigenous people in a hostile urban environment, and his subsequent suicide while incarcerated in a Toronto jail cell after a physical altercation with a police officer. This episode is then set in the larger context of Ontario's racist imagery as depicted in available social science literature and government publications.

An example of a violent altercation during an Indigenous protest at Ipperwash Provincial Park in 1995 during which one of the protesters, Dudley George, was shot and killed by OPP officer Kenneth Deane, is discussed at some length. An analysis of this incident is based on the Linden Inquiry of 2007 which was conducted over a decade after the initial park protest due to the political intransigence of the existing Conservative government.

This analysis is further utilized to illustrate the depth of racist attitudes toward Indigenous people in the Province from Ontario's Premier at the time, Mike Harris, down through the authority structure of the OPP and MPPs in the area and illustrates the prevalent depth of racist attitudes that exist in the governmental institutions of Canadian society.

Chapter Seven
King of the Grizzlies:
The Rise to Fame

The is no doubt that Johnny Yesno's claim to fame occurred because of his participation in the Walt Disney film *King of the Grizzlies* produced in 1970. This movie is an adventure film originally based on a loose adaptation of an earlier 1900 novel *Biography of a Grizzly* written by Earnest Thompson Seton. Aside from Johnny Yesno, the film also stars Chris Wiggins, Hugh Webster, and Jack Van Evera and was released by Buena Vista Distribution.

The film is based on the story of Moki, an Indigenous man of Cree heritage in the late 19th-century in Western North America. In the movie, Moki worked as a foreman on a ranch owned by his former army commanding officer, Colonel Pierson, and wore the sign of his tribal totem on his hand; a four-toed track, which is the mark of the grizzly bear.

As the story unfolds, a grizzly bear invades Pierson's ranch and kills a steer. As a consequence, Pierson shoots the marauding bear and one of her cubs but misses the other one. The surviving cub manages to avoid the fate of his mother and sibling when he falls over a cliff and into a river during which he is swept downstream.

While Moki was searching for the whereabouts of the surviving cub, he just happened to notice, when examining the cub's tracks, that it had only four toes on one of its paws. On this basis, Moki named the missing cub *Wahb*; meaning four-toed grizzly bear. Eventually, he succeeds in capturing the bear cub and then sets it free in the land that surrounds Pierson's property.

As fate would have it, Wahb managed to survive the perils of life without his mother and grow up to maturity. When he was just three years old, the young grizzly makes a reappearance on Pierson's ranch during which time he frightens a ranch hand. With this threat in mind, Pierson orders Moki to capture the bear, but Wahb manages to escape into the surrounding wilderness.

It was not until several years later that Waub reappears again, this time during an encounter with Moki in the mountains above the ranch. It was because of these different encounters that Moki formed in his mind the belief that he and Waub share a mystical bond and that the pair have a shared destiny on this earth. However, Waub reappears on the Pierson ranch which causes a herd of cattle to stampede.

This incident causes the owner to set out in an attempt to kill the bear, but in a strange twist of fate, Waub manages to circle around behind Pierson so that it is now the grizzly who is tracking his pursuer. Moki happens upon the scene of this strange reversal of events and as a consequence attempts to warn his boss about the possible impending danger but is not successful.

Pierson, who had been tracking Waub while riding on horseback, is thrown from his stead when he meets the bear in a head-on encounter. At this point in time, Moki arrives on the scene and runs to the side of his fallen boss. While attempting to ascertain Pierson's possible injuries, Waub appears, startling the men. Moki realizes that he is only armed with a small pistol, which is hardly sufficient to deter a charging grizzly bear.

Nonetheless, Waub leaves the two men alone and unharmed. Moki and Pierson then watch as Waub begins to claw away at a nearby tree. During this interval, Pierson draws a rifle from a holster on the side of the fallen horse and aims at the bear. Moki attempts to get him to stop by explaining that Waub is only marking the tree with his claws as a sign that he will not return to the ranch.

Pierson does not listen to this explanation but when the Colonel attempts to fire his rifle Moki shows him a handful of bullets that he had previously removed from Pierson's rifle. At this point, the grizzly turns and leaves the pair unharmed, never again returning to the Pierson ranch.

Some Reviewer's Comments

Reviewer 1: 14 March 2022

I am a big fan of nature documentaries, whether films or series, and there are many exceptional nature documentary series and films out there. Some are obvious, and some are not as well known today. Some people don't like it when animals are humanized, with the adjective "manipulative" sometimes coming up.

Mostly I don't have a problem with this myself. It is always interesting to see animals in life-like situations and behaving in a way that is relatable and it makes the animals easy to relate to as well.

This has been done better elsewhere than in *King of the Grizzlies*. Don't get me wrong, to me *King of the Grizzlies* was on the whole pretty good with many great things. Seeing grizzly bears portrayed in this way and that there is more to them than the dangerous ones often heard of was interesting and wouldn't say no to seeing this more. When it comes to documentaries on bears, there is a preference for the True-Life Adventures short film *Bear Country*.

King of the Grizzlies is a bit too over-deliberate in stretches, meaning that some parts drag. Personally, I didn't find the human element particularly necessary. Did think too that the narration writing was a touch too on the cutesy and too jokey side, which was also the case with some of the True-Life Adventures feature-length films.

However, *King of the Grizzlies* is beautifully shot, and also cannot complain about the scenery, the mountains look majestic. The music is atmospheric, haunting in the more dramatic moments, and tranquil when in softer moments (the latter of which there is more of).

While there were reservations about the narrative writing, there weren't any issues with Winston Hibler's delivery which was suitably good-natured. Suitably laidback at times and doesn't sound boring. Shorty is good fun too.

Really liked the gentle tone of the storytelling, though the film doesn't shy away from showing the challenges and not sugar-coating it. The journey of the grizzly bear is cute, moving, and relatable, as is the grizzly bear himself. Also found myself learning a good deal and the material felt fresh, did not find myself talked down to or talked at.

Concluding, worth seeing if not a must. 7/10.

Reviewer 2: Pleasant Wildlife Story for a Quiet Evening's Viewing: disbound 26 April 2002.

John Yesno as Moki, Chris Wiggins as The Colonel and Hugh Webster as Shorty is a pleasant enough family film, more of a grizzly life documentary with a sparse human element wrapped around it than an actual movie, about the life of a male grizzly from cub to adult. During his life as a cub, he loses his mother and is rescued from certain death by a Cree Indian, Moki, and released in the high mountains surrounding the ranch Moki works on for the Colonel.

The story shows the viewer a gentle, laidback view of the life of a typical bear with beautiful high mountain scenery and a glimpse of the rugged life of those intrepid souls who went west with a dream and established the big cattle ranches that eventually led to the settling of the wide-open country once owned by the Indians and animals, who unlike these, lived together in harmony.

Good for a time when you just want a quiet nature story and great mountain photography as not much in the way of excitement happens until near the end when the big bear's future becomes very uncertain after he crosses the tough rancher. 2 out of 4 stars db.

Reviewer 3: Movie for Science Class Rather than Family Movie Night: A Conflicted Recommendation.

I live near a used DVD store, and I purchase many of my DVDs there due to their closeness and great selection. King of the Grizzlies was there and it drew my attention for being an old Disney movie. My Grandma/guardian and I love old Disney movies like Swiss Family Robinson, Third Man on the Mountain, and The Ugly Dachshund, and she loves animal movies, so for that, and the $4 cost, I picked it up.

My Grandma and I just watched it, and it wasn't what we expected. It wasn't bad, keep that in mind, and I wouldn't mind seeing it again, but it was quite unusual for a Disney film.

King of the Grizzlies follows a grizzly bear with two cubs. We see them grow up and then befriend an Indian man named Moki who considers the male cub to be a brother. King of the Grizzlies has many cute moments with the bear cubs, and the human parts make for watchable drama. There were also some funny moments. In one part, the narrator tells us that male bears find a female to mate, and then abandon them after she gets pregnant.

My Grandma and I were both like:

"Human males aren't much different!"

However, the film did have some flaws. For one thing, there is way too much narration. The movie's cover made the movie look more like a drama, but it turns out it was more of a documentary. Comparing Disney movies, it felt more like

Earth, and we were expecting something like Rascal. And when I say 'too much narration', I mean about 97% of this movie's dialogue was the narration.

The other 3% is about a man the bears meet and some friends of his. I'm not saying there should have been NO narration (witness the mating part), but it was overkill for a movie that was supposed to entertain families.

Unless you don't mind a Disney movie being a documentary, this is fine. I like the Disney nature movies, like Earth, but this one was unexpected as a documentary and dull at times. King of the Grizzlies is sure to bore the target Disney audience as a result, but older Disney fans should give this a watch.

Like I said, King of the Grizzlies isn't bad, it just wasn't what I thought it would be. With different expectations in mind, I might like it more upon a second viewing. I don't usually recommend 7/10s, but for those who want to see cute bears and don't mind the narration, King of the Grizzlies is worth the 93 minutes of your time.

At best, this is better for a Science Nature class rather than a family movie night.

Indigenous People as Ecological Saviors

Reviewers are entitled to their opinions like everyone else. However, there is an old adage that people vote with their feet, or, in this case regarding movies, vote with their pocketbooks. Readers might be interested to know that for 2022 the gross income of Disney World was $82.7 billion U.S. dollars which was an increase of $15 billion over the previous year. Obviously, then, Disney films are immensely popular among its supportive fans, regardless of people's opinions of them one way or another.

Another factor that makes the *King of the Grizzlies* film interesting is Johnny Yesno's role in it. As an Indigenous person, Moki is portrayed as a sort of intermediary between the white, industrial world represented by Colonel Pierson, and Waub, the grizzly, representing the natural world.

In the film, Moki intercedes between the two worlds saving both from potential conflict, and in the process, the grizzly survives. Granted, this idea of an Indigenous person interceding between the two worlds, the modern and the natural, is somewhat of a clique. But it does suggest that Indigenous people are, as the saying goes, "more attuned to nature" than the European, colonial intruders.

In other words, Indigenous people are seen as ecological saviors providing a buttress against the intrusive industrial society whose members, out of fear one presumes, only want to kill problematic predators such as wolves, coyotes, lions, and grizzlies. This image of the "ecological Indian," which conveys the metaphor of the "one-with-nature" symbolism is particularly problematic because many people today—European and Indigenous, view such topics as environmental degradation and climate change as serious matters to be concerned about.

Shepard Krech (1999, 2005, 2010) has written extensively about ecological Indigenous imagery and in the process has become engaged in a controversial imbroglio. As Krech (2010) explains, "The image of North American Indians as first ecologists, conversationalists, and environmentalists, which can be called the Ecological Indian, became dominant in the 1960s. Today, many, including American Indians accept it as an accurate representation of Indian behavior through time."

In fact, a conference was organized in 2002 which was composed of both Indigenous people and academics that had the overt purpose of examining this Ecological Indian imagery. This conference, known as *Re-figuring the Ecological Indian*, was organized by the University of Wyoming's American Heritage Center.

Shepard Krech, the scholar deemed to have initiated the stereotypical controversy, was invited to give the keynote address and to explain his particular views on the subject. The organizers admitted that the conference invited controversy, and fully expected that Krech's imagery would be assailed as a problematic political tract.

Their angst was described as follows:

"We were, to put it mildly, unprepared for the reaction. And fortified by that particular variety of naïveté (cluelessness?) reserved for academics, we resolved to ride out (ignore?) the gathering storm" (Harkin and Lewis 2007: xii).

Perhaps, a change in political climate had occurred, or modern concerns for the environmental damage caused by modern industrial society have made people more aware of the ongoing ecological deterioration of the planet. But whatever the cause attendants at the conference, even the Indigenous people themselves, appeared at ease with the idea that Native societies were more respectful of Mother Earth than are today's (non-Native) inhabitants.

As the organizers of the conference admitted, "The controversy surrounding the *Ecological Indian* had become a multifaceted one, with the attendant fears that challenging the trope of the Ecological Indian somehow undermines Native self-image, the reality of Indian cultural distinctiveness, notions of sustainability versus the consequences of modern technological society, or just deeply held ideas about Indians and the environment" (ibid: xiii).

In other words, the organizers were fearful that any criticism of the Ecological Indian imagery, would therefore, consequently, imply that Indigenous people were not respectful of the environment, or worse; that they were just another exploiter of this planet's resources. As one would probably expect, the academics who were invited to deliver papers on their areas of expertise that could be related to the conference's main theme, and who probably had their papers prepared well in advance of the gathering, proved to be taken aback by the controversy which was reflected in their deliberations.

Even so, there appeared to be some agreement with Paul Nadasdy's (1999, 2005) position that environmentalism is a complex and at times contradictory continuum, which is to say, that environmentalism is in most ways more problematic than the ecological practices of Indigenous peoples. Furthermore, an important aspect of this problematic situation is that images of Indigenous people are organized around more than a few foci, such as *vanishing*, *violent*, and *wise* (Berkhofer 1978; Smith 2000). In turn, overriding these characteristics is the more prominent notion that the Indigenous people live (or lived?) in harmony with nature.

If this trope of equating Indigenous people with nature is pushed further, the consequences could be that Aboriginal people are, on the one hand, denied their own histories, while on the other hand, even deprived of their place in the modern world (Lewis 1995; Warren 2002).

Bears and the Anishinaabe

In the *King of the Grizzlies* movie, Moki relates that his grandfather told him about an Anishinaabe legend in which the Great Spirit (*Kitchi Manitou*) created both bears (*mukwa*) and people with the intention that they would consider each other as *brothers* (*nidjikwe*) and treat each other accordingly, this is, to treat each other with a special relationship of respect.

172

Thus, as far as the movie is concerned, Moki and Waub share a relationship with each other that would transcend any other relationship between fellow creatures, a relationship that was ordained by the Creator himself. As such, when Moki's boss tried to kill Waub, Moki felt it necessary to protect his "brother" from the impending assault. In turn, the grizzly bear would also comprehend this special relationship and act accordingly, to wit, agree not to transgress on the cattleman's territory.

In my own ethnographic fieldwork among the Anishinaabe of northern Ontario (Hedican 1986, 2001, 2023) that is, research conducted between Lake Nipigon and the Albany River, I was told by several elders that when a hunter met a bear in the bush he would begin to talk to this creature "as his brother."

That is, to speak to the bear in the Anishinaabe language because it would be assumed that the *mukwa* would understand the dialogue. There would be no fear on the part of the Anishinaabe hunter that the bear would harm him in any way. In fact, I was told, the bear would move its head back and forth as a gesture of comprehension, sometimes emitting his/her own grunts and growls in return.

"The Ojibways have great respect for the Bear. According to their legends, in the distant past, the Bear had a human form and was in fact an ancestor of the Ojibways. Therefore, he understands the Indian language and will never attack or fight any Indian if he is addressed properly."

Another aspect of the *mukwa-Anishinaabe* relationship concerns the so-called "bear walking" phenomenon. In the mid-1980s, I was asked to teach an anthropology course to Indigenous students in the Native Teacher Training Program at Lakehead University in Thunder Bay, Ontario.

After a lecture on Indigenous spirituality, a student approached me and said, 'Now I understand what my grandfather was talking about when he told me about his experience concerning walking bears. According to my grandfather, when he was a young man living in an Anishinaabe community in the Albany River area, he looked out of his cabin window one morning to see a bear, standing on its' hind legs.

"He said that he knew right away what was happening. Another man had taken over the body of a bear and wanted to hurt him. Evil people," he said, "could take over the body of a bear through magic spells. You could tell that the bear was inhabited by an evil person because it would always walk on its hind legs [like a person]."

"So," my grandfather said, "he rushed out of his cabin and struck the walking bear in the skull with his axe. As the bear was dying, it turned back into its' human form. Well, that's what my grandfather told me," related the student.

According to several sources, such as Basil Johnson's *The Bear-Walker* (1997), the post on Zhaawan Art, *Reawakening of the Medicine People: Return of the Bear Walker* (2024), A. Iving Hallowell, *The Role of Conjuring in Saulteaux Society* (1971 [1942]), Christopher Vecsey, *Traditional Ojibwa Religion* (1983), or more specifically, Robert Desjarait's, *The Bear Walkers* (2017):

"Although the Bear is a positive symbol in our culture, there is a negative, if not terrifying, side to her as well. Many Anishinaabeg believe that the *makwa bimose,* or bear walker, is a *maji-mide* (evil sorcerer) who walks at night and uses the Bear Medicine for selfish purposes, often leading to inflicting harm to people in the form of sickness and death."

In Northern Michigan, the Chippewa people have accounts about creatures called Bearwalkers. They are usually a shaman of some kind who gains the power of shapeshifting; almost always into the form of a bear. The Bear-Walker visits four times, four days apart. Around the victim's house, family members will see a light moving in the trees. After the fourth visit, the victim dies.

Four days after the victim is buried, the Bear-Walker must visit the grave and recover part of the body, usually one finger and the tip of the tongue; or they too will die, after four months have passed. Bearwalkers can be spotted when they're on their way to work their power, they breathe spectral fire.

Anyone who gets too close to a Bear-Walker will be paralyzed and fall to the ground unless they have the magic to counter it. If a person does manage to recover and can get their hands around the Bear-Walker, it will revert back to human form.

While in their bear form, they take on the strength of an actual bear, being able to lift objects two times their own weight. Despite all their supernatural abilities, Bearwalkers are still mortal and can be killed like any other human (*https://en.wiktionary.org/wiki/bear-walker*, accessed 22 June 2024).

In summary, the *King of the Grizzlies* movie was probably watched by many viewers as a mild form of entertainment, as a Disney nature film, fit for the children's channel on television. This is a shame because there are many aspects of this film that could have been explored in more depth, or in a more sophisticated manner.

As it is, some viewers will see in this film a presentation, or "trope" if you prefer, of the idea of Indigenous people as environmental saviors, or even ecological guardians, whether this relationship is applicable or not. Certainly, in this film, Moki has an inside track on the behavior of Waub the grizzly that other (Euro-American) people do not have.

Whether or not this esoteric insight is the result of Indigenous (Anishinaabe) traditions or specific personal knowledge of Moki himself is difficult to determine. Obviously, there is much more to this film than meets the eye, as they say, that could have been explained in the film for those who are not Indigenous scholars such as anthropologists. But even they, as my own personal experience suggests on the basis of my own research in northern Ontario, would have difficulty in providing a satisfactory interpretation of the Indigenous people-ecological relationship.

The Inbreaker (1974)

The next movie role for Johnny Yesno after the *King of the Grizzlies* was entitled *The Inbreaker* (1974) in which he played the role of Muskrat. The film was directed by George McCowan and the film location was Alert Bay, British Columbia. Essentially this movie is about a young man who takes a summer job in the west coast halibut fishery, only to find himself caught up in a conflict that he can neither calm nor comprehend. The description of the film below is an edited version of a review by Michael Walsh originally published in *Reeling Back* (*https://reelingback.com;* accessed 23 June 2024).

Former child star Johnny Crawford (remember *The Rifleman*?) plays Chris McKae, *The Inbreaker*. An Alberta university student, his education is being financed by his older brother, commercial fisherman Roy (Christopher George). The film opens with a cowboy-hatted Chris McKae arriving in brother Roy's B.C. fishing village.

In an attempt to assert his individuality and shoulder his own responsibilities, Chris has decided that he should work the summer on his brother's boat. The idea has less appeal to Roy, who explains that he is a simple two-man operation. To take Chris on, Roy will have to fire his deckhand Al (Al Kozlik). If he keeps Al and adds Chris to the crew, he will have to pay

Chris out of his own share of the catch, in which case Chris will still be dependent. As such, Chris agrees to look for a job elsewhere.

As luck would have it, he ends up as an *Inbreaker*—an unpaid apprentice—to Muskrat (Johnny Yesno), who just happens to be Roy's most hated rival. The film's best moments come during Chris's high-seas inbreaking, a period during which the gangling youth is desperately trying to convince his surly mentor of his competence. Adding to his anxiety is the fact that Muskrat, with ringing bravado, has challenged Roy to a fishing contest. Even with the handicap of an untrained crewman, Muskrat says he will catch more fish. Roy accepts, thus putting Chris under double pressure.

In *The Inbreaker*, the film's director McCowan brings together several effective elements: a finely-tuned interplay between actors Crawford and Yesno; a cheerful score by Vancouver composer Grant Horrocks (arranged by Curt Watts to blend in with the chug-chug-*chugga-chug*-chug-chug of the boat's motor); the visual menace of slashing blades and the random flicking of finger-sized hooks riding a high-speed line. All are combined to set filmgoers on the edge of their seats.

What follows is a series of incidents involving an accidental death, an attempted frame-up, a kidnapping, and a murderous chase. A basic unresolved question with the film is "Why does Roy so hate Indigenous people in general, and Muskrat with such particular vehemence?" In addition, why does Muskrat so fear the Mounted Police? "The cowboys," as he calls them.

That McCowan was able to make palatable entertainment out of *The Inbreaker* is important not only to this particular film's audience but also to the future of the B.C. film industry. It's worth mentioning that, with the exception of two of his three leading players, all of his resources, both technical and creative, are drawn from Canada's talent pool.

From co-star Johnny Yesno, an Ontario-born actor and broadcaster, to bit player Bonnie Carol Case, the performances are of uniformly high quality. In addition, another film review in *Box Office* (13 August 1973) includes the following quote by Johnny Yesno concerning his explanations for the problems encountered by Indigenous people who live in remote areas, such as that of BC's Alert Bay, the location of the *Inbreaker* film:

"Johnny Yesno, host of CBC Radio's *Our Native Land* when he's not working in films and an articulate spokesman on Indian problems, blames 'the government, politicians and the media too' for ignoring the plight of Indians in remote areas of this country. In defense of the drinking Indian, Yesno—who isn't opposed to an eyeopener himself—said the hotels themselves are culprits. 'They don't kick them out until they pass out or run out of money. At closing time, the police swoop down to fill their quota to impress on their headquarters how much they're needed in isolated Canadian towns,' Yesno said (*https://www.boxofficepro.com*; accessed 23 June 2024).

Cold Journey (1975)

Cold Journey, directed by Martin Defalco, is a National Film Board of Canada movie that includes a cast of Johnny Yesno, Buckley Petawabano, Noel Starblanket, and Willie Dunn (featuring his song "Walk On, Walk On") filmed mostly in the vicinity of The Pas, in northern Manitoba.

Aside from Johnny Yesno and the rest of the cast, this film also prominently features Chief Dan George (1899–1981) who was discussed at length in the previous chapter. In essence, this film portrays the attempts by a 15-year-old Indigenous youth (Buckley Petawabano, who starred in the *Adventures of Rainbow Country* for 26 episodes from 1969–1970) to find his place in life.

Buckley faces an experience of culture shock as the result of an educational system that teaches him to adapt to a Euro-Canadian way of life while at the same time trying to reconcile this way of life with his Indigenous culture and ancestry. As an example, when Buckley returns home from the residential school, where his time is spent longing for his home with dreams of hunting and fishing, he nonetheless feels like a stranger because he is forbidden to speak his Indigenous Cree language, or participate in a life focused on living off the land the same as his father and brothers.

It is for all of these various reasons that the film has been described by an anonymous reviewer as "a tragic story of unexpected pitfalls and disillusionment that are as cruel as the bitter wind that greets him on his cold and lonely journey."

At the residential school, Buckley is befriended by an Indigenous caretaker acted by Johnny Yesno who plays a role in introducing young Buckley to Indigenous history, knowledge, and culture. Later in the film, Johnny finds Buckley's frozen body in a snow bank and begins to unravel the tragic events of the boy's short existence on this earth which was characterized by such a tumultuous reality between the conflicting Euro-Canadian and Indigenous cultural traditions. It should also be indicated that *Cold Journey*'s narrative is similar in certain respects to the real-life story of Charlie Wenjack who, in 1966, also ran away from residential school and like Buckley froze to death on his fateful journey.

Cold Journey, as far as film genres are concerned, is termed a "docudrama" because it allows the audience to study actual, real-life social issues in the context of an engaging movie experience. In the case of *Cold Journey*, the film's director, Martin Defalco, was initially inspired by various accounts in which Indigenous children in Canada were taken away from their families and forced to attend residential schools all over Canada.

Thus, Defalco was emotionally influenced by these cases which, in time, formed the basis for the *Cold Journey* film and his decision to dedicate a film to this unfortunate phenomenon. In turn, the issue of Canadian colonial involvement with the Indigenous people of this country forms the wider context in which the issues in the film are explored.

Director Delfalco's interest in the emerging themes of the *Cold Journey* film was superseded by a previous documentary called "Northern Fisherman" that he was filming in the community of Pelican Narrows located in northern Saskatchewan during the mid-1960s. In an NFB blog that describes Delfalco's experience (Ohayon 2017), it was noted that "the reserve where he was filming was full of life, until one day, an airplane arrived and took all the children away to residential schools. Defalco was stunned to see just how desolate the reserve became after all the children left. This left a lasting impression on him."

It was a few years later that Noel Starblanket, who was a member of the NFB's Indian Film Training Program, came up with the suggestion that the NFB investigate the possibility of making a film that focused on Canada's residential schools and the experiences of Indigenous people in the Canadian educational system.

Defalco thought that this was a good idea and began to write an outline for such a film which he subsequently presented to the NFB. His opinion at the time was that such a film should mostly have fictional content although he insisted that the movie's cast should be comprised of Indigenous actors which led to Buckley Petawabano and Johnny Yesno being cast in the principal roles.

While several other professional actors such as Chief Dan George (who had just come off the great success of *Little Big Man*, for which he was nominated for an Academy Award as Best Supporting Actor) were also employed, most of the cast resided in the Pelican Narrows community. As the NFB blog indicates "Defalco felt that they would give his film an authentic look and feel." The film then was shot over the subsequent winter and summer months of 1971.

Initially, there was some disappointment expressed in the preliminary production of *Cold Journey*. As the NFB blog reiterated at the time, "NFB producers were very disappointed with the first cut of *Cold Journey*. They felt it was bleak and contained some terrible acting. Delfalco re-cut the film, but this did nothing to quell the voices who said the NFB should simply shelve it. [However,] Delfalco pointed out that this was a story about the realities of the Indigenous peoples of Canada" (Ohayon 2017).

The film might have been thrown in the garbage if it was not for filmmaker Alanis Obomsawin who was persuaded to watch the film and give her opinion. She told the producer that in her opinion *Cold Journey* had an important message about the manner in which Indigenous communities were treated in Canada and on that basis, it should be distributed.

As the *Canadian Encyclopedia* recounts (accessed 15 May 2024):

"Alanis Obomsawin is one of Canada's most distinguished documentary filmmakers. She began her career as a professional singer and storyteller before joining the National Film Board (NFB) in 1967. Her award-winning films address the struggles of Indigenous peoples in Canada from their perspective, giving prominence to voices that have long been marginalized.

She is a Companion of the *Order of Canada*. In 1971, she directed her first film, Christmas at Moose Factory, and in 1977 she became a permanent staff member at the NFB. Committed to redressing the invisibility of Indigenous peoples, Alanis Obomsawin's filmmaking style resides in the unique ability to pair Indigenous oral traditions with methods of documentary cinema.

Amisk and *Mother of Many Children*, produced and directed in 1977, combine interviews with music, dance, drawings, and archival images to validate the history of Indigenous peoples across Canada. Of her films on young people, *Richard Cardinal: Cry from a Diary of a Métis Child* (1986) is the best-known, and perhaps, the most striking. A dramatic account of a young boy's suicide led to a government report on social services for Indigenous foster children in Alberta."

One can, therefore, readily see that such a ringing endorsement by Alanis Obomsawin in the area of documentary films would carry great weight in the Canadian movie industry. Then, after this reprieve, *Cold Journey* was shown at the Cannes Film Market in May 1975, as a test of its commercial potential. Unfortunately, a *Variety* film critic suggested that the film was "a bleak undertaking."

After this presentation, the film was shown to members of the National Indian Brotherhood (now called the Assembly of First Nations). Their response was much more positive because they felt that the film was a fairly accurate portrayal of the realities that most Indigenous peoples faced who lived in Canada. However, the NFB was not able to secure a commercial distributor for the film in Canada, but nonetheless decided to distribute it in any event to local communities. As such, one year after the Cannes festival, in May 1976, the film had its premiere in The Pas, located in northern Manitoba, where it was an immediate success.

It then toured the prairie provinces where it was shown in both community centers and commercial cinemas where it was highly praised by Indigenous audiences. However, non-Indigenous audiences were left indifferent and unsympathetic for the most part.

It is entirely possible that Euro-Canadian audiences were less sympathetic to the plight of people who were subjected to the colonial pressures of the larger society. The film can be seen as a study of how European-based Canadian society pressured Indigenous education to assimilate Indigenous people, aiming to erase their cultural heritage and replace it with European norms, values, and language.

This situation results in a conflicting state of mind for Indigenous children, who on the one hand are often mercilessly beaten by the residential school teachers when heard to speak their Indigenous language. In turn, the students were often ridiculed by their local Elders for having insufficient knowledge of their local Indigenous language and culture. As a consequence, Buckley is neither accepted by his white Canadian classmates nor by other Indigenous students. It causes him to avoid his classes and take up drinking with the Indigenous school janitor who offers a sympathetic ear.

As director Defalco relates:

"The emotions that I experienced when watching the movie ranged from anger to sadness. I was impressed by the portrayal of Indigenous people's livelihood. At the same time, I was appalled by the events presented in the movie, namely, the case of the forced attendance of residential schools. I felt discomfort watching Buckley being laughed at and mocked by other Native people who did not consider him to be Indian…Thus, I consider the movie to be a way for the director to expose the colonial practices of the Canadian authorities" (Ohayon 2017).

Defalco also offers the opinion that school authorities did not listen to Buckley's concerns regarding his confused state of mind. This lack of support put him in a particularly vulnerable position because of his ensuing identity crisis; which was characterized by inner conflicts and attempts to solve this identity problem. In addition, Indigenous children in residential schools were denied the right to free expression because they were not treated as individuals. The Indigenous students were regarded by the school's authorities simply as objects to be manipulated; so that they would conform to the norms and values of the oppressive wider Euro-Canadian society.

The techniques that Defalco utilized to pursue an analysis of these themes of identity crisis and cultural conflict are based on a combination of fictional and non-fictional factors which are merged together in the plot's internal structure. As an example, the film features actual stories about the Canadian approach to the schooling of Indigenous children and young adults.

In comparison to the approach used toward the education of Indigenous students used in, say, the pre-1970s period, it was much less progressive than would be considered appropriate today. In recent times, schooling for Indigenous children is mostly carried out on the reserves themselves so that the children can live with their own families in their home communities.

In addition, there are reserves in northern Ontario that are teaching the Indigenous Anishinaabe and Cree languages in school. It is a far cry from the residential school approach which punished Indigenous children who were caught speaking their local language. Thus, the *Cold Journey* film uses non-fictional situations that demonstrate the repressive situations that the school authorities used to unfairly treat Indigenous students who were forced to spend most of the year away from their local communities and families all of which focus on the film's main topic of exploitive colonialism.

In this film for Buckley, the school situation is not one that he attends to receive knowledge and education but rather is a place of oppressive domination and an exercise in authoritarianism. In the school situation that

Buckley experiences, there are numerous attempts made by the school authorities to eliminate his cultural legacy and force alien norms, values, and cultural habits on him from the wider white society.

Interspersed with the real-life situations explored in *Cold Journey* are also various fictional portions of the plot that are added by the film's director. While some may disagree with this assessment, there are portions of the film that do not appear entirely realistic.

As an example, the situations in the film in which local Indigenous people refuse to teach Buckley his Indigenous language and culture appear inaccurate and unconvincing. From my own research experience among the Anishinaabe peoples living in northern Ontario, it is hard for me to believe from the Indigenous people that I interacted with that they did not want a youth such as Buckley to learn all the important aspects of their own culture and language that were possible for that time period.

On the other hand, what the film's director is attempting to achieve is a conflict situation in which the elders in Buckley's community are not necessarily rejecting Buckley as a person, but refusing to accept the various external norms, values, and cultural habits that he has absorbed through the residential school experience.

Of course, there is the disparaging description of some Indigenous people as "apples," which means that they are apparently red on the outside but white on the inside. Such a moniker, though, hardly does justice to the many Indigenous youths who did not choose to be forced into these situations of forced enculturation. So, when local elders ridicule Buckley in the film for not having sufficient knowledge of his culture, they are demonstrating resistance themselves to the various social, cultural, and political pressures to change their lifestyle that they themselves are experiencing in their own lifestyles.

All in all, then, the *Cold Journey* film could be considered a mechanism by which the director exposes the inequities in Canada's colonial heritage. In this context, the various themes explored in the film have a direct relevance to Canada's Indigenous policies today.

It is possible, then, to view the *Cold Journey* film as an educational success since the exploration of important historical themes in a Canadian context is certainly a valuable contribution. Yet, the film could hardly be regarded as a commercial success. There was much more viewer interest in the smaller (mainly Indigenous) community settings throughout the country than in the larger urban centers.

One of the reasons was probably the residential school experiences of the smaller, mostly northern Indigenous communities in which there was a greater cultural impact than in the larger centers. As an example, Johnny Yesno himself was removed by his father from the Sioux Lookout residential school from which the younger Yesno had also attempted to run away, to the school in Sault Ste. Marie which Johnny regarded as less repressive and authoritarian in its education approach toward Indigenous students.

In Johnny Yesno's case, he and a friend, both of whom were nine years old, attempted to run away in the winter months but eventually became lost and found themselves in Kenora. Once there the young students were rounded up by the local police, handcuffed, and returned to the Pelican Lake Residential School in Sioux Lookout. There, the headmaster informed them that the boys would have their heads shaved as a form of punishment. At this point, Johnny's father interceded to put an end to the punishment and subsequently transferred his son to the more southerly residential school of Shingwauk at Sault Ste. Marie.

In Johnny's obituary published in *Windspeaker* (Meili 2010), it was noted that "the transfer was good for the young boy because institution staff treated students better than those at Pelican Residential School. At Shingwauk, individuals really tried to help and support the students make their transition into the fast-changing white world. Johnny outdid himself in his new placement and proved to doubters that he could be academically successful. He carried on with his studies at the University of Waterloo, electing to enter the engineering faculty."

As such, as far as the various themes in *Cold Journey* are concerned, the reader must realize that the repressive, authoritarian experiences that Indigenous students experienced varied by the geographical locale and time periods involved. From Johnny's experience, residential schools in the northern part of Ontario were considered far more repressive than those farther south of the province.

There was also variations in time periods with the repressive tactics of school authorities of the 1940s tending to diminish as time went on. Another consideration was the changing composition of the residential schools' teachers and administrative structures from that run by various religious organizations to more secular personnel in later periods. However, regardless of time periods and staff, a primary goal of the educational organizations nonetheless was geared toward inculcating in Indigenous students the norms and values more in line with those of the larger Euro-Canadian society than with those of their original reserve cultural heritage.

In Johnny Yesno's case, he no doubt regarded certain aspects of his educational experience in a positive light. Many of these experiences certainly allowed his access into the larger society, especially in the so-called performing arts while at the same time maintaining cultural themes important to his Indigenous cultural background.

It must be remembered that all peoples and cultures are constantly changing, so in this light, it is unreasonable that people should regard Indigenous cultures as stagnant phenomena. However, maintaining certain cultural themes and values of Indigenous societies is also important in maintaining the self-esteem of Indigenous people, so one can expect varied mixtures of such themes from location to location around the world. It would be ethnocentric to think otherwise.

Review from *On Stranger Tides* (2 August 2020)

Generally speaking, this is a solid film. It traces the tragic loss of a young man caught between two worlds. The protagonist, a Cree teenager from a northern reserve, struggles to find and maintain his identity in the face of the residential school system. He feels out of place in his family because he can't speak Cree and because he must spend his winters in school instead of in the bush with his father and older brothers.

The scenes of Buckley (main character) and his dad hunting and fishing at their summer camp are poignant—made more so by the fact their entire livelihood, and, by extension, the livelihood of their entire community, is threatened by mercury-poisoned lakes. This prompts a journey, aided by the older Ojibwe maintenance man [played by Johnny Yesno] at the school, into the city, to powwows, and eventually to a winter trapping camp in the bush.

The Native cast, though not trained actors, is one of the strengths. In the end, however, the movie suffers from unfulfilled potential. The depths of trauma resulting from the residential school system are not mined to the fullest effect. In addition, the inclusion of a narrative voice is distancing and awkward.

A film worth watching, but the end result is not what it could have been. Execution and a simplified view of a complex subject keep it from reaching the highest of heights.

Therefore, as a way of summing up, we can ask "What are the central themes of *Cold Journey?*"

Of course, different people could have varied opinions, so anyone's thoughts on the film are bound to be subjective. Nonetheless, two of the most important themes of the film that must be considered, particularly those relating to Buckley Petawabano, are *anxiety* and *alienation*.

The concept of *alienation* has a long history in the social sciences, specifically in relation to 19th-century sociologist Emile Durkheim's concept of *anomie*. *Anomie* can have many characteristics, such as a feeling of normlessness, apathy, powerlessness, and pessimism, among others. It is a feeling of anxiety, involving a fear of the unknown, estrangement, detachment from self and others, or a loss of self, are several of the chief characteristics of this condition.

In the movie *Cold Journey,* there are many scenes that highlight the feelings that Buckley experiences that pertain to Durkheim's concept of *anomie*. Take, as an example, the classroom scene in which a prissy teacher lectures the Indigenous students at the residential school on the concept of the *iambic pentameter* in English literature. This concept dates back to Geoffrey Chaucer's 14th-century and is used in poetry in relation to five measured beats.

I watched this scene with incredulity. "What," I thought, "could be more irrelevant to the Indigenous way of life in northern Manitoba than a discussion of the iambic petameter?" As a way of ridiculing his classroom experience, Buckley annoys Johnny Yesno by trying to speak using this concept.

Another important theme concerns Buckley's disassociation from both his Cree (or Anishinaabe) culture and that of the Euro-Canadian people. In one scene, Buckley watches from the shoreline as his family paddles away in their canoe to spend the winter on their trapline.

His father turns around and orders his son to "get back to school." Possibly, his father realizes that in the future Buckley will need to know something about the white man's society and educational system to survive. Regardless of his father's intentions, the young man seems stranded in a no man's land. Then, Buckley ventures out to Johnny Yesno's trapping cabin; a cramped little place lit with an oil lamp and no other apparent modern amenities. Buckly takes

Johnny's rifle and heads out to hunt. Spotting a wolf, he aims and fires, but only wounds the animals.

He then returns to the cabin only to be admonished by Johnny, "You can't leave a wounded wolf wandering around here in the bush!" he says.

There are also several scenes in which Buckley is placed in a Euro-Canadian foster home. The father is a drunkard. Later, it is revealed that his foster parents' only interest in Buckley concerns the money they receive for his care. The parents then tell him that they must give him up because it is more expensive to keep him than the money they receive. Buckley then learns that the foster parents' daughter has committed suicide. Buckley says that "he feels like a whipped dog with no place to go."

In *Cold Journey*, Chief Dan George plays Johnny Yesno's uncle John. Perhaps, the most important scene in the entire movie occurs when Uncle John takes Buckley aside in order to give him some friendly advice about Indigenous dances at the pow-wow. As Uncle John explains, "The Indian dance is very simple, if the spirit is healthy. When you dance, you must dance proudly". He then broadens the discussion more broadly. "If you quit school now, what are you going to do," asks Uncle John.

Buckley then responds with, "I'm an Indian, I'll do it the Indian way!"

Uncle John, then explains, "Buckley, there is no true Indian way for you. An Indian must be taught from the first year."

Buckley then asks, [do you mean that] "I should become like a white man?"

Uncle John responds, "I don't know what an Indian should be. I don't know the answer. I only know that many Indians will die before the land becomes friendly again."

Unfortunately, Uncle John does not elaborate on this rather cryptic explanation. We are left wondering what Chief Dan George meant by "friendly again"?

The Chanie "Charlie" Wenjack Tragedy

In 1964, Chanie "Charlie" Wenjack was taken from his home in Ogoki Post, close to Fort Hope in northern Ontario where Johnny Yesno was born. He was forcibly brought to the Cecilia Jeffrey Indian Residential School in Kenora which was over six hundred miles away from his reserve community when he was just nine years old. It was two years later, that Chanie arrived back home in a casket.

Chanie was not of course the only Indigenous child who was removed from their homes and forced to attend residential schools. While the true number will probably never be known, there were thousands of children who died at these schools, many of whom died of abuse, disease, or exposure while attempting to run away.

Many children who died at residential schools were simply buried in unmarked graves since proper records were hardly ever kept by the school administrators. Thus far, there have been over six thousand Indigenous children's names uncovered but this is by far only a small percentage of those who have died in the unmarked graves of residential schools.

Chanie "Charlie" Wenjack's death was first brought to the public's attention when *Macleans* published an article written by Ian Adams in 1967, entitled "The Lonely Death of Charlie Wenjack."

The article indicates that:

"It's not so unusual for Indian children to run away from the residential schools they are sent to. They do it all the time, and they lose their toes and their fingers to frostbite. Sometimes they lose a leg or an arm trying to climb aboard freight trains. Occasionally, one of them dies. And perhaps, they are Indians, no one seems to care very much. So, this, then, is the story of how a little boy met a terrible and lonely death, of the handful of people who became involved, and a town that hardly noticed."

The author goes on to explain that the village where Chanie (teachers at the residential school misnamed him "Charlie") was born, called Ogoki Post on the Martin Falls Reserve, did not have a school. The Cecilia Jeffrey School in Kenora was run by the Presbyterian Church and paid for by the federal government.

About 150 Indigenous children lived at the school for 10 months of the year, which means that the school is not much more than a large dormitory. Chanie could hardly speak any English when he arrived at the residential school and as a result, needed to spend his first two years in grade one. After this period, he was placed in what was called a junior opportunity class, which is a euphemistic name for a class of slow learners who were given special instruction in English and arithmetic.

His progress was still not satisfactory for the school authorities, so, he was subsequently enrolled in the senior opportunity class, rather than placed back into the regular grade system. The principal of the school, Velda MacMillan, commented that "Chanie was not a slow learner and had a great sense of humor. The thing we remember most about him was his sense of humor. If the teacher in the class made a joke, a play on words, he was always the first to catch on."

After his frozen body was discovered, a post-mortem was later performed by Dr. Peter Pan. The report showed that Chanie's lungs were infected at the time of his death. Kenora's public health doctor, P.F. Playfair, noted in Adams' article that "Indian children's early medical records are practically impossible to track down." In fact, it was only discovered at the time of the post-mortem that in Chanie's early childhood, his chest had been opened and there was an enormous scar that ran in a loop from high on his right chest, down and up over his back.

Chanie ran away from the Cecilia Jeffrey school grounds with his two friends, Ralph (age 13) and Jackie (age 11) MacDonald, who were all only wearing light clothing. The same day nine other children also ran away but were caught within the next 24 hours. The destination for the boys was a small town called Redditt. It was not much more than an isolated railroad stop on the CNR line, 20 miles north of Kenora.

After walking for eight hours, the boys finally arrived in Redditt. One of the MacDonald brothers knew a "Mister Benson" who fed them and allowed them to spend the night on the floor of his house. The same morning the boys met up with another of Charlie's friends from the residential school, Eddie Cameron, who had also run away from the school.

Chanie's three friends, Ralph, Jackie, and Eddie decided to stay in Redditt, so Charlie left by himself. Apparently, Chanie had little idea of where he was going or the location of his home reserve, as Eddie later remembered, "Chanie only knew that his dad lived a long way. And it was beside a lot of water."

Chanie did not realize that he had nearly half a province to cross before reaching Ogoki Post. During Chanie's walk along the railway tracks, there were snow squalls and freezing rain with the temperature hovering about -6 degrees C. In the end, Chanie had only covered a little more than 12 miles. When he was discovered, Chanie was covered in bruises probably from falling down on the rock and railway tracks. Chanie was lying on his back when the members of a section crew found him, probably as a result of a fall, and he never got up again.

On 17 November of that year, an inquest was conducted in Kenora's Magistrate's Court. After spending more than two hours deliberating, a written verdict was produced along with several recommendations. The jury found that "the Indian education system causes tremendous emotional and adjustment problems."

There was also a suggestion made that the school be staffed adequately so that children could develop personal relationships with the staff, and that more effort be given to boarding children in private homes. The report ended with the poignant suggestion that "A study be made of the present Indian education and philosophy. Is it right?"

Later, in 2016, Giller Prize-winning author Joseph Boyden published a relatively short novel about Chanie's tragic demise entitled simply "*Wenjack*." In addition, Gord Downie leader of the Tragically Hip band, who passed away in October of 2017, began work on his *Secret Path* project which included an album and animated film. As Downie indicated, the rationale for this project was initiated because,

"Chanie haunts me. His story is Canada's story. This is about Canada. We are not the country we thought we were. History will be rewritten. We are all accountable, but this begins in the late 1800s and goes on to 1996. *White* Canada knew—on somebody's purpose—nothing about this.

We weren't taught it; it was hardly ever mentioned. All of those governments, and all of those churches, for all of those years, misused themselves. They hurt many children. They broke up many families. They eased entire communities.

It will take seven generations to fix this. *Seven.* Seven is not arbitrary. This is far from over. Things up north have never been harder. Canada is not Canada. We are not the country we think we are (Statement made at Ogoki Post, Ontario, 9 September 2016 *https://secretpath.ca*).

The Courage of Kavik, the Wolf Dog (1980)

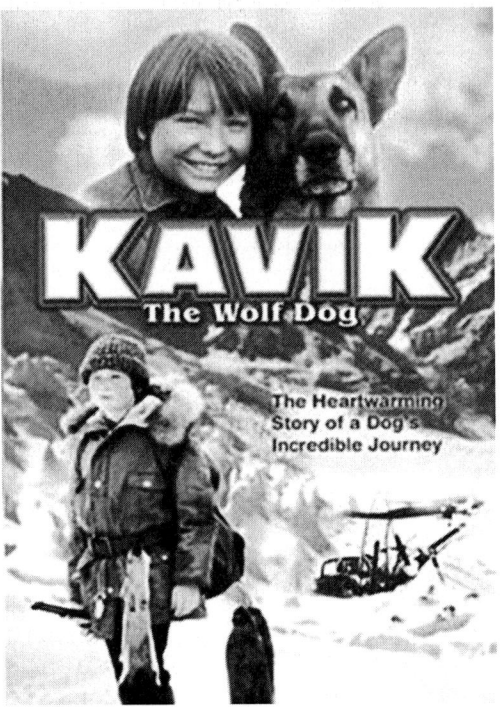

Source: National Broadcasting Corporation Movie Poster, 1980

This movie is based on the 1893 novel *Kävik the Wolf Dog* written by author Walt Morey which was re-published in 1968. Johnny Yesno plays the role of Charlie One-Eye and John Candy as Pinky. A made-for-TV movie called *The Courage of Kävik the Wolf Dog* based on the book aired under the *Sunday Big Event* umbrella on NBC in 1980.

Kävik is an Alaskan malamute sled dog who gets sold from Charlie One-eye to Mr. Hunter for $2,000 after winning the North American sled dog race and is loaded on a plane in an iron-barred cage. In the middle of the trip, something goes wrong and the plane crashes into the ground, killing pilot Smiley Johnson before he even has time to undo his seatbelt.

Kävik's cage makes a gaping hole in the side of the plane as it crashes in the eye of a storm. After being trapped in a cage for three days while starving, freezing, and getting multiple wounds from neighboring animals, Kävik is found by young Andy Evans, a teenage boy whose trap line was near the location of the wreck.

Andy uses his belt axe to open the cage and uses a piece of the plane's wing to create a sled to carry the injured dog until they reach a cave where Andy and Kävik spend the night. The next morning, Andy is shaken awake by his father, Kurt Evans, and they take Kävik back to their house where he is later treated by Dr. Walker on the advice of Andy's mother, Laura Evans.

Over the period of a few weeks, Kävik almost fully recovers and heals. Andy notices he is as good as new when he climbs up the stairs and is able to open his door. One day, while Andy is at his job downtown, Kävik escapes to town and gets chased by a pack of dogs led by Blackie. It turns out he has lost his fighting courage due to the horrible plane wreck. A few weeks later, Andy comes home and notices that Kävik is nowhere to be found.

His dad tells Andy that Mr. Hunter came by earlier that day and took Kävik back with him to his home in Washington, despite being told by Andy's father that Kävik is a complete coward and that he had lost his wolflike courage. When Mr. Hunter goes to show Kävik off, Kävik escapes out of a window and sets out over 2,000 miles to return to Andy, the only person who ever loved him enough to take care of him. While he was traveling, he found a mate who later got killed. The return journey comprises most of the second half of the novel.

The Movie

Kävik, a champion sled dog, who has just won a race in Alaska is sold for $2000 to George Hunter, a ruthless businessman from Seattle, who has local business interests. The plane carrying the dog crashes into the snow-covered wilderness; the pilot is killed, and the dog is more dead than alive.

The crash site is found by Andy Evans, a young boy who lives in the nearby fishing settlement of Copper City. He struggles to get the dog home and begs his parents to let him ask the local doctor to take a look at Kävik. Dr. Walker does, initially reluctantly, have a look and does his best to deal with Kävik's multiple injuries.

The dog slowly recovers and starts to bond with Andy. However, due to its near-death experience, Kävik is terrified of other dogs and is quick to run away when confronted. In a turn of events, Hunter arrives on a regular trip and claims back the dog, taking him to a kennel in his palatial Seattle home.

Hunter's kennel manager, seeing that the dog is unhappy and unlikely to be a champion racer, allows him to escape. Kävik manages to stow away on a coastal ferry and travels north. He struggles over inhospitable terrain, learning to fight other dogs and wolves for his food. Barely alive, he makes it back to Copper City and reunites with Andy.

Hunter arrives, angrily demanding the return of the dog. Andy's father, Kurt, equally angrily claims that the dog will be happier with them than with Hunter. Hunter, who employs Evans and practically owns the whole town, gives in with ill grace, selling Kävik to the Evans family for a token sum.

Reviews: The Nerdy Book Club

Review by Kim Campbell:

Like many Nerdy Book Club members, I regularly shop at thrift stores for books for my students. I'm always hoping to spot one of my favorites on the shelves: Kavik the Wolf Dog by Walt Morey. The author also wrote Gentle Ben. I've always wanted to read that famous book, but haven't, perhaps, because I feel I know the author well through Kävik.

"This book is dedicated to all young people from 6 to 60 who have known the love of an animal," explains Morey in the opening pages.

Kävik takes place in one of Morey's favorite settings—Alaska—and in the Pacific Northwest, where he lived. I wish I had discovered Kävik when I was younger and fallen for novels about the natural world, such as Jack London's White Fang. Morey's writing easily fits alongside London's—and Jean Craighead George's and Gary Paulsen's.

His appreciation for nature is obvious in his description of everything from Kävik's build to thawing snowpack. Aiding the imagery is a handful of drawings by well-known illustrator Peter Parnall.

In the book, the boy and the dog first meet after a small plane carrying a prize sled dog goes missing. Andy stumbles upon the crash and decides to put the barely surviving animal out of its misery:

"He was about to pull the trigger when the dog's eyes opened and looked at the boy," Morey writes. "The blue eyes of the boy and the yellow ones of the dog studied each other. His eyes held the boy's with as direct a gaze as Andy had ever known. Scarcely realizing what he was doing, Andy tilted the rifle muzzle away and eased back the bolt."

Andy and Kävik form a strong bond, but problems arise when the dog's wealthy owner, who lives out of state, wants him returned. Kävik builds to a satisfying conclusion, one that doesn't require too many tissues. It is a book for dog lovers, nature lovers, and good-story lovers.

Review by Diane Pendergraft:

Charlie One-Eye [Johnny Yesno] raises sled dogs to sell. The fight and intelligence he sees in the new puppy, several parts wolf, inspire Charlie to make one more attempt at winning the North American Sled Dog Derby in Fairbanks, Alaska. He names the puppy Kävik, Eskimo for Wolverine. Two years later, Charlie and Kävik win the race.

George C. Hunter, a wealthy businessman, collects objects of interest in the north and ships them home to Seattle. He sees Charlie and Kävik win the North American and pays Charlie $2,000 for Kävik. Hunter puts Kävik on a plane headed for Hunter's cannery where the dog can then be put on a ship to Washington.

The plane crashes before it gets to the cannery, Kävik, in his cage, is thrown from the plane and nearly dies. He is rescued by Andy, a 14-year-old boy, the first person ever to show Kävik affection.

When Hunter comes back to Alaska the next spring, he finds that the dog he thought was dead is alive, strong, and healthy. He insists on taking Kävik home to Washington. Living in a cage, surrounded by the sounds and smells of the city. Kävik can think of nothing but somehow heading north back to the boy. He takes advantage of his first opportunity to escape, which is the start of a 2,000-mile endurance trek.

I suspect that during the time when I was devouring books about animals, these books were exemplifying virtues that I did not see in adults in my life. Couldn't every lonely, disappointed child do with a dog so devoted that he would risk his life to cross rugged, glacier-filled mountains in order to get back home? Such loyalty, such stamina, such heart!

While the human characters in this story are a bit like unfinished coloring book pages, they are not entirely incidental. Some help shape Kävik's early life, some help save his life, and some are necessary to the success of his journey. Though the people who make Kävik's life difficult are more selfish and thoughtless than serious bad guys, the difference between them and those who behave selflessly and virtuously is clearly defined.

Honesty and integrity are highly valued. When it is clear that Kävik is going to recover from the injuries sustained in the plane crash, Andy hopes he won't have to tell Mr. Hunter. Andy's dad insists that Kävik rightfully belongs to Mr. Hunter and that they must be completely honest with him and let him decide what to do with his dog.

They face the same dilemma again when Kävik finds his way back to them. Andy's dad, this time firmly on Kävik and Andy's side, still insists on being completely honest with Mr. Hunter.

Charlie One-Eye raises Kävik to be a fighter, but Andy finds out that the plane crash and subsequent suffering have taken the fight out of the dog. When Kävik is confronted by the town's stray dog pack, he turns tail and runs home, much to Andy's humiliation. Andy's dad explains that, because of a tragedy that happened in his own life, he can understand how Kävik could be so beaten down as to lose his courage.

Through the suffering and challenges of the long journey home, driven by his love for the boy, Kävik regains his courage. The enormity of what the dog must have gone through inspires Andy's dad to stand up to Mr. Hunter and convince him that Kävik belongs in the north and with Andy. The dog's example also brings Andy's dad to a place where he knows it is time to overcome his own fear and go back to doing what he once loved.

"This book is dedicated to all young people from 6 to 60 who have known the love of an animal," writes Walt Morey.

Matt and Jenny (1980)

Matt and Jenny was a television series in which Johnny Yesno played the role of Joe for one episode in 1980. The episode (S1. E26) was titled The *Ghost of Pocomoonshine Swamp* set in 1850. Matt and Jenny (or Matt and Jenny on the Wilderness Trail) is a Canadian television series of 26 episodes of 25 minutes each, broadcast on Global starting 21 October 1979.

The series was essentially about two English children, Matt (Derrik Jones) and Jenny Tanner (Megan Follows, who won Gemini Awards for Best Performer for *Anne of Green Gables* in 1986 and for *Anne of Avonlea* in 1988), and their mother as they depart for the New World from Bristol, England. During the voyage, their mother dies of typhoid fever.

The two children arrive in Canada and begin a search for their uncle Bill Tanner, who arrived before they had. While Matt and Jenny are on their way to meet their uncle, they hear strange, unearthly cries in the swamp. They lose their way while trying to solve the mystery.

In the final episode, (aired on 20 April, 1980) Matt and Jenny are exploring Pocomoonshine Swamp. The episode begins by showing the many animals who live in the swamp and how Matt and Jenny are drawn further into it by their delight in the new creatures they find. When a wild cry sends them scurrying back toward their camp. In their haste, they both fall and Jenny scrapes her arm.

As they get up, they are startled to find an Aboriginal man named Joe (Johnny Yesno) standing over them. He tends to Jenny's injured arm with remedies that he finds in the nearby forest and then tells them a strange story about an Indigenous man named Jean Big Canoe.

He was murdered many years before, and whose ghostly cry can still be heard echoing through the swamp while he paddles around at night. As Joe tells the children, this swamp is the "resting place of lost spirits. I've seen even the strongest men grow weak with fear in this swamp."

As night comes on, their rescuer takes them to Jean Big Canoe's cabin. The two children bed down, but they hear footsteps on the roof accompanied by an unearthly roar. When they emerge with billets of wood in their hands to fight off the menace, they see nothing, but they decide that Matt should take the first watch. Joe rejoins him by the fire. Time passes and then Matt sees a figure in a canoe on the misty moonlit water.

He wakens Joe, but there is no one there. Later, after Joe shows Matt how to paint his face with mud to repel mosquitoes, Jenny teases him:

"Some kind of war paint?"

Eventually, the children's uncle, who is leading a search party with two other men, finds the children in the accompany of Joe. Suddenly a panther appears, and Bill Tanner prepares to shoot the wild cat, but Joe stops him.

As Joe explains, "It has been the panther all along who has been making the eerie noise, although it was never made clear how this big cat is able to emit such a sound."

The story about Jean Big Canoe and the various spiritual sightings were all concocted in an attempt to "keep poachers out of the swamp", Joe tells the group. Joe goes on to explain that it had been the cougar on the roof in the night, but he had been nearby to make sure it did not hurt Matt or Jenny.

There was, indeed, a murdered man called Jean Big Canoe but there is no ghost. However, the camera shows the canoe and its paddler in the mist independently of Matt's point of view.

As Miller (2008: 129) states, "At least he [Johnny Yesno] uses English, not *Tonto speak*." It's also worth noting that the series won an award for Best Television Series from the Canadian Film and Television Association in 1979 (Toronto *Globe and Mail*, 20 October, 1979).

(Note: this episode of Matt and Jenny is still available at no cost on "YouTube. Vintage Canada"; accessed 29 June, 2024).

Conclusion

There are so many important themes that one could discuss in Johnny Yesno's television and movie career, however it is difficult to mention them all. Certainly, his career did not have the length that other of his compatriots were able to achieve in the film industry, yet it is necessary to state that Johnny Yesno also had another media career in the radio business as well that was, perhaps, as equally significant as his movie career.

Having stated this qualification, one should start by noting that Johnny Yesno's film career was based to a large extent on his own personal experience. This was particularly the case with his involvement in Ontario's residential schools. As with Buckley's life and death in *Cold Journey*, he also ran away but fortunately did not freeze to death on the rail tracks.

There is a theme in this film which is essentially a continuation of that discussed in the last chapter concerning the high suicide rates among Indigenous people in Canada, which is especially the case for Indigenous youth. As we follow Buckley's journey through the film it would appear that he was becoming more desperate as his life continued. His feelings of desperation were becoming more intense as time went on.

The main question raised by *Cold Journey* is "Where do Indigenous youth fit in modern Canadian society?" The elder Indigenous people in northern areas have their hunting and trapping, but how about the younger population? If we use Buckley as an example, he does not fit into the older Indigenous lifestyle, yet he also doesn't seem to fit into the Euro-Canadian society either. His feelings of desperation become accentuated, resulting in a sense of alienation and disassociation, or, to use Durkheim's term, *anomie*.

Johnny Yesno, on the other hand, seems to be able to fit into both worlds. He is able to pursue the trapping life, although not very successfully. He is a hit on the pow-wow dance circuit, winning a world championship with his rendition of the hoop dance. Yesno appears able to maintain a sense of his Indigenous identity without living in a state of cultural and personal disassociation and turmoil. In real life, he seems far removed from a state where he would want to commit suicide in order to escape the torment of modern life.

Chapter Eight
Our Native Land

By the time that the Disney movie *King of the Grizzlies* was released in 1970, Johnny Yesno had already moved into radio. Initially, he hosted and produced CBC Radio's *Indian Magazine*, first created in 1965, which was touted as Canada's first radio program that focused on Indigenous people in the country.

Seven years later, in 1972, this show evolved into a program called *Our Native Land* (1972–1985). A holiday edition of CBC Radio (18 December 2014) reminisced:

"From the mid-1960s to the mid-1980s, Saturday afternoon on CBC Radio meant time for a weekly serving of bannock and tea along with a look at Aboriginal issues. For more than 20 years, Our Native Land gave voice to Aboriginal stories. The show grew up alongside a resurgent native rights movement in Canada, becoming a provocative, politicized, all-native current affairs show [which eventually] morphed into Our Native Land in 1970.

In 1971, host Johnny Yesno called Our Native Land "Canada's only national radio program for native peoples. I realize that programs about Indian, Metis, and Eskimo people have been done before, but not with native peoples participating. They were being used, studied, analyzed, and classified like rare butterflies." Our Native Land was different.

It was, as its producers said, 'all-red, all the time'."

These radio programs demonstrated Johnny Yesno's versatility as he moved comfortably away from personal achievement in the film industry to social and cultural awareness. This phase of his life developed into a career in broadcast journalism with the inauguration of a CBC newsmagazine show called *Take 30*.

It was at this point that Johnny became quite critical of Canada's media treatment of Indigenous people, criticizing for example, the CBC, which he suggested was out of touch with the concerns of the country's first peoples and failed to represent them in an accurate manner.

In 1968, an edition of the *Indian Record* newspaper noted Johnny Yesno's involvement in CBC's *Indian Magazine* (vol. 31, no. 9) with the headline "Radio's Leading Role in the Quiet Revolution."

The article notes that "One of the reasons Tecumseh, Pontiac, and other great native leaders failed to come to an understanding with the non-Indian and with each other was that they didn't have radio. No tom-tom or runner carrying the wampum-belt messages can beat the immediacy, intimacy, and impact of instant wireless communications, as the CBC's Northern Services program, *Indian Magazine*, has been proving on many Canadian stations since 1964."

The article goes on to suggest that during the 1960s there was a "quiet revolution" occurring among Canada's Indigenous population which gave native people "the courage, and facts to help them work together for a better deal." Progress toward achieving this "better deal" was facilitated by radio shows such as that hosted by Johnny Yesno's *Indian Magazine*.

Rather than focus on the individual concerns of the Inuit, Metis, and status Indian populations in Canada. Johnny Yesno's program aims to link these separated groups in such a manner that their commonalities are explored, thereby, reducing the divisiveness of the social and political pressures that these individual populations must cope with.

Thus, as the *Indian Record* suggests, by seeking to find what these separated groups radio shows such as that hosted by Johnny Yesno can further "help them organize themselves to conquer passivity, fear, and confusion. It's also a means of letting non-Indians hear the Indian viewpoint, and better understand the loneliness of geographical isolation, prejudice, and misunderstanding."

Remembering the Bad Old Days in the Residential School

In 1972, Johnny Yesno hosted an edition of *Our Native Land* in which the topic of discussion with two former classmates concerned their experiences in Canada's residential school system. The following is a verbatim transcript of this show comprising about 25 minutes meant to preserve the tone and nuances of Johnny and his guests' reminiscences using their own language (Note: punctuation marks made at the author's prerogative):

"I got together with a few of my school chums who I first met when I was about four or five years old. We're going to reminisce about residential school days. You know hundreds of thousands of Indian children were sent away to attend Indian residential schools, they don't call them anymore by that name, now they call them student residences.

Now, these schools are administered by the federal government, excuse me, sponsored by the federal government, and administered by a church organization, in my case it was the Anglican Church of Canada. At one time, the government of Canada was sponsoring 66 Indian residential schools across the country.

They refer to these schools now as Indian student residences because of some of the changes made to fit the role that they function now. Presently, they have been reduced to 45 with the enrollment around 4,500 students so that's an average of about a hundred students per school. In my day, there were 10,000 Indian children going to these schools ranging in age from 5 to 16 years.

The first one that I went to was Pelican School at Sioux Lookout Ontario that's near the Ontario-Manitoba border on the CNR [Canadian National Railway] line. Then I was later transferred to Shingwauk [Indian Residential] school at Sault Ste. Marie. So, when I get to talk with my guests Pelican at Sioux Lookout and Shingwauk is within the city of Sault Ste. Marie.

By the way, I entitled this 'Education is a War' and I'll be talking with Ronald Weslie who works with metropolitan Toronto as a survey technician and has been for seven years, and Kelly Bull a CNR electrical technician in Toronto for nine years. Ron and Kelly both come from Lac Seul, which is Ontario's largest Indian reservation, I believe it has about 105 thousand acres. I first asked Ronnie if he could remember his first day:

Ronnie: I was rather young when I first went in because of some unfortunate circumstances my parents, and my three older brothers had already enrolled at the Pelican [Residential] School and because of the separation from my parents I was enrolled when I was only four years old but—

Johnny: That's quite a tender age.

Ronnie: Like I said, I had three older brothers there, I was more or less too young to even know what I was being put into.

200

Johnny: Were you able to speak English when you first went to school Ron?

Ronnie: No, I don't think I did, well I was more or less just at home because my father was unable to look after me while he was working at trapping. He thought it was better if I was with my brothers [who could] look after me better as I was too young to be enrolled in normal classes so I guess some sort of kinder garden was set up.

Johnny: Getting to you Kelly, when did you first attend an Indian residential school?

Kelly: Well Johnny you know we're going back something like 28 years I believe—

Johnny: He's giving his age away [laughter]

Ronnie: And I believe at this time I was sick that summer and I remember my parents taking me to school and I suppose the first thing that hit me was the thought of being without my parents.

Johnny: Probably the most tragic thing about the Indian children going to a school is the separation from their parents and the mileage that they have to go shall we think about five miles or 10 miles as a long distance, but we are talking about Indian children who had to go hundreds of miles.

In the United States, I believe they take them from the Alaskan territory and put them to school in the Oklahoma which I believe is over two thousand miles and these kids have to attend school. I thought to attend, and this still goes on and it's not as if we're not older but maybe we get into well some of the routines that we used to have to go through.

The teachers and supervisors couldn't pronounce your name, so you were known by a number. I was not known as Johnny Yesno at school, and I believe that my number was 241. Ronnie, what was your number?

Ronnie: My number was 278 and I think we were pretty well in the same group...when some of the older boys quit school you got his number. In my case, I was the only kid left, and his number, instead of going up into the thousands they tried to keep within 500 or so which is what I think; they did because Kelly had gone to school for two years.

Johnny: Let's get into a sort of routine day. You would get up at about what? 7:00, 7:30? Now we would go down and line up in the play room in a line and get ready to have our breakfast. I don't know if you recall breakfast like I do but...Kelly, do you remember breakfast?

201

Kelly: They didn't vary, and they still don't, well our breakfasts were the same for the 10 minutes we were there were the same. We had porridge, slabs of bread, and a glass of milk and that was it.

Johnny: Lumpy porridge if I remember at all.

Kelly: Watery.

Johnny: That's right, they used to add water to the milk. Before each meal and after we used to have to say a prayer…there was great emphasis placed on a prayer before a meal and all that.

Kelly: Almost anything we did we started with a prayer and ended with one.

Johnny: That sort of put callouses on the knees, didn't it? You were either going to be a missionary or a farmer. We're going to get to the farming after a while. Now, we would get to about 8:30 and we had chores to do. My chores used to be if I recall sweeping the stairs and making the bed and I guess my most memorable job was at Shingwauk in Sault Ste. Marie where I used to have to fill up the coal bin every morning. What was your favorite job, Ron?

Ronnie: Oh, I don't know. The most memorable one that comes to mind was on Saturdays we used to have to scrub the dining room, and I remember there were probably about seven of us there. I don't know how many squares of tile there were across the dining room, and of course at one time every two days, they would switch you around and give the boys an opportunity to wash the dishes from all the cooking and everything.

Johnny: The boys used to deliberately drop the dishes on the floor so that they would get out of the job.

Ronnie: I don't know but I wouldn't doubt it if…I don't think any of them liked that type of job, that sort of domestic work.

Johnny: Being a married man do you do that now? All that training that you got in residential school like washing floors, waxing.

Ronnie: It comes in handy in pacifying my wife, well because of having to do it at residential school I don't mind it because it's something that had been instilled in me.

Johnny: Actually, I find it very easy myself. I ended up washing dishes and waxing the floor and because of that training that I got.

Ronnie: We used to do it 10 months of the year.

Johnny: What was your job, Kelly?

Kelly: Well, the job that I liked most when I was at Shingwauk was…this was every Saturday morning…my colleague in this department; we used to have to cut the boy's hair. I kinda liked that [laughter].

Ronnie: Cutting or butchering? Yeah, we ended up doing that too…the kitchen dishes. I often wonder about that, if they weren't going to educate the children why did they move them hundreds of miles just to work to keep this building going…they could cut wood at home, staying on the reservations…going to school, the education portion…there should have been another system.

Johnny: What other system would you advocate? What changes would you make?

Ronnie: Well, I think they should have, to begin with, let them home automatically set them back a bit and if it was possible to have the schools near home like the Anglo-Saxon children go home every day after school. I think that this would go toward educating the children better.

Johnny: Would you have sent your children to a residential school?

Ronnie: No, I don't think so. My daughter went to school like any other child here. She comes home every night and evening and like the other boys and girls. What went wrong there? About having the children closer to home…well, if you take our situation, I don't think that it was possible because our parents were some 35 miles away. We didn't have access to schools on a day-to-day basis and get to go home at night so the next best thing I suppose was to have the children go to these residential schools.

Johnny: That helps to explain it. Happened on the other side of the line, why I say 'the other side of the line' is in a school there was a divisionary point where the school was divided with the boys on one side and the girls on the other. Well, Kelly had a sister and so did I, just tell me how often did you get a chance to see your sister?

Ronnie: We used to see her across this imaginary line that you are talking about but we were never allowed to cross that line…just smiling at her, and returning a smile. I suppose, there was a conveyance of something there and we were still; there was something there, that we still had each other. But they used to have what were called social evenings. These were on every Saturday night, of course, what I'm talking about was when I was 10 years old to 12. I suppose so, this was the only time that we had with our sisters.

Johnny: Which was not quite often as I recall, once a week was a rarity in fact that was a little too frequent, once a month would be closer for a chance to see our sisters, let alone girlfriends.

Ronnie: That was a real no-no.

Johnny: A no-no, I want to say they put saltpeter in our food I often wonder about that, gee I can remember too before we had oil heating at Pelican school and this was real child labor I can remember cutting cordwood, skidding logs, and all of that, do you remember that, Ron?

Ronnie: I think, well as you said before we used to go to school in the morning, and perhaps, less than half a day, and in the afternoon, we had to go into the bush for say about five miles. There was this old man cutting logs for us and we had to take a team of horses and skid them out to the road for the boys to put them on to the sleighs and take them back to the school. There is one story that I remember quite well.

Johnny: How old were you then?

Ronnie: Well, I would be about 12 or 13 years old. There were big trees there about 14 or 15 inches in diameter.

Johnny: Do you remember milking cows in the morning? Milking cows at 10 o'clock in the morning because we had to have milk for the kids.

Ronnie: We used to have to get up at something like 6 o'clock in the morning. We used to have to go out in the fields to bring the cows in and by the time that we got them in it was something like 7 o'clock and we had to milk I don't know about 30 cows I would imagine. It was a lot of hard work for a 12-year-old boy to do.

Johnny: I remember getting lickins for, well, speaking Indian. We got it for being late if you didn't make your bed right or if you didn't eat your meal.

Ronnie: Hmm, I thought they were a little bit harsh on that subject there because how can you expect a 7-year-old boy to go up there and make a bed like a nurse would, that was something that I didn't like about it.

How can you expect to break a 7-year-old boy and break into an established routine? It was a bad thing for us. For the smaller children, of course, they didn't have any conception as to what was going on or what was expected of them so the regimentation did not come easy for them because for the smaller children they had to learn from when they were young.

Johnny: Would you agree that we were never treated as individuals but rather as a herd of sheep?

Ronnie: I would go along with that.

Johnny: They get one order and that was it for everybody.

Ronnie: And I remember the way they used to punish the kids. Well, if one boy did not make the bed right then the whole room of kids would suffer on account, and I thought that was wrong.

Johnny: Do you remember some of the lickings that you witnessed and had to stand up and watch? When you had to stand up and watch?

Ronnie: There was one [instance] that I recall that still sticks in my mind very much and I think it had to do with some of the boys running away from school. About a week went by, I guess and eventually, they got them back in school and I suppose this was the principal's way of conveying a message to us.

They used to punish the individuals in front of everybody, which was very cruel. That should be an example of how much these young Indian kids who were taken to these schools hate it. You never hear about kids running away from Upper Canada College or anything like that.

Johnny: Let's talk about teacher-student relationships, how do you think this was sort of worked out? How close do you think the teachers worked with us?

Ronnie: I thought that the teachers, that I remember, could not get close to any individual child because they had up to five different grades in one classroom; depending upon which row you sat in, you were in a different grade. But she had to reach them as a whole and there were no individual tutors, so to speak, that you might have been bound to another group; so, I don't think you were ever thought of as an individual.

That system still exists, when you had two or three grades in one classroom, they still get away with it, and there's still no way of getting away from it. Definitely, the teachers know when they're handicapped. How I was ever taught at home was in Indian, so coming to a school like this was a completely different experience.

Johnny: Do you remember writing letters home Kelly?

Kelly: Well, I remember that the teacher used to put the letter up on the board. I was just talking to a friend of mine the other day about how we used to write letters. He just shook his head because I told him the teacher used to just write the letter on the board and we used to have to copy it and sign our name at the end. That was it; so, we didn't get to express our feelings, like that we were well, or that they were treating us nice, and then out the letter went.

Johnny: It was censorship, wasn't it? I used to think that the teachers didn't even know that most of our parents couldn't even read English in the first place [laughter] and there were a number of kids who didn't even have any parents, didn't have a mom or a father.

What do you feel was the difference between say the Pelican school and the Shingwauk school? The Pelican school was sort of isolated, was about 12 miles out of town, and was in a rather remote area, whereas Shingwauk was within the bounds of a city.

Ronnie: Remember too at the time that we were a bit older so when we went to Shingwauk I was already in grade eight and therefore, had an idea as to what was going on. While at Pelican, I had no idea at all about the facts of life and, of course, I felt that they were a little bit more lenient because Shingwauk being that it was in town.

So, Pelican by comparison as you mentioned earlier Pelican was so isolated. The relationship between the teacher and the student was a little bit homier than it was in Sioux Lookout because in my case seven years had passed and I was getting to the age where I could understand. Anyway, they had a different group of supervisors and teachers weren't as hard as the ones we had in Sioux Lookout, I thought.

Johnny: You have some notes there; do you just want to go through them?

Ronnie: I never got around to finishing them.

Johnny: What headings do you have?

Ronnie: One of the headings is that I remember going for walks and the thing that I recall was that we all had to march in pairs, and there wasn't much freedom to roam around in the bush but the older kids I believe could run around in the woods and things like this.

Johnny: I think that they were afraid of us running away, but I do recall that we had to walk like an army. What else do you have there?

Ronnie: Yes, it was almost like the military. Well, I have another heading under recreation and, of course, there were games depending on our age. We had a choice the smaller kids could just puddle around in the water and the older children could be playing ball.

Johnny: I guess our favorite sport was making slingshots. I remember that very well too. We had trapping one year if I recall do you recall trapping Ron?

Ronnie: No, but some of the older boys there at Pelican were going trapping. They couldn't keep goodies in their pocket, it was kept in the office and doled out by the principal. The goodies that you could buy any candies that you wanted.

Johnny: I remember the trapping there and learned a little about it. I set a trap line down in Young Street in Toronto but fortunately, didn't get any fur like you say [laughter], but what else you got there, Kelly?

Kelly: Getting back to the individual number system again, as I said my number was 278, but I was just trying to think of why they gave these numbers? I think was to help keep track of our clothes more than anything else. There were a lot of children, and I remember some of their names which were difficult to pronounce so they would just call a number, and you had to reply of course.

Johnny: You get a fellow like Archie Achnepenushkum, so you just call him number 21 and that's it [laughter] front and center, grab that wheelbarrow and clean up the pet barn, that's what they used to tell you. I'm with my friends here Kelly Bull and Ronald Wesleyan and really thank them for coming on the air to reminisce about the good old days.

We were practically born in those places when I was five and Kelly was seven, and possibly why we succeeded more than anybody else, is probably, the fact that we stuck together. When we first went in and then we were transferred from Sioux Lookout to Shingwauk in Sault Ste. Marie and we gave each other moral support, and then we attended high school, which was probably the first integrated school that we all went to.

Like I said there have been changes but some of this still goes on. The changes by the Department of Indian Affairs which involved more Indian people supervising and trying to get Native teachers, they have eliminated roughly about 20 of these schools I believe most of them I regret to say, that they eliminated those ones which were close to the cities.

Initially, when these schools were first started, they were to make the healthy Indian children make the transition from the reserve. From the reservation type of life to the so-called Western civilization, you take a case like Sioux Lookout which is roughly 12 miles out of town sort of like a Howard Hughes private health spa.

It transformed into an island caught between two worlds. When Indian children attended these schools, they lost the cultural practices that could support them upon returning to their reservations. Additionally, if they ventured into larger cities, they found themselves unprepared, lacking the academic training necessary for success. The fundamental issue was that their schooling was limited to just half a day, resulting in a profoundly inadequate educational experience.

Now, they call these places student residences in September 1972, next fall in Fort George Quebec they hope to have the Fort George school up there completely staffed by Indian personnel. The church people have until 1 April 1973, to get out of the education business and hand it over to the Indian people. So long for now."

Follow-Up: Truth and Reconciliation

At the time of the writing of this book, it has now been well over 50 years since Johnny Yesno conducted this interview about residential schools with his school friends. There is much that has happened since then. Perhaps the major development was the establishment of Canada's *Truth and Reconciliation Commission* on 2 June 2008 into the country's residential school system.

In Canada, the residential school system is often considered the most outstanding act of cultural genocide ever inflicted on the Indigenous peoples of this country. The truth and reconciliation approach is often seen as a form of restorative justice, rather than an approach that differs from the form of adversarial and retributive justice which is based primarily on fault finding and punishment of the perceived guilty parties (see Hedican 2013:46–47, 2016: 153–159; Niezen 2013).

Shortly after the *Truth and Reconciliation Commission* (TRC) had been constituted, Prime Minister Stephen Harper delivered a historic speech in the House of Commons on 11 June 2008. In this, he apologized on behalf of all Canadians for the hardship that had been done to the Indigenous people of this country because of the Indian residential school system.

In this speech, Prime Minister Harper said, "The government of Canada sincerely apologizes and asks the forgiveness of the Aboriginal peoples of this country for failing them so profoundly. We are sorry". He also stated, "Today, we recognize that this policy of assimilation was wrong, has caused great harm, and has no place in our country".

The TRC was part of a court-approved Residential School Settlement Agreement which was negotiated between the legal counsel of former students, government representatives, church members, the Assembly of First Nations, and other Aboriginal organizations.

In addition, in March 2008, Aboriginal peoples and church officials embarked on the "Remembering the Children" tour, which went from city to city listening to Indigenous people's experiences with the residential school system. In addition, in January 2009, King's University College of Edmonton, Alberta, convened an interdisciplinary conference on the subject of the findings of the *Truth and Reconciliation Committee.*

As far as the former students at residential schools are concerned, remembering these past horrific events was not easy. As the various hearings across the country revealed, physical and sexual abuse of Aboriginal students took place on a wide scale. Indigenous students in residential schools often spent long periods of time away from their parents, other siblings, and community members. As a result, the trauma that these students experienced has come to be termed *cultural disassociation*, which had the long-term effect of preventing traditions from being passed down to succeeding generations in the Indigenous society.

The TRC hearings were conceived as a process or approach that seeks to heal or restore the relationships between offenders, community members, and the victims of the offenses that have taken place. This approach was especially favored by Canada's Indigenous people who were living in small, relatively isolated communities.

It was also recognized that offending persons needed to be forgiven for their offenses because they often return to the communities and need, in turn, to be reintegrated back into their social and cultural settings. However, not everyone agreed with the TRC approach which emphasized healing over retribution. As an example, Harry LaForme, who was a Justice of the Ontario Court of Appeal and was appointed as the first commission chair, resigned shortly after his appointment in October 2008.

Justice LaForme, who was a member of the New Credit First Nation in Southern Ontario, claimed that the commission hearings were being unduly influenced in a political manner by the existing Grand Chief of the Assembly of First Nations, Phil Fontaine, a national organization which represents all of the status Indigenous people in Canada.

As far as Justice LaForme was concerned, he claimed that Grand Chief Fontaine wanted the TRC to abandon the reconciliation approach and by so doing take a more political stance against the federal government in Ottawa. As a result, in the midst of this controversy, several of the TRC commissioners resigned.

However, in June 2009, a reconstituted commission was subsequently established, headed by Justice Murray Sinclair, the first Aboriginal judge in Manitoba's history. One of the conclusions that could be made then about such truth and reconciliation commissions is that they are bound to have important political dimensions that are bound to affect the course of the eventual hearings. Or, as one commentator stated, "Public apologies and truth and reconciliation commissions have become like confessionals for the states" (Niezen 2010: 179).

Thus, as far as Johnny Yesno and his friends from the Pelican Lake and Shingwauk residential schools are concerned, their radio program in 1970, which was aired over half a century ago, can be seen as an important forerunner of the eventual truth and reconciliation process. They foresaw the need for a public inquiry into the events, abuses, and other hardships that were inflicted upon the Indigenous students at the time.

While their short radio program of less than half an hour did not highlight all of the problems that they experienced in the residential school system, they did bring to the public's attention the need for discussion of the Aboriginal student's ongoing mental, social and cultural issues that resulted from their participation in this repressive system.

One of the most prolific writers promoting anti-Indigenous tropes is Frances Widdowson of Winnipeg's Frontier Center for Public Policy (FCPP). One of the main activities of this 'think tank' is to promote climate change denial. In September 2018, the Frontier Center also ran a radio ad claiming to debunk myths about the Indian residential school system that resulted in the deaths of 6000 Indigenous children.

The Assembly of First Nations National Chief, Perry Bellegarde denounced the ad because "it knowingly turned its back on the facts" (*CBC News*, 24 September 2018).

The ad begins with the question: "Are Canadians being told the whole truth about residential schools?" A professor at the University of Regina, James Daschuk, comments "I honestly do not understand why they would devalue their own brand by coming out with an advertisement that's so egregiously wrong."

A spokesperson for the FCPP attempted to distance itself from the ad by saying that it had "no editorial control over the piece." Frances Widdowson is listed as a Senior Fellow with the FCPP who uses a political economy perspective in her research on Aboriginal policy, as well as the politics of religion.

She is known for several controversial books on Indigenous issues, such as *Disrobing the Aboriginal Industry: The Deception Behind Cultural Preservation* (2008, with husband Albert Howard). The main point of the book, according to its publication blurb, is "to expose the industry that has grown up around land claims settlements, showing that Aboriginal policy development over the last 30 years has been manipulated by non-Aboriginal lawyers and consultants." The authors singled out the clergy, consultants, lawyers, and anthropologists who "have used the plight of Aboriginal peoples to justify a self-serving agenda" (2008: 9).

Within an Indigenous community, "Privileged leaders live in luxury and are paid huge salaries, while most Aboriginal people rely on social assistance. The vanity and arrogance of an unprincipled native leadership is supported by…the bureaucrats and academics whose careers would be jeopardized by exposing the non-performance of current Aboriginal policies…The result is a squandering of billions of dollars each year" (ibid: 9–10).

In a book review, well-known political scientist Peter H. Russell, professor emeritus of the University of Toronto, concluded that: The first thing to be said about the book is that it is not based on well-researched empirical political science. Most of the evidence for their thesis is anecdotal. Careful empirical research of any First Nation community, on or off-reserve is totally lacking. Broad historical propositions are advanced that distort history and provide an ill-informed basis for appraising current policy in relation to Aboriginal peoples (2010: 785). In addition, he "profoundly disagrees with the assumptions of these authors and their empirical characterizations of Aboriginal people's culture and capacities past and present" (ibid: 786).

Debunking Residential School "Myths"

There are those in Canadian society who are attempting to promote the idea that the harsh conditions of the residential schools have been greatly exaggerated. As an example, *CBC News* reported in 2018 on a radio ad claiming to debunk the "myths" of residential schools and the subsequent

211

criticism that this ad evoked and the following accusation that the producers of this ad "knowingly turned their backs on the facts" according to one professor who has knowledge of the facts involved (*CBC News*, 24 September 2018).

This ad which was aired in Saskatchewan has prompted angry reactions across the country. The ad was aired on the Manitoba-based Golden West Radio which operates stations in Swift Current, Humboldt, Moose Jaw, Estevan, Weyburn, and Rosetown/Kindersley which, as such, has a wide coverage in the prairie provinces, possibly indicating a widespread Indigenous bias in this area.

The ad which comprised a two-minute piece made by the Winnipeg-based Frontier Center for Public Policy (FCPP) was aired across multiple private radio stations and began with the question: "Are Canadians being told the whole truth about residential schools?" In the ad veteran prairie broadcaster, Roger Currie says "We have been told that the residential school system deserves the blame for many of the dysfunctions in Indigenous society; abuse of alcohol and drugs, domestic violence and educational failures can all be blamed on the school system which did not finally end until 1990."

Here is a list of the so-called *myths* that the radio ad claims to be true:

Residential schools robbed native kids of their childhood. In fact, the average stay was less than five years, and the vast majority of Aboriginal youth never attended a residential school.

The harm that was done to those attending residential schools has been passed on to today's generation. In fact, there is little evidence that abuse that was suffered by a grandparent had any effect on the academic success of the generations that followed. A spokesperson for the radio station indicated that the ad was a "commentary" that was aired in a paid spot on Fridays.

Condemnation of the ad did not take long in coming. A media relations specialist, Tammy Robert, who is based in Saskatoon said that "I sat there and listened to the entire thing, kind of in disbelief" as she heard the commentary in a coffee shop. Robert said that she was stunned at the presentation of residential school-related trauma as myths, and the use of the word *fact*. She further stated, "I'm an advocate of free speech and opinion but you have to be grounded in fact, and at this stage, there's not a chance that those were facts. That's what struck me the most."

The reader should be reminded that the Truth and Reconciliation Commission heard from more than 6,000 witnesses over six years and its final report which was released in 2015 found that residential schools amounted to cultural genocide. In terms of the "facts" involved, around 150,000 Indigenous children went to residential schools, and it has been estimated that about 6,000 children died while in the care of the school's custodial staff which included religious authorities, teachers, and administrators.

Previously, in 2008, Prime Minister Stephen Harper issued an apology to the former students at residential schools; saying that it was "a sad chapter in Canada's history and that the policy of assimilation that had been promoted during this era was wrong."

Robert said that she thought the piece was particularly problematic because it was aired in an area of rural Saskatchewan which is an area that she believes has a "racism issue." As she explains, "we've seen it play out time and time again and most prominently with the Gerald Stanley trial which created even more rural tension and racial tension in Saskatchewan. I just don't see the point of [the broadcast]."

For those not familiar with the Gerald Stanley trial (*CBC News*, 14 February 2018), it involved Stanley's acquittal when a jury in Battleford, Saskatchewan found Stanley not guilty of second-degree murder in the death of Colten Boushie, 22.

As a prominent civil rights lawyer, Julian Falconer explained, "Stanley's acquittal was an outrage because it was the result of centuries of oppression...centuries of treatment of Indigenous people as less than worthy victims. The outrage felt and expressed across the country following the verdict in the Gerald Stanley trial comes from years of injustice that have deeply eroded the confidence of Indigenous peoples in Canada's justice system."

The *outrage* that Falconer refers to stems from the verdict of a Battleford jury which found Stanley not guilty of second-degree murder in the death of Colten Boushie, 22, who was shot and killed after he and four other men from the Red Cree Nation drove onto Stanley's rural property near Biggar Saskatchewan in August 2016.

Furthermore, commentary on the Stanley case and on the wider implications that it entailed was also provided by Christina Gray, a senior research associate with the International Law Research Program in Waterloo,

Ontario. She said that Indigenous peoples face systemic failures in the justice system that range from the police officer on the street all the way through the court system and into the corrections system. "There is a history of resentment toward Indigenous people and stereotypes," Gray suggests.

In this context, the negative comments concerning the findings of Canada's Truth and Reconciliation Commission report of 2015 can be seen as an extension of an anti-Indigenous backlash. It's concerning that a respected organization like the Frontier Center for Public Policy (FCPP) is spreading false information about the negative effects of the residential school system through a radio broadcast.

Then, in a specious attempt to distance itself from the broadcast, the FFPP said in a statement that its radio commentaries are "designed to reach a wider non-traditional audience" and that they're based on the items published by the center (*CBC News*, 24 September 2018). The FFPP statement further indicated that Currie, the man who voiced the piece, had "no editorial control" over the piece and was "simply a paid professional." However, the statement did not address concerns raised in reaction to the ad.

James Daschuk, who is a professor at the University of Regina specializing in the study of Indigenous health issues, expressed concern that the FFPP who he regards as "a legitimate, right-wing think tank", would have ever developed such a commentary so negatively situated against Indigenous people because it tends to "undermine their credibility."

"Furthermore, I honestly do not understand why they would devalue their own brand by coming out with an advertisement that's so egregiously wrong. There is so much overwhelming evidence, it is undeniable," Daschuk asserts. "The producers of that segment were knowingly turning their backs on the facts."

As far as Currie, the person who voiced the ad is concerned, he referred to his role as "regretful" and went on to apologize "for any hurt and offense that my participation may have caused. These are not my thoughts, but that's not a real, valid excuse." He went on to indicate that "I have not read the Truth and Reconciliation report. Very few people have." Nonetheless, it is apparent that both Currie and the FCPP personnel have not taken real ownership of the harm that spreading false information about Indigenous peoples has caused, especially the fundamental issues that gave rise to the residential school system in the first place.

As Assembly of First Nations, National Chief Perry Bellegarde said in a statement issued concerning the broadcast, "Overwhelming research and evidence shows that harmful, negative impacts of residential school on First Nation children, families, and culture" are a fact, not a "myth" as some Canadians are led to believe.

As Mr. Bellegarde further states, "Trying to downplay the impacts of the residential schools on the thousands of children that attended, and their families, is wrong and it's shameful." In addition, as Ry Moran, director of the National Center for Truth and Reconciliation in Winnipeg said, "the ad's perspective is not surprising. Canadians are hanging onto this narrative that the residential school system was good with a few bad apples in it. That's not the case" (*CBC News*, 25, 30 September 2018).

Fifty Years Later

Johnny Yesno's original broadcast on CBC's "Our Native Land" concerning his experiences at the Pelican Lake and Shingwauk Residential schools took place in 1972. Now, over 50 years later, the reverberations of this broadcast echo through Canadian history.

Johnny brought attention to an issue that was rarely discussed in the early 1970s but certainly gained momentum through time resulting in Prime Minister Stephen Harper's apology to Indigenous people in 2008 and in the Truth and Reconciliation Commission of 2018.

It was his foresight, and other Indigenous people with his vision of the future, that brought such an important historical investigation to the forefront. Without people such as Johnny Yesno, one wonders if such an investigation would ever have occurred at all, given the sentiment of some Canadians who would deny the historical facts of such colonial suppression.

Toronto's *Globe and Mail* (13 October 2023) has now reported on how horrific the abuse of Indigenous children actually was in an article entitled "97-Year-Old Nun Charged with Historical Sexual Assaults at Residential Schools."

This article is a report of the criminal occurrences at St. Anne's Indian Residential School at Fort Albany, which is situated on the Hudson Bay coast at the headwaters of the Albany River system; home also of the Eabametoong First Nation (Fort Hope). This was the First Nation where Johnny Yesno was born and spent his childhood, years before he was brought to the residential school at Sioux Lookout.

As this article indicates, "A group of survivors from the school fought for years to have a document about recorded abuses at the school released, which they say would support their claims for federal compensation, under the Indian Residential Schools Settlement Agreement [IRSSA] of 2006. [However], the Supreme Court of Canada refused to hear their case last year."

Previously, the *CBC* (29 March 2018) reported on the many cases of the sexual, emotional, and physical abuse of Indigenous students in "The Horrors of St. Annes." As this *CBC* report indicated:

"The preteen girls would take turns with the towel in the bathroom of St. Anne's Indian. Residential School. On at a time, they would wrap it around their throats and pull it tight. 'We called it getting high. We'd get dizzy, lightheaded,' one of them said nearly two decades later, on 3 August 1993, during an interview with Ontario Provincial Police investigators in Room 251 of the Howard Johnson Hotel in London, Ont. 'We looked forward to it,' said the residential school survivor, whose name is redacted in the OPP transcript. 'It was an escape'.

The woman, by then in her mid-30s, was describing her horrific nine-year stay at the school on Fort Albany First Nation, near the James Bay coast, as part of an indecent assault investigation of one of the former nuns. What we needed to escape, she told investigators, were the constant strappings and whippings, and the sexual assaults by a man she knew only as *the gardener*. "This shouldn't have happened to us. They're God's workers, they were to look after us."

The transcript of the interview is among thousands of pages of OPP records from a sprawling investigation into abuse at St. Annes's obtained by *CBC News*. The investigation began on 9 November 1992, after Fort Albany First Nation Chief Edmund Metatawabin presented evidence to police following a healing conference attended by St. Anne's survivors. Over the next six years, the OPP would interview 700 victims and witnesses. They also gathered 900 statements about assaults, sexual assaults, suspicious deaths, and a multitude of abuses alleged to have occurred at the school between 1941 and 1972.

Investigators identified 74 suspects and charged seven people. Fiver [the "gardener"] was convicted of crimes committed at the residential school. However, from 2008 to 2014, the federal government omitted references to the

OPP investigation. It included the convictions, from the official St. Annes's record, known as the "school narrative," used during compensation hearings created by the 2006 Indian Residential Schools Settlement Agreement.

The school narrative is a key piece of evidence for compensation cases heard under the agreement's Independent Assessment Process (IAP). Adjudicators who hear survivors' stories can refer to the school narrative as one way to determine the veracity of a claim. In the case of St. Anne's, adjudicators relied on a school narrative that said there was no record of sexual assaults or student-on-student abuse cases.

The school narrative referred to only four recorded cases of physical abuse found in St. Anne's records in the Indian Affairs Department archives. Yet, the federal Justice Department obtained the OPP files from the investigation in 2003 after a group of St. Anne's survivors filed an abuse lawsuit in Cochrane, Ont., against Ottawa and the Catholic entities that ran the school. The case ended with a settlement.

Indian Affairs also included a reference to the OPP case and the convictions in the St. Anne's school narrative used during the Alternative Dispute Resolution process for settling compensation claims. The case ran from November 2003 to September 2007, when it was replaced by the IAP.

A 2014 ruling from the Ontario Superior Court forced the Harper government to disclose the OPP files and documents from the civil action in Cochrane to St. Anne's survivors. The school narrative used in the IAP hearings grew from 12 pages to about 1,200 pages referring to more than 12,000 documents.

Litigation has continued following the ruling as it emerged some St. Anne's survivors lost compensation cases because adjudicators doubted the veracity of their claims as a result of the incomplete record. Survivors want the Ontario Court of Appeal to force the government to turn over testimony transcripts from the Cochrane hearing. They are also seeking a process to deal with St. Anne's claims that were heard before the government turned over the OPP files.

Grey Nuns and a Priest with Students at St. Anne's in the 1940s

Photo Credit: Algoma University/Edmund Metatawabin Collection.

Some survivors have spoken out and written books about their experiences at the school, including in some cases, being shocked in a homemade electric chair. The OPP investigation also received national media coverage at the time. However, the investigation files obtained by CBC News contain the raw evidence gathered by the OPP during its investigation into one of the most notorious residential schools—evidence that has never been shared with the public. While the names of the victims and perpetrators are largely redacted from the OPP files, they reveal the depth of abuse and torture at the school.

This school was run by the Catholic order of Oblates of Mary Immaculate and the Grey Sisters of the Cross from 1902 until 1976. The federal government began funding the school in 1906. Only a small shack remains of St. Anne's today. The school, the nun's residence, and the rectory burned down separately over the past 15 years. The site which is owned by the band, is now a water treatment plant and a storage depot for housing material.

All of the survivors interviewed by the OPP during the investigation described suffering or witnessing multiple abuses—physical, sexual, and psychological. This was the case with the survivor interviewed at the Howard Johnson Hotel. At one point in the transcript, she described a straitjacket. She

218

told investigators it was a grayish-beige color and made from rough material like denim, with zippers down the back and front. The sleeves had fringes to bind the arms together across the front and bindings to secure the hands together behind the neck, she said during her second interview with the OPP on 10 August 1994:

"Sometimes students would be tied to the bed," she said. "It depended on how bad you were acting up." She remembered one time while having her first period, she resisted a nun who was rubbing her breasts and stomach before going down between her legs.

"A confused angry look came over her face," she told investigators. "That's when she said, you know the devils inside you, and that they had to get the devil out. The nun then restrained her in the straitjacket and continued to sexually assault her," she said. "She didn't even mind the mess or anything. It was almost like she got a thrill out of it or something," the survivor said.

Nuns, priests, and lay brothers would hit students with large straps, small whips, beaver snare wire, boards, books, rules, yardsticks, fists, and open hands, survivors told investigators. Sometimes, students were locked away in the dark basement for hours at a time.

They also told investigators about being force-fed porridge, spoiled fish, cod liver oil, and rancid horse meat that made students sick to the point of vomiting on their plates. They said they were often forced to then eat their own vomit. There were numerous allegations of sexual abuse involving nuns, priests, lay brothers, and other staff, ranging from fondling and forced kissing to violent attacks and night time molestation.

One survivor, who was in her 50s at the time of her August 1993 interview with OPP investigators, said she remembered a staff member who targeted five girls for sexual abuse during her time at St. Anne's, which lasted from 1951 to 1955. The survivor, who began attending the school at age 11, said the staff member took a different girl every night.

She said that she once sneaked upstairs with her cousin and a friend to the boys' section and peeked through the door. She said two boys were lying naked on separate beds. "I remember hearing the boys screaming," she told investigators at the Taykwa Tagamou Nation band office near Cochrane, located about 120 kilometers north of Timmins.

A survivor who attended St. Anne's in the 1960s said an older student once lured him into the basement with the promise of a surprise. "I thought it was gonna be a good surprise like a cake or something," he said, according to transcripts of his statements to police in July 1993 and November 1994. The survivor described a life of harsh punishment at the school that was made worse by his dyslexia. He said a staff member once broke a yardstick across his back. But nothing prepared him for the brutal surprise waiting for him in the basement. He remembered between 30 and 50 students were gathered there.

After he was beaten by about 15 students, six of them then held him down and tied his hands and feet together. They wrapped a rope around his neck. The students started playing tug of war with him, with one group pulling at his feet and the other pulling at his neck, he told the OPP. He said he kept his neck from breaking by grabbing onto the rope with his bound hands.

Then one of the students told the others to throw the rope attached to his neck over a pipe running across the ceiling. "I remember being pulled up once and when I was off the ground I blacked out," he said. "When I came to, all the boys were gone. The rope was taken off by...the supervisor."

He said he was taken to the hospital, given ointment, and returned to class with a neck collar over some gauze. Neither the supervisor who found him nor the nun who treated him at the hospital ever asked him what happened, he said. The OPP contacted the former supervisor, but he claimed he could not remember the attack. Investigators also found the former nun who worked at the hospital. She said she could not remember the boy.

The investigation record is replete with allegations of staff activity participating in or facilitating student-on-student physical and sexual abuse. There are also stories of student-on-student gang rapes and beatings. Some of the suspect profiles reveal student abusers were often themselves abused.

In one OPP interview, a male supervisor recalled that during the 1956–57 school year, a nun ordered eight boys to hold him down as she strapped him 27 times. In another interview, a woman who attended St. Anne's between 1963 and 1971 described how a school supervisor would pick on certain children she considered slow and how she humiliated a girl by forcing her to wear toilet paper around her neck to class.

"It got to the point where older girls would beat up the younger girls," she told the OPP. "I beat up my younger sister...we did this to get rid of our frustration." One survivor, known in court records as H-15019, lost his compensation claim because he wasn't believed. During his IAP hearing in

July 2014, Justice Department lawyers relied on the incomplete school narrative despite possessing proof a priest mentioned in the compensation claim was a serial sex abuser, the survivor later alleged in court documents. The court granted him a new hearing and he eventually secured his compensation.

The federal government's handling of St. Anne's-related documents is part of a pattern, according to filings before the Ontario Court of Appeal in the St. Anne's disclosure case. The survivors say the federal government has a history of "reluctant, contradictory, and inconsistent disclosure of documentation of abuse in residential schools."

They provide several examples, including a case from 1998 where a former student of Port Alberni Indian Residential School on Vancouver Island sued Ottawa over abuse he suffered at the school. During the case, which reached the Supreme Court, Indian Affairs claimed it only knew of five cases of sexual assault at residential schools across the country over a 50-year period. However, between 1994 and 1996, the department had identified a possible 91 cases of physical and sexual abuse at the schools and asked the RCMP to investigate.

In 1994, the Indian and Northern Affairs Department refused to hand over documentation to the RCMP task force investigating cases in British Columbia, forcing the Mounties to obtain multiple search warrants for the department's head offices in Hull, Que., according to the Court of Appeal filings.

Even the Truth and Reconciliation Commission (TRC) faced difficulty obtaining records of criminal convictions related to residential school abuse from Indian Affairs. The department told the commission it didn't have them. The TRC concluded otherwise but was forced to complete its final report without them.

The description of the electric chair varied but it appeared to have been used between the mid-to-late 1950s and the mid-1960s, according to OPP transcripts and reports. Some said it was metal while others said it was made of dark green wood, like a wheelchair without wheels. They all said it had straps on the armrests and wires attached to a battery.

"I can remember we tall girls were in the girl's recreation group and [redacted] came in and had the chair with him," a survivor said in an interview with OPP on Dec. 18, 1992. "Then one by one [redacted] and [redacted] would make the girls sit on the electric chair. If you didn't want to [redacted] would push you into the chair and hold your arms onto the arms of the chair."

The survivor told the OPP she was forced to sit on the chair in 1964 or 1965. "I was scared," she said. "[Redacted] hit the switch two or three times while I sat in the chair. I was shocked. It felt like my whole body tingled. It's hard to describe. It was painful." She then started to cry.

The OPP records indicate one former student said she was put in the chair and shocked until she passed out. Another said he was told to sit in the chair if he wanted to speak to his mother. One survivor, in an interview with police on 27 February 1993, said two lay brothers made the students stand in a circle holding on to the armrests as one student sat in the chair. One of the brothers flicked the switch. "It felt like a whole bunch of needles going up your arms," the former student said. "The two brothers started to laugh…and shocked us again. I then started to cry because it really hurt."

There were stories about the death of a boy who fell from a swing in 1933. Another boy drowned after falling through the ice while skating in the 1940s. One survivor told police a boy was beaten to death in the 1940s or 1950s for stealing a communion wafer.

Then there was the disappearance of three boys: John Kioki, 14, and Michel Matinas, 11, both from Attawapiskat, and Michael Sutherland, 13, from Weemisk. The trio left St, Anne's with a fourth boy in the early morning hours of 19 April 1941, but he returned to the school because he was told by the others that he was too young to make the journey to Attawapiskat.

The boys had planned their escape in whispers at night, according to various interviews conducted by the OPP. They told the other students to keep the plan quiet as they gathered leftovers from meals to store in a flour bag they kept hidden for their escape. The boys also had a bow and 10 arrows to hunt rabbits and partridge.

The boys ran away because they were sick of being strapped, said a former classmate, who also told police the boys snuck out at 5 o'clock in the morning. in stocking feet, holding their boots. He said he and four other boys snuck out of the school three hours after the first group. It was foggy that morning and it took them some time to find the first group's trail that led north on the Albany River.

"The river wasn't open yet, but it was getting wet on top of the river," he told the OPP. The group of five eventually returned to the school after another student caught up with them and told them a priest had noticed they were gone and ordered them back. A St. Anne's staff member was later sent out to look for the missing trio but turned back after it got dark. A storm hit on the second day of searching.

The RCMP and an Indian Affairs official were not informed of the boy's disappearance until weeks later, on 6 June 1941. Eventually, some of the local Cree who were out hunting said, they came across a small wigwam and arrows about 16 kilometers away near the Chickney River. The boys were assumed to have drowned since their bodies were never recovered.

"The whole affair is regrettable, and the parents' indignation is understandable," an RCMP constable said in a dispatch to superiors on 27 June 1941. "There does not seem to be anything further that can be done at this late date. In my view of this, the file is being considered closed." A public inquiry was held the following year and reached the same conclusion.

The legacy of St. Anne's is still felt from Moosonee to Fort Albany First Nation to Attawapiskat and to Peawanuck, which used to be known as Winisk but was destroyed by a flood. Surrounded by deaths and disappearances, constant fear, and violence, the survivors interviewed by the OPP spoke about attempted suicides, struggles with addictions, and broken lives. Lives crippled by a childhood living at school. "I craved…and was sick for love," a survivor told an OPP investigator.

The Five People convicted following the OPP investigation included:

Anne Wesley, a Cree nun born in Attawapiskat, who attended St. Anne's as a child, was convicted of three counts of common assault, three counts of administering a noxious substance, and one count of assault causing bodily harm. She received an 11-month conditional sentence.

Jane Kakaychawan, an Ojibway nun born in Ogoki Post, Ont., who as a child attended the McIntosh Indian Residential school north of Vermillion Bay, Ont., was convicted of three counts of assault causing bodily harm. She was given a six-month conditional sentence.

John Moses Rodrique, a cook and later employed by Indian Affairs, pleaded guilty to five counts of indecent assault. He was sentenced to 18 months in jail.

Claude Lambert, a child-care worker at St. Anne's, pleaded guilty to one count of indecent assault and was sentenced to eight months in jail.

Marcel Blais, who worked in the kitchen, pleaded guilty to one count of indecent assault on a male. He did not receive jail time.

In addition, as indicated earlier in a *Globe and Mail* (13 October 2023) article, a 97-year-old nun, Francoise Seguin of Ottawa, has been criminally charged with three counts of gross indecency and is scheduled to appear in Moosonee court later in the year.

According to the press release, the Jame Bay OPP was contacted about incidents that allegedly occurred in the 1960s and 1970s at St. Anne's Indian Residential School in Fort Albany in Moosonee which operated until 1976. In a related *CBC News* (19 October 2023) report, former Fort Albany Chief Edmund Metatawabin said that "many people will be relieved" by the charges of abuse by the St. Anne's nuns.

They are among the 180 alleged perpetrators listed by 152 survivors in 61 lawsuits, filed against the Canadian government and Catholic Church in the early 2000s. According to Charlie Angus, new Democratic MP for Timmins-James Bay, whose riding encompasses Fort Albany where St. Anne's operated, "This was supposed to be a school. Instead, it was a torture chamber, a place for pedophiles…If the police believe that there's enough to charge her, that case should go ahead [to trial]," Angus said.

Francoise Seguin is the third nun to face criminal charges stemming from her work at St. Anne's with the Sisters of Charity of Ottawa. Previously, two Sisters of Charity of Ottawa nuns were charged and convicted following a 1990s OPP probe into suspected criminal conduct at St. Anne's. Anne Wesley, a Cree nun who had attended St. Anne's herself, was convicted in 1999 of administering a noxious substance and assault.

Jane Kakeychewan was convicted in 1998 of three counts of assault causing bodily harm to female students. Between 1992 and 1997, police interviewed more than 700 people, and took 900 sworn statements. And also, seized more than 7,000 documents from several church organizations, eventually laying charges against seven former school workers, among whom five were convicted.

"When it comes to these types of testimonies, it's very difficult," says Anna Betty Achneepineskum, Deputy Grand Chief of the Nishnawbe Aski Nation. She commended the former students for coming forward and is grateful to the police for pursuing the investigation. "It takes a lot of courage because there's been many times where no one believed them. And also, the court system has not been kind to First Nation citizens in this country, in order for them to acquire that sense of justice. So, this is very significant in terms of validation," she said.

The Chiefs of Ontario Response

The Chiefs of Ontario, an organization in which Johnny Yesno was a founding member, provided additional recent information on residential schools. Many First Nations have been working for years to recover the remains of the lives taken in Residential Schools, Day Schools, Indian Hospitals, and Industrial Schools. These ongoing efforts have received national attention and recognition as a result of the hundreds of unmarked graves that were confirmed across Canada in the summer of 2021.

On 1 August 2023, the Ontario government launched the new Indian Residential School Community Engagement Fund (IRSCEF), which will provide up to $7.075 M in support to organizations and communities for community engagement and related activities. It was in response to planned or ongoing burial investigations at former Residential Schools, as well as for mental health support for survivors and their families.

This new funding opportunity was created after hearing from Indigenous communities and leadership that more support is needed for the broader network of communities and organizations involved in, or impacted by, ongoing investigations at Indian Residential School sites. To that end, the IRSCEF will allow for the funding of even more Indigenous-led supports and survivor-centered, culturally sensitive programs and services that are as flexible as possible in responding to and supporting the needs of survivors and their families.

A National Indian Residential School Crisis Line has been set up to provide support for former Residential School students. You can access emotional and crisis referral services by calling the 24-hour National Crisis Line: 1-866-925-4419.

The Indian Residential Schools Resolution Health Support Program provides mental health, emotional, and cultural support services to eligible former Indian Residential School students and their families throughout all phases of the Indian Residential School Settlement Agreement. This program included all former Indian Residential School students, regardless of the individual's status or place of residence within Canada, who attended an Indian

Residential School listed in the 2006 Indian Residential Schools Settlement Agreement, and are eligible to receive services from the Resolution Health Support Program.

In recognition of the intergenerational impacts that the Indian Residential Schools had on families, Resolution Health Support Program services are also available to family members of former Indian Residential Schools students. The family of former students is defined as a spouse or partner, and those raised by or raised in the household of a former Indian Residential School student. The program also is available to any relation who has experienced the effects of intergenerational trauma associated with a family member's time at an Indian Residential School.

Indigenous Services Canada verifies the eligibility of persons requesting Indian Residential Schools Resolution Health Support Program services with Crown-Indigenous Relations and Northern Affairs Canada. It holds data on former students who attended those Indian Residential Schools that are part of the Indian Residential Schools Settlement Agreement.

Cultural support is provided by local Indigenous organizations who coordinate the services of Elders or traditional healers. Cultural supports seek to assist former students and their families to safely address issues related to Indian Residential Schools as well as the disclosure of abuse during the Settlement Agreement process.

Specific services are chosen by the former student or family member and can include traditional healing, ceremonies, teachings, and dialogue. Emotional support is also provided in terms of services available through local Indigenous organizations and is designed to help former students. Their families safely address issues related to the negative impacts of the Indian Residential Schools as well as the disclosure of abuse during the Settlement Agreement process.

A Resolution Health Support worker will listen, talk, and provide support to former students and their family members through all phases of the Settlement Agreement process. In addition, both cultural and emotional support programs are augmented by professional counseling. Professional counselors are psychologists and social workers who are registered with Indigenous Services Canada, for individual or family counseling. A professional counselor will listen, talk, and assist individuals to find ways of healing from Indian Residential School experiences.

Indigenous Services Canada's Non-Insured Health Benefits (NIHB) and Indian Residential Schools Resolution Health Support Program developed a joint Guide to Mental Health Counseling Services which outlines the criteria, guidelines, and policies. Under this arrangement the NIHB program's Mental Health Counseling benefit and the Individual and Family Counseling component of the Indian Residential Schools Resolution Health Support Program operate.

Conclusion

One may describe the plight of Indigenous people in Canada using different terms, such as racial profiling, suffering from discrimination, or stereotypes, yet none of these designations come close to depicting the horrors of the residential school system in this country.

The very people in various religious organizations who were designated to protect the innocent Indigenous children; were the very ones who inflicted such indescribable atrocities on these innocent victims.

It has now been over 50 years since various Indigenous people, such as Johnny Yesno, began to speak out about their experiences in Canada's residential schools. Even today, there has been little judicial action taken on the perpetrators of these unforgivable assaults on innocent children. The residential school system in Canada will no doubt go down in history as the great shame of our nation.

Chapter Nine
The Order of Canada

Johnny Yesno was made a member of the *Order of Canada* on 23 June 1976, for his services to broadcasting in Canada. His investiture in the Order makes note of his following contributions,

"Actor, broadcaster, and producer, who has taken part in many television and radio programs and has been concerned with satellite programming to the North and ensuring that Canadians have a better understanding of the Indian people" (*https://www.gg.ca/en/honours/recipients*).

Also, as noted in a newspaper article titled "Johnny Yesno: Survivor to Star" (*Sootoday* 5 December 2021):

"Yesno's career in both film and journalism was recognized and acknowledged in 1976 when he was made a member of the Order of Canada…With his experience and success, it should come as no surprise that Johnny Yesno became a leading voice in Indigenous and government relations.

Following his call to the Order of Canada, he became the director for the Chiefs of Ontario and went on to hold the position of Aboriginal advisor with the former Ministry of Northern Development and Mines here in Sault Ste. Marie until his retirement in 2002."

Nishnawbe Aski Nation Grand Chief Stan Beardy furthermore noted that Johnny Yesno can be credited with inspiring a generation of Aboriginal people to follow their own dreams as he did.

"Yesno," Beardy continues, "blazed a lot of trails for us…(he) pushed our priorities to the forefront…he worked to improve satellite communications in far northern communities…[Johnny Yesno] educated society at a time when the Lone Ranger and Tonto were on television, about not stereotyping First Nation people."

Director: Chiefs of Ontario

After his call to the *Order of Canada*, Johnny Yesno became an even more vocal advocate of Indigenous rights especially as this pertains to various governmental relationships. This was particularly the case when he became director for the Chiefs of Ontario in March of 1975 during which he met Queen Elizabeth II shortly after. He then went on to hold the position of Aboriginal Advisor with the former Ministry of Northern Development and Mines in 1988, now called the Ministry of Northern Development. It was a position that he held until his retirement in 2002.

Johnny Yesno (L) in Business Suite

Photo Courtesy of Caroline Yesno

The Chiefs of Ontario organization began with the First Annual "All Ontario Chiefs Conference," which was initially formed as a joint First Nations

Association Coordinating Committee; constituted as a federation of the four major Ontario First Nations organizations. The purpose of the committee was to provide a single Ontario representative to the Assembly of First Nations (then, the National Indian Brotherhood).

From this committee emerged the Chiefs of Ontario office whose basic purpose was to enable political leadership. It was a forum to discuss and eventually decide on various regional, provincial, and national priorities that affect all the First Nations people who live in Ontario and, hopefully, provide a unified voice on these issues.

The Chiefs of Ontario use a logo comprising five feathers around a circle with a picture of a map of Ontario. As indicated on their website *https://chiefs-of-ontario.org/*. The circle and map represent the continuity, strength, and harmony of the First Nations peoples of Ontario. The five feathers signify the four political organizations of the Chiefs of Ontario. The fifth feather represents the independent nations and First Nation peoples living off-reserve, First Nations who are not forgotten. The overall symbol represents the continuance of the First Nations peoples of Ontario's struggle for pride, culture, self-determination, and spirituality (as indicated in organization's web page above.)

Ministry of Northern Development

Mining, along with forestry, is one of the major concerns of Ontario's Ministry of Northern Development. Johnny Yesno was well aware of the importance of mining in Ontario's northern economy, especially because he was a band member of the Eabametoong (Fort Hope) First Nation, situated on the Albany River which is a mineral-rich portion of the province.

Thus, he realized the importance of an Aboriginal advisor to this ministry when the Ontario government was in the process of making decisions regarding mining development and the impact that these decisions would have on the First Nations of this region.

In other words, this Aboriginal advisor role was a natural continuation of his previous activities as Director of the Chiefs of Ontario in providing a liaison between the Indigenous and non-Indigenous decision-making bodies of regional governments.

As an example, the Chiefs of Ontario hosted a panel event in Toronto that highlighted the importance of First Nations consultation and engagement in the mining sector. Here is a summary of the news release which explains the importance of this panel discussion:

(6 March 2024, Toronto, ON) Yesterday, First Nations Leaders joined together alongside industry experts and media to spur discussion on First Nation mining priorities, including the Mining Lands Administration System (MLAS) Moratorium and the importance of First Nations consultation and engagement. "To call for a moratorium on the MLAS is both a critical and timely issue that demands our attention," said Ontario Regional Chief Glen Hare in his opening comments to the event attendees yesterday afternoon. "The government of Ontario must be speaking directly with the rights holders" he indicated.

On 24 January 2024, Ontario Regional Chief Glen Hare called on the provincial government to implement a 365-day moratorium on the MLAS, detailing the need for a pause on the system, due to an exponential and ever-growing number of mining and exploration claims being staked within First Nations territories. As it stands, First Nations communities do not have the capacity nor the resources necessary to fully assess claims and analyze the potential impacts that they may have on their traditional territories.

"In Anishinabek Nation, we have seen upwards of 26%-30% of an increase in the number of claims being made in our territories," said Grand Council Chief Reg Niganobe, Anishinabek Nation. "We have been limited in resources to act upon and assess these claims—not by our own choices, but by the government's interference in these processes, which have been occurring for far too long."

As Jason Batise, Executive Director of Wabun Tribal Council, explained during the panel, the impact on First Nations begins on the first day that the claim is staked. Mining prospectors must acknowledge the impact that their activities have on communities and must ensure that they involve First Nations in a meaningful capacity from the beginning of any processes that they wish to undertake in relation to mining and exploration.

As the Chiefs of Ontario and ORC Hare have acknowledged, there are widely varying stances on mining throughout the 133 First Nations communities across Ontario. Yesterday's event prompted conversation and created a platform for First Nations to voice opinions on claim staking, implementation of First Nations consultation and engagement, and ensure that the standard of Free, Prior, and Informed Consent is integrated into the current system.

"The only way to have any certainty in moving forward with such developments is to create and build that relationship with us," said Chief Shelley Moore-Frappier, Temagami First Nation, "we are the rights holders, and we are going to exercise our jurisdiction over our own lands."

Northern Ontario's Mining Controversies

When Johnny Yesno joined the Ministry of Northern Development in 1988 in the Aboriginal Advisor capacity, a role that he would occupy for the next four years until his retirement in 2002, he was probably not fully aware of the brewing controversies developing in the very country in the Albany River area that he was born into. Of course, the controversies were multifaceted as many of these issues had to do with mineral and treaty rights, provincial and federal responsibilities, and other jurisdictional matters.

For the most part, the controversies are mining-related focusing on what has come to be termed the *Ring of Fire* area. One may initially think that the term *Ring of Fire* refers to the vitriolic controversy that occurred between the First Nations of northern Ontario and the various government officials who were involved in the decision-making of the area's mining sector.

However, the *Ring of Fire* term is the name given to a vast region of mineral deposits in northern Ontario, situated some 400 kilometers northeast of Thunder Bay, in the James Bay Lowlands. The *Ring of Fire* region was named after Johnny Cash's famous country and western ballad; when Richard Nemis, founder and president of Noront Resources, first made significant mineral finds in the area.

The region is near Attawapiskat River in the Kenora District, extending about 70 kilometers east of the First Nations community of Webequie and due north of the Albany River, west of James Bay.

There are three First Nations communities in this area that are directly impacted by mineral exploration and development, namely Marten Falls, Webequie, and Neskantaga (Lansdowne House). There are other First Nations on the edge of the *Ring of Fire* that would also be influenced to one degree or another by the proposed mineral development, such as Constance Lake, Nibinamik (Summer Beaver), Aroland, Long Lake 58, Ginoogaming (Long Lake), Eabametoong (Fort Hope), and Mishkeegogaming (Osnaburgh House).

For the most part, all of these First Nations suffer from depressed economic conditions in one way or another, such as high unemployment, low per-capita incomes, and lack of employment opportunities. As an example, as Tony Clement, former Treasury Board president, and FedNor minister, acknowledged in an interview on 4 February 2013, "The *Ring of Fire* area is home to some of the most socioeconomically disadvantaged communities in all of Canada."

Clement stated further that "chronic housing shortages, low education outcomes and lack of access to clean drinking water jeopardize the ability of local First Nation to benefit from significant economic, employment and business development opportunities associated with the *Ring of Fire* developments." Nonetheless, the *Ring of Fire*, according to Clement, represents a "once-in-a-life time opportunity to create jobs and generate growth and long-term prosperity for northern Ontario and the nation" (Ontario Ministry of Natural Resources, 2013).

The *Ring of Fire* development, therefore, could be seen as a possible significant economic benefit to this area of northern Ontario, but there are also infrastructural challenges that could blunt the possible economic benefits that the mining activities could bring to the region. In an effort to facilitate the mining developments, the former Ontario Premier, Bob Rae, was appointed to represent the First Nations whose members would be impacted by the mining developments; to act as their chief negotiator (*Globe and Mail*, 24 June 2013).

However, even with Bob Rae's participation in the negotiation process there nonetheless remained major questions about the development and its supposed benefits to the Indigenous people of northern Ontario. How prepared, for example, were the region's First Nations people for the possible employment opportunities that were expected to be available? According to the Grand Chief of the Nishnawbe Aski Nation, Mr. Les Louttit, two or three years were evidently not enough time he claimed for the skills training that would be required to prepare local workers for the construction jobs in the mining industry.

He also noted that there was a significant gap in the secondary and post-secondary educational levels between First Nations people in northern Ontario and the rest of Canada. The implication of Mr. Louttit's comments was that the *Ring of Fire* mining proposals would not benefit the First Nations people of northern Ontario as much as originally hoped (*CBC News*, 29 June 2013).

As such, the *Ring of Fire's* potential for economic development in northern Aboriginal communities may be derailed by political conflicts among the various parties involved (Wightman and Wightman 1997; Bray and Epp 1984).

The Hudson Bay Lowlands

If the First Nations people who live in the *Ring of Fire* region of northern Ontario were to have any chance of benefiting from the mining proposals presented by the provincial government, then there was a long road ahead. Potential developers, for example, are required to negotiate an Impact Benefit Agreement (IBA) with the First Nations communities before any mining development can take place. There is also other legislation that could potentially benefit the First Nations' bargaining position.

As an example, the government of Ontario's Far North Act received assent and became law on 25 October 2010. The Far North Act provides a "legislative foundation to support Far North land use between First Nations and Ontario." According to the Ontario government, the Hudson Bay Lowlands, which is the primary region affected by the mining proposals, is the "third largest wetland in the world," with a population of 24,000 First Nations residents in 34 communities.

Negotiations between the mining companies and the First Nations residents initially did not go smoothly. In 2003, Noront Resources began using two frozen lakes as landing strips without consulting Marten Falls and Webequie First Nations for prior permission. The Ontario Mining Act only allows exploration activities, rather than the construction of permanent structures.

In 2010, Martin Falls Chief Eli Moonias explained that Noront Resources did not have "permits to construct landing strips on the string bog or roads to the nearby airstrip." The chief also described how, over a seven-year period, Noront Resources "sunk machines here and they have done outrageous acts here" (Garrick 2010, *Wawatay News*, 4 February).

In response, members of the Marten Falls and Webequie First Nations set up a blockade on the landing strips at Koper and McFaulds Lakes. Further impediments to the negotiating process developed when, on 20 October 2011, Mattawa First Nations management, a regional chiefs council, removed its support for the *Ring of Fire* development.

The situation remained unless the federal government agreed to a joint review of the Environmental Assessment process, which would allow First Nations communities in the area to have a voice in the assessment. The problem with the Environmental Assessment process, according to a notice posted on the Neskantaga (Landsdowne House) First Nation website, is that it "is a generic public process with no distinct or government-to-government engagement with the First Nations that will be affected by the proposed projects…All who have something to say should be given an opportunity to speak and have their say in our own language, in our own communities." The website also mentions that the Ontario government decides "what's best for First Nations and implements policies and programs in line with that determination," rather than consulting directly with the First Nations involved (*www.neskantaga.com*/ retrieved 5 May 2024).

However, despite these various issues raised by members of the Neskantaga First Nation, on 26 March 2014, nine Matawa-member First Nations and the Province of Ontario moved toward reaching an agreement that would ensure First Nation communities would benefit from the proposed *Ring of Fire* development. The regional framework agreement was a first step in a community-based negotiation process that began in July 2013, at the request of Matawa-member First Nations. The agreement ensured that First Nations and Ontario would work together to advance *Ring of Fire* opportunities.

Key aspects of the agreement were the regional long-term environmental monitoring and enhanced participation in Environmental Assessment processes, resource revenue sharing, economic support, and regional and community infrastructure (Ginoogaming First Nation, 2014).

The Chiefs of Ontario Response

The province of Ontario continues to expedite the rate at which mineral exploration and development occurs at the expense of First Nations. Thus far, many concerns of the impacted First Nations have gone unresolved as the province continues to neglect the duty to consult, their fiduciary responsibilities to First Nations, and the United Nations Declaration on the Rights of Indigenous Peoples, including the principle of Free, Prior, and Informed Consent.

Resolution 23/30S: Mining Encroachment in First Nations Traditional Homelands and Territories was passed by the Chiefs in Assembly at the 2023

Fall Chiefs Assembly. This Resolution directed the Chiefs of Ontario Secretariat to coordinate a technical review and feasibility assessment; focused on the legal mechanisms executed in similar cases to the issue of the MLAS and First Nations in Ontario. The Resolution mandates that decisions including the Landore Decision (2018), the Saugeen SON Decision (2017), and the Gitxaala v. British Columbia (2023) be considered when addressing the series of questions prepared by the TWGM's technicians and COO Secretariat.

Additionally, the Resolution initiated the establishment of a TWGM as a part of the mandated Mining Sector Strategy. This group brings together technicians from First Nations across Ontario to facilitate wholesome discussion on the mining activities; impacting the land and infringing on Aboriginal inherent treaty rights. A series of questions was drafted by the TWGM that addresses the key concerns of the technicians regarding mining and the rights of First Nations and can be found in full within the downloadable RFP as attached above (*https://chiefs-of-ontario.org*).

The Landore Decision (2018)

Headline News: Robert Hiltz, *CIM Magazine*, "Ontario Court Dismisses Junior Miner's Exploration Permit Over Failure to Consult" (8 August 2018). According to this court decision Landore Resources and Ontario Mines Ministry failed to properly consult Eabametoong First Nation over the drilling permit, court rules.

The Ontario Superior Court threw out a junior mining company's permit for drilling work on Eabametoong First Nation's traditional territory in northern Ontario. It was after ruling that the company and the province had failed in their duty to adequately consult with the Nation.

Justice Harriet Sachs wrote in a mid-July ruling that Landore Resources Canada and Ontario's Ministry of Northern Development and Mines (MNDM) did not meet the required level of consultation to be seen as *upholding the honor of the Crown*, when dealing with Eabametoong (see also *CBC News*, 28 September 2018).

The judge wrote that both Landore and the MNDM dealt with Eabametoong in an opaque way that left the First Nation in the dark about why and how decisions were being made and excluded them from parts of the process. Sachs remitted the exploration permit back to the government *pending completion of adequate consultation* with the First Nation:

"Certain clear expectations were created by the Crown and its delegate, Landore, as to how the duty to consult would be fulfilled in this case and then, without meeting those expectations, or offering an explanation as to why they could not be met—the Crown changed the process in such a way as to render it one that could not reasonably be considered to be a genuine attempt at *talking together for mutual understanding*," Sachs wrote in her judgment.

One of the lawyers who represented Eabametoong, Krista Robertson, said the ruling is a relief to the people of the community:

- It's terrible for a First Nation to have to go through a case like this. It's expensive.
- It's stressful.
- "Nobody wants these cases to end up in the courts," Robertson said. "So, I do hope that everyone pulls their socks up on the proponent and government side and does a better job so that First Nations don't have to go through the court process."
- Cameron Ferguson, a spokesman for the MNDM, said, "The government would not appeal and will move forward with obligations set out in the Divisional Court's decision."

"The ministry values our relationship with Eabametoong First Nation. We look forward to working with the community in the future," Ferguson said. "The government continues to review and evaluate Ontario's approach to mineral exploration and development, including the duty to consult, through collaboration with Indigenous communities, industry partners, and other stakeholders."

The company's exploration permit is for claims on Treaty 9 lands near the Miminiska and Keezhik Lakes, some 40 kilometers west of Eabametoong First Nation, which is used extensively by members of the Nation for fishing, hunting, and spiritual purposes. Relations between Landore and Eabametoong began amicably, with Landore telling the First Nation at the beginning of the permit process, in 2013, that the company would not go forward with drilling without first agreeing on a memorandum of understanding (MOU). After two face-to-face meetings with the community, a third was promised by Landore's CEO to address some of Eabametoong's concerns.

Eabametoong hoped to review the company's drilling plans and work on the MOU, but Landore never responded to an email from the First Nation proposing a date for the third meeting. Both the ministry and Landore stopped trying to set up a meeting with Eabametoong. Landore had a private meeting with the ministry in January 2016. During the meeting, the company revealed they were in preliminary acquisition talks with Barrick Gold, the judgment said, and began to push the ministry to approve the permit as soon as possible, because of the negotiations.

The MNDM eventually emailed the First Nation with a deadline of five business days to approve a list of proposed conditions on Landore's permit. Despite Eabametoong's objections to the deadline and the conditions, Ontario approved the permit. During the process, the First Nation had sent a list of its concerns to the Ontario government but never heard anything back. In court, it came out that the ministry had done a detailed review of the concerns, but never took their analysis back to the community.

All of these factors added up to a lack of consultation, as Sachs wrote:

There was no real and genuine attempt by the Ministry or Landore to listen to Eabametoong's concerns, provide feedback about those concerns, and discuss ways to meet those concerns (if possible), the ruling says. "Instead, the concerns were noted, the expected opportunity for discussion was foreclosed without explanation and the Ministry proceeded in a unilateral way (without seeking or giving real feedback) to make its decision."

Sachs added that the ministry's conduct "cannot reasonably be considered to be the type of conduct that would promote reconciliation between the Crown and Indigenous peoples." In addition, Robertson said that "an overview of the process might look quite impressive, but it really actually wasn't responsive consultation or genuine consultation, and I think that happened particularly with Landore, but also with Ontario."

She said she thinks the conclusion that the substance of the consultation should go beyond ticking boxes will have broader impacts on the industry. "I think this is a case that requires Ontario and mining companies to be mindful that their consultation processes in any case can be judicially reviewed and put under a microscope. And if they are not genuine, they will not stand," Robertson said.

Ontario Court Dismisses Junior Miner's Exploration Permit over Failure to Consult

Headline News: Aria Laskin, 2018. Ontario Court Reaffirms that the Duty to Consult Requires "Real Engagement Aimed at Promoting Reconciliation," *JFK Law-Canada*, 19 July. Accessed 1 July 2024 (see also McKiernan 2012; Ross 2018)

In another summary of the important Landore case regarding Indigenous mining challenges in northern Ontario Eabametoong First Nation, represented by Robert J. M. Janes, QC, and Krista Robertson of Ontario Court reaffirmed that the duty to consult requires "real engagement aimed at promoting…reconciliation."

JFK Law has succeeded in its application to set aside a mining exploration permit issued by the Ontario Ministry of Northern Development and Mines to Landore Resources Canada. In reaching its decision, the Divisional Court of Ontario found that the Crown failed to discharge its duty to consult. The decision provides important guidance about how courts will assess the adequacy of consultation in the future.

The exploration drilling site authorized by the permit is located on important lands within Eabametoong's traditional territory. In 2013, Landore applied for the permit and contacted Eabametoong to discuss the proposed site. From 2013–2016, Landore and Eabametoong engaged in intermittent discussions about the project and the consultation process. In 2014, Eabametoong provided the Ministry with a list of concerns they had about the proposed project, but it never received a response.

In January 2016, the Ministry and Landore had a private meeting in which Landore told the Ministry that it had entered into negotiations with a major mining company and needed to get the permit approved *as soon as possible*. Eabametoong was never told about the meeting and did not learn about this development until the start of the litigation. After that meeting, the Crown and Landore unilaterally changed their approach to the consultation process.

They refused to enter into any meaningful dialogue. Eabametoong expressed concern about this change in approach, but those concerns were not addressed. Instead, the Crown approved the permit in March 2016. According to the court, this conduct breached the duty to consult. In response to the Crown's and Landore's arguments that consultation was sufficient, the court held that it had to "look beyond form to substance," and that in substance, there was no real and genuine attempt to engage in meaningful discussion with Eabametoong.

The court also found that the unilateral change in the consultation process without notice to Eabametoong was inconsistent with the Honor of the Crown. As a result, the court set aside the decision to approve the permit. Although the Crown asked the court to issue a direction for more consultation, it declined to do so. It reiterated that the duty to consult had to be discharged before, not after, a decision is made. This decision reinforces that the duty to consult involves more than "the use of words or the appearance of listening." Going through the motions is not enough. Instead, the consultation process must proceed "in a way that fosters trust as opposed to misunderstanding and betrayal," which did not happen in this case.

Who Carries the Duty to Consult?

Headline News: Michael McKiernan, 2012. Who Carries the Duty to Consult? *Canadian Lawyer*, 17 December.

When members of the northern Ontario Wahgoshig First Nation stumbled across an exploratory drilling team preparing to clear the forest and bulldoze access routes on its traditional land in the spring of 2011, the work crew was unwilling to disclose whom they were working for. It had been almost two years since their employers, junior miner Solid Gold Resources Corp., received instructions from the Crown to contact the band for consultation over its plans for a 22,000-hectare patch of unpatented mining claims, and none had occurred.

When the Wahgoshig finally figured out who they were dealing with, they tried in vain to contact Solid Gold to get the consultation belatedly started. By November 2011, the province was moved to intervene with a letter that repeated its earlier instructions. The next day, the First Nation turned to the courts, initiating a claim against the province and Solid Gold, and later won an injunction that prevented any further drilling by the company.

With regards to a related case, in its 2004 decision, in Haida Nation v. British Columbia, the Supreme Court of Canada said the Crown bears legal responsibility for the duty to consult and accommodate Aboriginal groups but confirmed that procedural aspects of the duty may be delegated to third parties.

Lawyers representing both First Nations and mining companies say Ontario has taken delegation to the extreme, appearing determined to stay out of the fray; and in the process injecting uncertainty into the exploratory mining regime. For them, the Solid Gold case is emblematic.

"I think sometimes they can be charged with abdicating their responsibilities," says Sara Mainville, a Fort Frances, Ontario lawyer who represents First Nations in the consultation process. "They don't really get involved unless there's a dispute. Just being present would help, but it's like they're waiting for a fight." Cindy Blancher-Smith, assistant deputy minister at the Ministry of Northern Development and Mines, admits there may be something to Mainville's characterization.

Solid Gold isn't the only matter where the Crown has run into trouble.

"I can think of a few others," she says. "We haven't had the regulatory tools in the past to have that more hands-on approach." Blancher-Smith hopes that will all change with the recent introduction of new regulations under the Mining Act. Three years in the making, the new rules came into force on Nov. 1., sweeping away the province's old "free entry" mining system and enshrining the duty to consult at the exploratory stage.

"We want to encourage that development and exploration in a manner that is consistent with Aboriginal rights," says Blancher-Smith, acknowledging that it will mean more work for mining industry players. "We intend to work very hard with them to help overcome obstacles," she says. "We've developed policies to provide clarity on what we're expecting when it comes to Aboriginal consultation."

By 1 April 2013, all prospectors must provide an exploration plan to the ministry and all affected groups for comment when carrying out certain low-impact activities, including geophysical surveys using a generator, line-cutting, and drilling for mineral samples. Anything more significant, such as when the drill used weighs over 150 kg, or when the line cut measures more than 1.5 m, requires the proponent to apply for an exploration permit from the ministry.

Blancher-Smith is keen to emphasize that this is "not a consent regime," but says the ministry will be able to attach terms and conditions to a permit that address First Nations concerns about the adverse impact of exploration. The decision on whether or not to grant the permit will consider whether consultations have occurred and if any arrangements have been reached between the players. If an agreement can't be reached, the province can refer the application to a dispute resolution provider.

Neal Smitheman, the Toronto partner at Fasken Martineau DuMoulin LLP who represented Solid Gold in its court fight with the Wahgoshig, says the new rules reinforce the image of a province washing its hands of its own duty to consult. "They've simply pulled a Pontius Pilate and downloaded the obligation to consult to the industry," he says. Smitheman warns junior mining companies have neither the time nor the money to invest in consultation efforts at the exploration stage that he argues should be the government's responsibility and says it could turn investors off pumping money into the province. "They should stamp the new act with something like *investors beware*," he says. "The more obstacles and difficulties you have in a certain jurisdiction, the less the money flows. If you look at other jurisdictions in Canada, exploration is certainly a lot more encouraged."

Mainville also has her doubts about the new regulations. She says a number of her First Nations clients have independently developed their own frameworks for dealing with mining companies, involving early talks over resource benefit sharing.

"Those are being ignored under the new regulations because the process doesn't accommodate them in the consultation process," she says. "Permitting almost gets in the way of those types of relationships being developed." She commends Osisko Mining Corporation and Rainy River Resources Ltd. for their culturally sensitive and cooperative approach to First Nations affected by their projects in northwestern Ontario. "I think that in a lot of ways, there are already some best practices that the ministry should have taken notice of," she says.

At McCarthy Tétrault LLP, Vancouver-based Aboriginal law group head Thomas Isaac takes a more optimistic view of Ontario's new exploratory rules. "On their face, they read very well. The issue will be whether or not they're implemented and carried out in a fair and transparent way. I go in totally optimistic," he says. Isaac says uncertainty over the rules of consultation has traditionally made Ontario one of the most challenging jurisdictions in Canada for mineral exploration. He says junior miners are willing to take on more of the heavy lifting if it means they can better predict the outcome of a permit application. "If that's the result, then it will be a good investment for companies," he says. "But if it's the same old situation, where the decision depends on the First Nation, what part of the province you're in. Or the political sensitivities of this particular week, then you haven't got a level playing field. It's just another additional burden with little light at end of the tunnel…the proof is in the pudding."

Blake Cassels and Graydon LLP partner Charles Kazaz says Ontario lags behind Quebec when it comes to mineral exploration. He credits 1975's James Bay and Northern Quebec Agreement reached between the Crown, the Cree, and the Inuit of the region for giving all players a set of realistic expectations about the exploration process. "There is a clear path, and yes, it takes some time to get through, but you can predict it to a certain degree," he says. "For the first couple of years, there was a lot of mistrust between parties, but I think over the years, the relationship has evolved."

Martin Ignasiak, a partner in Osler Hoskin and Harcourt LLP's Calgary office, says many of his clients, which include oil sands players and electrical generation companies, prefer to err on the side of caution when it comes to consultation with First Nations, in order to minimize the risk their projects will fail to get approved. "The reality is that having local support is always a positive thing, and something most companies strive for," he says. He calls government involvement in the process a *double-edged sword* since they often operate on their own timetable, one which "may not always align with your own."

However, Smitheman says, it's unfair to expect junior miners to invest large sums in consultation ahead of exploratory work, in the same way a larger, more established company might. "Most of these companies are not much more than a couple of guys with a shovel. They're hanging by a financial thread and they can't afford to pay significant amounts of money to put in accommodations," he says.

In September, Solid Gold won the right to appeal the Wahgoshig's injunction at Ontario's Divisional Court after a judge decided there was reason to doubt whether any duty to consult existed under the Mining Act in force at the time. The new regulations clear up that confusion by making clear that a duty to consult would now exist, but Jocelyn Kearney, a lawyer at Norton Rose Canada in Toronto, says the appeal will still be useful for companies that deal with consultation issues. "Hopefully it will help clarify parameters of appropriate delegation by the government," she says. "These new rules help to do that, but they only apply in the context of exploration, so there are other industries affected by the duty to consult where there isn't such a framework in place."

243

The Wabauskang Challenge

Another important mining development in northern Ontario was first reported in the *Kenora Daily Miner* in 2014. It is related to the Wabauskang First Nation near Kenora in northwestern Ontario near the Manitoba border. It used its hearing with the Supreme Court of Canada to challenge the Province of Ontario's ability to delegate the carrying out of Aboriginal consultation to mining companies, rather than having the Ministry of Mining and Northern Development deal with First Nations themselves. The hearing at the Supreme Court was granted to Wabauskang First Nation so that it might settle its long-standing dispute with Rubicon Minerals over a proposed mining project inside the First Nation's territory.

Wabauskang, the provincial government, and Rubicon Minerals all submitted outlines of their arguments to the court for the justices to consider (*Kenora Daily Miner and News,* 11 March 2014). This situation was complicated by the fact that federal government approval is required before treaty lands can be appropriated for development use, something the Crown is allowed to do according to the provisions of Treaty No. 3.

In this context, First Nations lawyers argued that the provincial government of Ontario went too far when it delegated the responsibility for conducting mandatory consultations with them. So, the plan for the Rubicon mine project, which had been approved by Ontario, was presumed to be invalid because of this jurisdictional issue. According to the Rubicon submission, the delegation of aspects of the process did not deprive the Indigenous community of the consultation they are entitled to. However, Wabauskang's Chief Leslie Cameron disagreed, saying that giving the proponents of the project the responsibility to consult with First Nations is very problematic.

As Chief Cameron indicated, "it makes for a very one-sided form of consultation process there the provincial government just takes for granted what the company [Rubicon] is telling them, saying they've dealt with us. And some of the things they say happened [during consultation] are out-and-out lies" (*Kenora Daily Miner and News,* 11 March 2014).

What then followed was a landmark decision on treaty rights by the Supreme Court of Canada on 11 July 2014, when it decided that the Province of Ontario is burdened with legal responsibilities when making land-use decisions in the Treaty No. 3 area. This decision is a result of the challenge brought by the Wabauskang First Nation to the Ontario Court of Appeal. This indicated that there is no role for the federal government in ensuring the protection of treaty rights when Ontario makes decisions about lands and resources in the Treaty No. 3 region.

Furthermore, the Supreme Court also disagreed with Ontario's position, arguing that Ontario was directly responsible for ensuring that treaty rights were protected. According to Wabauskang spokesperson, Martine Petiquan, "Our Treaty is with Canada. It is Canada that is responsible for fulfilling the promises made to the people of Treaty 3. We have always maintained, and will continue to affirm, that the federal government needs to be involved in ensuring that our treaty rights are respected" (*Wabauskang First Nation*, 11 July 2014).

In conclusion, the Wabauskang First Nation challenge clearly indicates that Ontario has an obligation to respect treaty rights in the province. It also points to the complicated jurisdictional concerns involving Ontario's First Nations, the federal government, and provincial/territorial responsibilities.

Conclusion

Johnny Yesno was awarded the Order of Canada for "ensuring that Canadians have a better understanding of Indian people." Then, as a *Sootoday* (5 December 2021) article indicated, "With his experience and success, Johnny Yesno became a leading voice in Indigenous and government relations." In the later years of his life, Johnny Yesno became the *Aboriginal advisor* with the former Ministry of Northern Development and Mines.

As the various discussions in this chapter are meant to illustrate, the mining situation in northern Ontario, especially relating to the Eabametoong First Nation where he was born, has become a complicated matter in recent years. Partly the problems stem from jurisdictional issues between the Province of Ontario, and the First Nations communities which are situated on federal government lands.

There is much at stake in the various court decisions that have been made in recent years, and those to be made in the future. Johnny Yesno was no doubt a key figure as Ontario's Aboriginal advisor in situations in which the First Nations communities, the government of Ontario, and the federal government all have an important role to play, all of which will influence the prosperity of Indigenous people who live in northern Ontario for many years to come.

Chapter Ten
A Life Well-Lived

One wonders at times how it is that certain individuals seem to overcome insurmountable obstacles in life. They not only survive but keep achieving goals that seem quite improbable. Johnny Yesno did not just achieve respectable goals in his life but did so in many different fields: movie star, broadcast personality, champion dancer, political leader, and government consultant.

The achievement of these various roles would have been no less remarkable if he had been born into a wealthy, well-connected class in Canadian society. Instead, Johnny Yesno rose into the national spotlight from a remote area of the country, a place where the people largely spoke a language different from the national majority. His background and customs were quite different from those prevalent in the outside world of Indigenous people in the Canadian north.

You could call this a Horatio Alger story of rags to riches if you want, but even he did not have to contend with the cultural, linguistic, and social obstacles that Johnny Yesno was able to overcome. In any event, Johnny Yesno's goals were not to achieve riches and rise up in the hierarchy of an alien society. Instead, he wanted to inform those in the larger Euro-Canadian society about Indigenous people; their history, their concerns in life, and the suppression and the impediments that the larger society placed in their way.

Johnny Yesno knew first-hand what it was like to feel the lash of the teachers in the residential schools, the beatings for speaking your own language, and the intense pressure to conform to the expectations of a repressive educational system. As some have pointed out, the residential schools were more like prison camps than places of learning and scholastic achievement.

Yet, even in such suppressive environments, Johnny Yesno managed to excel, earning an engineering degree from Waterloo University and then studying acting at the Toronto Workshop Production which laid the foundation for his multifaceted roles in the movie and television industry.

His roles in the television hit series *Wojeck* in the late 1960s, and in the 1970s films such as *The King of the Grizzlies*, *Cold Journey,* and the *Inbreaker* brought international attention to the plight of Indigenous people in Canada. The issues that were the focus of his various films, such as racial suppression and media stereotyping, were then further discussed and brought to the forefront of a national audience in his long-running radio show *Our Native Land*. On this basis, he was then able to consolidate a political focus with the Chiefs of Ontario organization in 1975, which tended to transcend various divisions in the Indigenous political community.

In 1988, he became an Aboriginal Advisor at Ontario's Ministry of Northern Development, dedicated to voicing the perspectives and concerns of Indigenous communities. His primary focus was the emerging mining industry in what would later be recognized as the *Ring of Fire*, ensuring that government officials were aware of the implications for these communities.

His time on this earth, and the improbable achievements that Johnny Yesno overcame and then excelled in, certainly could be called *a life well-lived*. His achievements in life were certainly worthy of recognition with the Order of Canada as one of this country's outstanding citizens of his time.

Appendix One
The James Bay Treaty No. 9

The James Bay Treaty, (Treaty No. 9) is an agreement between Ojibway (Anishinaabe), Cree (including the Omushkegowuk), and other Indigenous Nations (Algonquin) and the Crown (represented by two commissioners appointed by Canada and one commissioner appointed by Ontario). The treaty, first entered into in 1905–1906, covers the James Bay and Hudson Bay watersheds in Ontario, about two-thirds of the province's total landmass. The treaty embodies the nation-to-nation relationship between First Nations and the Crown (see Long 2010).

A treaty is a formal agreement between two or more nations about sharing the land and resources and living together in peace and in friendship. Treaties between Indigenous peoples and the Crown are solemn agreements that set out promises, obligations, and benefits for both parties. Treaty and Indigenous rights that flow from such agreements are constitutionally recognized in Canada. The text of Treaty No. 9 is included below.

Articles of a Treaty made and concluded at the several dates mentioned therein, in the year of Our Lord 1905, between His Most Gracious Majesty the King of Great Britain and Ireland, by His Commissioners Duncan Campbell Scott, of Ottawa, Ontario, Esquire, and Samuel Stewart, of Ottawa, Ontario, Esquire; and Daniel George MacMartin of Perth, Ontario.

Esquire, representing the Province of Ontario, of the one part; and the Ojibeway Cree and other Indians [including] the inhabitants of the territory within the limits, hereinafter, defined and described [in original] by their Chiefs and Headmen, hereunto subscribed, of the other part.

Whereas the Indians inhabiting the territory hereinafter defined have been convened to meet a commission representing His Majesty's government of the Dominion of Canada at certain places in the said territory in this present year of 1905, to deliberate upon certain matters of interest to His Most Gracious Majesty, of the one part, and the said Indians of the other.

And whereas the said Indians have been notified and informed by His Majesty's said Commission that it is His desire to open for settlement, immigration, trade, travel, mining, and lumbering and such other purposes as to His Majesty may seem to meet, a tract of country bounded and described as hereinafter mentioned.

Also, to obtain the consent thereto of His Indian subjects inhabiting the said tract, and to make a treaty and arrange with them; so that there may be peace and goodwill between them and His Majesty's other subjects. Also, His Indian people may know and be assured of what allowances they are to count upon and receive from His Majesty's bounty and benevolence.

The Native Americans from the specified region, having convened in council at the designated locations listed below, were requested by His Majesty's Commissioners to appoint certain Chiefs and Headmen. These leaders would be empowered to represent them in negotiations and to sign any resulting treaty. Furthermore, they would be accountable to His Majesty for ensuring that their respective groups uphold the obligations agreed upon. Thus, the Native Americans have recognized the Chiefs and Headmen who have signed below for this purpose.

And whereas the said Commissioners have proceeded to negotiate a treaty with the Ojibeway, Cree, and other Indians, inhabiting the district hereinafter defined and described, and the same has been agreed upon. It was concluded by the respective bands on the dates mentioned hereunder. The said Indians do hereby cede, release, surrender, and yield up to the Government of the Dominion of Canada, for His Majesty the King and His Successors forever, all their rights, titles, and privileges whatsoever, to the lands included within the following limits, that is to say:

That portion or tract of land lying and being in the Province of Ontario bounded on the south by the height of land and the northern boundaries of the territory ceded by the Robinson-Superior Treaty of 1850, and the Robinson-Huron Treaty of 1850.

It is bounded on the East and North by the boundaries of the said Province of Ontario as defined by law, and on the West by a part of the eastern boundary of the territory 9 by the Northwest Angle Treaty No. 3; the said land containing an area of 90 thousand square miles, more or less. [end of page 1 in Ontario's copy]

And also the said Indian rights, titles, and privileges whatsoever to all other lands wherever situated in Ontario, Quebec, Manitoba, the District of Keewatin, or in any other portion of the Dominion of Canada. To have and to hold the same to His Majesty the King and His Successors forever. [end of page 1 in federal copy]

And His Majesty the King hereby agrees with the said Indians that they shall have the right to pursue their usual vocations of hunting, trapping, and fishing throughout the tract surrendered as heretofore described; subject to such regulations as may from time to time be made by the government of the country acting under the authority of His Majesty and saving and excepting such tracts formal treaty documents.

As may be required or taken up from time to time for settlement, mining, lumbering, trading, or other purposes. And His Majesty the King hereby agrees and undertakes to lay aside reserves for each band, the same not to exceed in all one square mile for each family of five, or in that proportion for larger or smaller families.

The location of the said reserves having been arranged between His Majesty's Commissioners and the Chiefs and Headmen as described in the schedule of Reserves hereto attached, the boundaries thereof to be hereafter surveyed and defined, the said reserves; when confirmed, shall be held and administered by His Majesty for the benefit of the Indians free of all claims, liens or trusts by Ontario.

Provided, however, that His Majesty reserves the right to deal with any settlers within the bounds of any lands reserved for any band as He may see fit; and also, that the aforesaid reserves of land, or any interest therein, may be sold or otherwise disposed of by His Majesty's government.

Particularly, for the use and benefit of the said Indians entitled thereto with their consent first had and obtained; but in no wise shall the said Indians, or any of them, be entitled to sell or otherwise alienate any of the lands allotted to them as reserves.

His Majesty and the aforementioned Indian subjects have reached a mutual agreement regarding the reserves and lands specified. Should any portions of these reserves be needed for public works, including buildings, railways, or roads of any kind, His Majesty's government of the Dominion of Canada may appropriate such areas. In return, fair compensation will be provided to the Indian communities for the value of any improvements made, along with equivalent compensation in land, monetary, or other forms for the area of the reserve that is appropriated.

And with a view to show the satisfaction of His Majesty with the behavior and good conduct of His Indians, and in extinguishment of all their past claims, He hereby, through His Commissioners, agrees to make each Indian a present of eight dollars in cash.

His Majesty also agrees that next year, and annually afterward forever, He will cause to be paid to the said Indians in cash, at suitable places and dates, of which the said Indians shall be duly notified, four dollars, the same unless there be some exceptional reason, to be paid only to the heads of families for those belonging thereto.

Further, His Majesty agrees that each chief, after signing the treaty, shall receive a suitable flag and a copy of this treaty to be for the use of his band. Further, His Majesty agrees to pay such salaries of teachers to instruct the children of said Indians and also to provide such school buildings and educational equipment as may seem advisable to His Majesty's government of Canada. [end of page 2 of Ontario copy]

And the undersigned Ojibeway Cree and other Chiefs and Headmen, on their own behalf and on behalf of all the Indians whom they represent, do hereby solemnly promise and engage to strictly observe this Treaty and also to conduct and behave themselves as good and loyal subjects of His Majesty the King.

They promise and engage that they will, in all respects, obey and abide by the law; that they will maintain peace between each other, and between themselves and other tribes of Indians, and between themselves and others of His Majesty's subjects, whether Indians, Half-breeds or Whites, this year inhabiting and hereafter to inhabit any part of the said ceded territory.

And that they will not molest the person or property of any inhabitant of such ceded tract, or of any other district or country, or interfere with or trouble any person passing or traveling through the [end of page 2 of federal copy] said tract or any part thereof, and that they will assist the officers of His Majesty in bringing to justice and punishment any Indian offending against the stipulations of this Treaty or infringing the law in force in the country so ceded.

251

It is further understood that this Treaty is made and entered into subject to an agreement dated the third day of July between the Dominion of Canada and the Province of Ontario, which is hereto attached. In Witness Whereof His Majesty's said Commissioners and the said Chiefs and Headmen have hereunto set their hands at the places and times set forth in the year herein first above written.

Appendix Two
Caroline Remembers

22 January 2021

Johnny was a private person. He never talked about the movies he made.

Even about the time he spent at the residential school.

He was just a little boy about 4 years old when his mom Sarah passed on tuberculosis. She's buried in Selkirk Manitoba. My dad didn't know what to do with the two little kids he had after his wife died.

My dad's friend Rev Ahab suggested to Dad to have someone look after them at the Pelican Indian Residential School.

That's where Johnny and Barbara were for a while. I have no idea how long.

Anyway, Johnny's first wife has passed. He married four times, I think.

Barbara lives in Thunder Bay now. Maybe you can get a hold of her. Her last name is Elie. The oldest brother on my mom's side is Andy. He lives in FH [Fort Hope]with his family.

Johnny told me that his buddies were dying. They drank a lot he said and I am scared too he said. I told him to just slow down and to never do cold turkey.

16 May 2021

I miss Johnny so much. I miss his calls. He'd call my office; he'd say Hello Eabametoong Education. That's how I answer calls. Silly guy. We were very close. He's my stepbrother. My dad married twice. He had two from his first wife Sarah. Johnny and Barbara.

My dad wanted to name all his sons John until my mom Jane said something.

Actually, Dad had a child before he married his first wife Sarah Head. His love child was Naomi Yesno-Papah.

Then there's Johnny and Barbara from Sarah n Dad.

With his second wife Jane Okeese who is my mom. Athlee is deceased Andy Peter is deceased Caroline Margaret Sidney is deceased Harvey is currently Fort Hope Chief Ida John Ray, deceased Ruth Lewis Edward 15 in all.

Johnny spent much of his time away from home. I don't remember at home except when he almost drowned. The only memory I have of him. Same with Barbara but I communicated with Barb when I was very young. Writing letters to each other.

Johnny was close to his cousin Sarah Patience-Demaria.

Sarah n her family live in Brantford.

Sarah is deceased. Her husband as well. But their kids would probably know of Johnny as well. I think he frequently visited them in Brantford.

He lived in TO for a number of years.

Yes. My dad John had a store. He traded fish. Also had tourist business.

Fur, not fish.

There was a small sawmill close to where our home stood. I don't remember who owned and operated the sawmill. Dad told a story about Johnny being an interpreter for the native workers. Johnny was fluent in Ojibway. The employer said to Johnny, "Tell the workers they will need to pay for room and board. Johnny says to the men in Ojibway."

"Guys, you need to pay for your dwelling and lumber." Men questioned Johnny Why are we paying for the lumber. Johnny didn't know what *board* meant in terms of room and board. Board means lumber in Ojibway.

That was so funny. Do you understand, Ed?

Saul Okeese is my uncle. My mom is Jane's brother. Yes. Elizabeth Patience is my dad John's sister. Aunt Liz's children are Donald, Peter, Hamish, and Sarah. Jon John would be my late brother John Ray.

Wow. I didn't know Aunt Liz had twins.

Maggie Yesno-Oskineegish is Dad's sister. Maggie had Andrew, Thomas (Tommy), Victoria, Barbara, and another daughter there.

Margaret and Sarah are my aunties; Mom's sisters.

Yes. Elsie is also my auntie.

I don't know who Gilbert's dad is. George Ooshag is my step-grandfather. Sarah and Elsie are George's daughters.

My mom's father was George Okeese.

My dad's father is George Cooper from Scotland. Hudson's Bay manager. Peter Yesno raised him.

My dad used to call him Uncle Peter. My dad took his dad's name. John Cooper Yesno.

I don't know who Jim Ooshag is.

Sounds so complicated lol.

Yes. That's my dad.

Johnny, apparently, got abused badly but he never talked about it. My bro Andrew went to school there and he doesn't talk about it either.

The only reason I know Andrew was abused is because the Nate girls told me. Quite vivid too.

Andrew Nate is also George Cooper's son.

Dad and Andrew are half-brothers.

I didn't know about the Pelican Lake article.

My dad John Cooper Yesno and Andrew Nate are half-brothers.

Yes. I'd like to read that copy and paste didn't work; need to send it as an attachment.

1 June 2021

Elizabeth Goose is my grandmother. My dad's mom.

Oh. Sorry. Barbara Goose is my grandmother. Elizabeth Goose is Edward and Andrew Nate's mom.

I was at Pelican when I was very young. My sis Barbara was working there. Andrew was attending there.

I think Johnny was at Shingwauk because I don't remember him.

My grandmother Barbara Goose had a child, my dad with George Cooper

He must've gone back to Scotland. I really have no idea. He had kids whenever he went, I heard.

Andrew Nate is George Cooper's son. So is Erland Vincent. Those are my dad's half-brothers or step-brothers.

Erland was taken away and adopted. He was raised in Moose Factory. He came to visit my dad one summer.

Edward and Erland were not Barbara Goose's sons.

That is likely what happened to Aunt Liz's twin.

There's a grave in Fort Hope that belongs to Mary Yesno. I have no idea who that would be.

I just knew of the Order of Canada that Johnny received.

2 June 2021

John Yesno my dad married twice.

First wife was Sarah Head and they had Johnny and Barbara.

Second wife is Jane Okeese who is my mom.

I've never heard of Allen Yesno myself.

But there's Allen Vincent who is my dad's half-brother. Son of George Cooper.

Apparently, that was Peter Yesno my dad's uncle.

Andy my bro might know more about all this because he did research in Winnipeg. Hudson's Bay archives.

I know for sure George had three sons. My dad, Andrew Nate, and Erland (Allen) Yesno Vincent.

I wonder where he went from Fort Hope. HBC managers moved around.

My sis Ida was telling me that Nayaneekeesics might be related to Yesno.

9 June 2021

I came across your question about Rosemary King. She's Johnny's common-law partner. He met her when she hired her to clean his place. This is after he got transferred from Geraldton to Sault Ste Marie.

He said, "Yes, she cleaned and she's still here." Lol

He wanted to marry her but divorce from Dorothy Ross took a while. Okay.

Rosemary King lives in Wequekonmekong. Idk how it's spelled. It's on Manitoulin Island. We lost touch.

10 June 2021

Dorothy Ross is the second wife he had. That was short-lived. Two days before the wedding he came to see me. He didn't think he should go through with it. I asked him what was going on. Dorothy started drinking. She'd been sobered for a long time because she was an alcoholic. Because Johnny drank, she decided to start drinking.

Well, one time she attacked Johnny and destroyed his stuff including the Order of Canada he had on a wall. I told him you needed to decide and you need to notify all the guests. He got married. It lasted about a month. That was so sad.

I don't know how he met her. When he was in Manitoba working, he said he met someone and wrote him a letter. He said she went through a lot of traumas in life.

Sad of Johnny's life personal life is his daughters didn't like his choices. I suppose the girls wanted him to go back with their mom. Myself I like them. He always was at his first wife's place. They separated because Sharon had an affair and had a son from that relationship.

14 June 2021

He was a hoop dancer. His wife Sharon was a princess. Later on, his girls went into dancing. A lot of times he'd put them on flights to wherever there are powwows across Canada.

29 June 2021

Andy has been ill. Bypass surgery was successful yesterday. Also, two toes were amputated at the same time.

I have lost count of how many bypass surgeries he's had. Amazing. He has solid faith in God.

Autumn Yesno is Johnny's granddaughter. Her mom Wanda passed away several years ago. I gave her your email and she sent it her write-up of her grampa.

Also, Bradford Yesno is the grandson. Her mom Debbie passed away as well. I also gave him your email. He says he'd rather talk to you.

257

2 July 2021

I contacted Carla Fabisiak. That would be Johnny's second cousin, I think. They live in Brandford. Johnny spent a lot of time with them.

21 July 2021

My sis Ida was just telling me this evening that my dad had a lot of sisters. One was Caroline, the other Margaret, and another Mary.

While she was in Winnipeg, Ida said she went to see and read some of the archives written about Yesnos.

Donald Patience's partner Elsie Drake is very ill. I really wanted to talk to her. She's in the ICU.

My bro Andy has been in the hospital for about three weeks now. Heart disease.

25 July 2021

Yes, Josie. She passed away.

My mom Jane's brother is Saul. Margaret is the bio-sister of Mom and Saul.

My mom Jane is bio sis Sarah Ron Goodwin's wife.

There is Sarah Okeese and Sarah Oshag. My mom's sister Sarah Oshag is stepsister to Sarah Okeese. Complicated

Oops.

My mom's sister Sarah Okeese (Ron) is stepsister to Sarah Oshag.

I was thinking about Johnny while I was in Sault last week. I remember Johnny telling me to go visit the radio station when I was at the residential school. I was shy to go. I think he visited the radio station while he was staying at the residential school. That was before I was there. He kept in touch with them too.

Johnny has a son in the James Bay area. I forget the name of the reserve. We've met him. His name is Johnny as well. He contacted us when Johnny passed. We met his mom to be.

20 June 2022

I got a hold of one of Johnny's best friends. His name is Michael Cachagee. Michael and Kelly Bull are the only ones still alive. Chris Cromarty just passed away last week. Chris was Johnny's best man when he married his first wife Sharon. They had two girls, Debbie and Wanda. Both girls have passed on.

26 June 2022

I was in Prince Rupert BC a few years ago for work and was a speaker. A man came up to me afterward and said he danced with Johnny at the 1976 Montreal Olympic Games opening ceremonies.

2 July 2022

Apparently, Johnny was misbehaving super badly because he was being abused. A story he didn't want to talk about.
He'd clam up if he was asked.

19 April 2023

I had asked Andy about Johnny, but he didn't provide me the information. Us siblings didn't really know Johnny. He rarely came home. I only remember once that he did with his first wife and their first daughter. I will ask around again.

29 March 2024

Delia wasn't his first wife. They didn't have kids. Sharon Stonefish was his first wife. She's deceased. They had two girls. Deborah and Wanda. Both deceased. Wanda was still alive when her dad passed. He passed away in Sault. Last place he lived.

30 March 2024

Good morning Johnny was a hoop dancer. About the same time his wife Sharon was the princess for her First Nations. I think it's Six Nations where she was from. My dad had pictures, but I don't know what happened to them. I think it was last fall there was this FB post about hoop dancing.

This guy mentions Johnny being a hoop dancer. I contacted him. He said he didn't know Johnny. I saw him dancing, I guess. There was an article about Johnny hoop dancing. I don't remember where it was taken. If it was on Toronto Star, I don't know.

24 April 2024

Johnny didn't talk about what he was doing to us. We found out later. Such as movies he made. He rarely came home. He visited one of his buddies more than us. Mike Cagachee was telling me he visited him at his home many times. There were four of them hanging out like brothers, Mike was telling me. Johnny was a quiet guy.

The one time he came home was when he and Delia paddled from Auden, Ontario to Fort Hope. At the time, Delia was studying to be a lawyer. During their trip, one of them broke a paddle. Johnny made a paddle using an axe. The paddle was heavy, but it worked. I saw the paddle. Delia had a couple of thick books she was reading. Johnny came home when Dad passed. That was just before Christmas.

He bought a headstone for Dad. He insisted he purchase it himself. Almost looks like a marble stone. When Delia was leaving him, he called me to talk to Delia. I did talk to her, but the relationship was beyond repair she said. Anyway. Thinking of Johnny.

2 April 2024

I saw Delia not too long ago. She had made it up there alright.

Johnny and Delia wanted an outdoor experience. We had already had an airstrip.

Glossary

Note: While there are many other Indigenous organizations in Ontario and Canada that could be mentioned and discussed here, the organizations and communities listed below are those that have a more direct influence on Johnny Yesno's life (see *Aboriginal Culture* www.ontariotravel.net.en/play/Aboriginal-experiences/Aboriginal-culture).

This website is sponsored by the Ontario government through Travel Ontario. It is designed to direct interested parties to various Aboriginal experiences, such as powwows and outdoor activities. Also, included are resource centers on Aboriginal culture such as heritage organizations, guided tours, eco-travel, Indigenous art collections, and traditional foods.

Assembly of First Nations (www.afn.ca)

The Assembly of First Nations is a national organization representing First Nations citizens in Canada, which includes more than 900,000 living in 634 First Nations communities and in cities and towns across the country. The national executive of the organization is comprised of the National Chief, 10 Regional Chiefs, and the chairs of the Elders, women, and youth councils.

Regional chiefs are elected every three years by chiefs in their regions, who are elected by the citizens and members of their respective communities. The National Chief is also elected every three years. The Assembly of First Nations is also designated to present the views of the various First Nations (Aboriginal people with status under the Indian Act) through their leaders in such areas as Aboriginal and treaty rights, economic development, education, and justice issues.

Attawapiskat (www.attawapiskat.org)

This First Nation is named after the Cree *Ahtawapiskatowi ininiwak*, which means "people of the parting of the rocks." It is located in the Kenora District of northern Ontario, at the mouth of the Attawapiskat River at James Bay. The people live on two reserves: one 165 kilometers west of James Bay on both banks of the Ekwan River, and the other near the west shore of James Bay on the left bank of the Attawapiskat River.

The total registered population is approximately 3,500 people of whom about 2,000 live on-reserve. The people are members of the Mushkegowuk Tribal Council, which represents six First Nations of primarily Cree speakers from Moose Factory to Cochrane.

In 2008, the De Beers Victor Mine was opened, which generates about $400 million in annual revenue for the company. Although De Beers has acknowledged that the mine is on Attawapiskat traditional land, the royalties from the Victor Mine flow to the Province of Ontario, not to the Attawapiskat First Nation.

However, the mine does employ about 100 Attawapiskat persons. As of 2011, the De Beers company has also transferred about $10.5 million to a trust fund held by the Attawapiskat First Nation. The beneficiaries of the trust fund include "all members of Attawapiskat on a collective and undivided basis" (see Attawapiskat First Nation 2012: 4).

Big Trout Lake, See also *Kitchenuhmaykoosib Inninuwag*

Bill C-31 (www.thecanadianencyclopedia.ca)

Bill C-31 is a significant amendment to Canada's Indian Act made in 1985 that allowed for the reinstatement of Indian status under application for Aboriginal persons who had previously lost their status. Under this amendment to the Indian Act, Indigenous people would no longer lose their Indian status. In 1985, parliament responded to the appeals of Indigenous peoples by changing discriminatory sections of the Indian Act.

This amendment reinstated Indian Status to women who had lost it through marriage to men without status. Among other changes, the bill also enabled all first-generation children of these marriages and individuals who had been enfranchised to regain their legal status. More than 114,000 people gained or regained their Indian status as a result of Bill C-31.

Canadian Indigenous/Native Studies Association (CINSA) (*www.ccednet-rcdec.ca*)

CINSA is a community of scholars committed to fostering the development of Aboriginal studies as a discipline informed by, and respectful of Indigenous intellectual traditions, in order to create a place of respect and dignity for Aboriginal peoples within Canada and the world. Among its objectives are the dissemination of research and the facilitation of communication among members through such means as conferences, journals, and other publications.

Canadian Journal of Native Studies (www.brandonu.ca/native-studies/cjns)

The Canadian Journal of Native Studies (CJNS) is the official publication of the Canadian Indian/Native Studies Association. The journal publishes research in the fields of Native Studies, although the majority of articles deal with Indigenous peoples in Canada. It also publishes articles dealing with Indigenous peoples worldwide. It comes out on a bi-annual basis and publishes original scholarly activity, which is refereed by peer review.

Center for Indigenous Theater (www.indigenoustheatre.com)

The Center for Indigenous Theater (CIT) was founded in 1974 by the late James Butler, with the goal of providing a viable Aboriginal theater school whereby Aboriginal actors, playwrights, and directors would have a forum for exploration and exchange with the goal that the results of this exchange would have a measurable impact on the Aboriginal theater community.

Today, CIT offers a three-year full-time program, as well as summer programs in Peterborough, Ontario, and Lethbridge, Alberta, which embrace the spirit, energy and inspiration derived from the culture, values, and traditions of Indigenous people. The purpose of the program is to develop contemporary performance skills for a distinctly Indigenous cultural foundation.

Chiefs of Ontario (www.chiefs-of-ontario.org)

The Chiefs of Ontario is a political forum and secretariat for collective decision-making, political action, and advocacy for the various First Nations communities located in Ontario. It recognizes the self-determination efforts of the Anishinabek (Ojibwa), Mushkegowuk (Cree), Onkwehon:we, and Lenape peoples in protecting and exercising their inherent treaty rights. The Chiefs of Ontario originated in 1975 as a federation of the major Ontario First Nations whose purpose was to provide a unified voice on provincial issues and a single Ontario representative to the Assembly of First Nations according to the following goals.

Understanding First Nations Sovereignty:

As distinct and independent nations, we possess inherent rights to self-determination. These inherent rights were not endowed by any other state or Nation, but are passed on through birthright, are collective, and flow from the connection to the Creator and our lands.

They cannot be taken away. Self-determination means we freely and independently determine and exercise our own political, legal, economic, social, and cultural systems without external interference. In other words, we have jurisdiction over all aspects of our livelihood.

The land is our source of identity as Nations, and the Creator has laid out our responsibilities to these lands. Our traditional territories stretch across Turtle Island. We possess a relationship to the lands, water, and air as reflected in our ceremonies and our laws for our protection and perpetual use.

These lands are different from lands reserved for Indians, whose borders were imposed by the Canadian government. We possess Inherent and Treaty rights to utilize our traditional territories today.

Treaties were made to establish how nations would co-exist and granted rights and permission to the settlers. Treaties are agreements made between our Indigenous Nations and also with the Crown. They were negotiated on the basis of mutual respect and the principles of Peace and Friendship and determined how lands and resources are to be shared. Treaties also outline responsibilities in areas such as education and health.

The Spirit and Intent of the Treaties refers to the original oral agreements made between First Nations and the British Crown, agreements which were altered when written in English. All Canadians and First Nations are party to the Treaties.

Treaties are living, international agreements, which remain valid today and continue to affirm our sovereign relationships. We are and always have been original nations that have never relinquished our title, rights, language, culture, and governance by way of Treaty to the British Crown or the successor state of Canada.

This is why we continually seek to work with state bodies on the basis of a government-to-government relationship. This is why the development or utilization of lands requires our free, prior, and informed consent, or when decisions are made that may impact our Inherent and Treaty rights. While Indigenous Nations are forced to use colonial systems and laws, this does not supersede our inherent rights.

Indigenous peoples have been tireless in ensuring Inherent and Treaty rights are recognized through non-Indigenous vehicles such as the Constitution Act, case law, and court decisions. The United Nations Declaration on the Rights of Indigenous Peoples is another powerful international instrument that creates the minimum standards and principles for the survival, dignity, and well-being of Indigenous peoples and their rights.

We are the Anishinaabek, Mushkegowuk, Onkwehon:we, and Lenape peoples—the Indigenous peoples located within the artificial borders of Ontario. As the sovereign nations of Turtle Island, we possess inherent rights to self-determination.

Our right to self-determination means we have jurisdiction (the right, power, and authority) to administer and operate our own political, legal, economic, social, and cultural systems. The recognition of our Nationhood through treaty-making is why the successor state of Canada must work with our nations on the basis of a government-to-government relationship.

Treaties were made between nations, establishing how treaty partners would co-exist, therefore, granting rights and permissions to the settlers and their colonial governments, on areas such as land and resources. The Spirit and Intent of the made Treaties must be honored, respected, and implemented (practiced) by all Treaty people.

The land is the founding source of our identity and culture. Great responsibilities to protect and preserve the land have been bestowed upon us by the Creator and are captured in each Nations Laws. Through the Treaty our Nations agreed to share the land, therefore, our free, prior, and informed consent is required before any development or decisions are made that may impact our Inherent and Treaty rights to land.

As sovereign Nations, we have never surrendered our rights or titles in the right of the Crown or the successor state of Canada but, have maintained and solidified their inherency through the treaty-making process.

Congress of Aboriginal Peoples (https://obo-peoples.org)

The Congress of Aboriginal Peoples is a national-level organization representing non-status and Métis people founded in 1994. It was formerly known as the Native Council of Canada, which was established in 1971. As of 2011, more than 70% of Aboriginal people live off-reserve.

Its head office is located in the capital, Ottawa, Ontario. The congress works with its affiliate organizations on issues that affect the Aboriginal peoples of Canada who live off-reserve. Affiliates of the congress have their own constitutions with some being separately funded through the Métis and Non-Status Indian Relations Directorate of the Department of Aboriginal Affairs and Northern Development Canada.

The Métis and Non-Status Indian Relations Directorate works primarily with Aboriginal political organizations that represent the interests of Métis and Non-Status Indians (MNSI) and other off-reserve Aboriginal organizations.

Constance Lake (www.clfn.on.ca)

This First Nation is situated on the shores of Constance Lake, near Hearst in the Cochrane District of northeastern Ontario. In 2014, it was home to 1,672 people of Cree and Anishinaabe ancestry, with approximately 860 people living on two reserves. One of these, Constance Lake 92, is located on the Kabinakagami River, and the other, English River 66, is situated on the east bank of the Kenogami River.

Both communities are members of the Nishnawbe Aski Nation, a tribal political organization representing many of the First Nations in northern and northwestern Ontario, especially those who are living in the Treaty No. 9 area.

The community is also a member of the Matawa First Nations Management, which represents 10 First Nations in northwestern Ontario. This First Nation is also situated in the mineral-rich *Ring of Fire* region, and there is a proposed massive chromite mining and smelting development project in the James Bay Lowlands.

Tony Clement, former president of Ontario's Treasury Board, has claimed that the *Ring of Fire* area will be the economic equivalent of the Athabasca oil sands project, with a potential to generate $120 billion. This development would be of immense economic benefit to the First Nations people of the area as they are some of the most socioeconomically disadvantaged communities in all of Canada, according to Mr. Clement.

In addition, former Ontario Premier Bob Rae has been appointed as the chief negotiator to represent the different First Nations governments (Marten Falls, Webequie, Neskantaga, Nabinamik, Aroland, Long Lake 58, Ginoogaming, Eabametoong, Mishkeegogamang, and Constance Lake) in this region.

Eabametoong (www.eabametoong.firstnation.ca)

This First Nation consists of one reserve (Fort Hope 64) which is located in the Kenora District of northern Ontario, on the shore of Eabamet Lake in the Albany River system, approximately 300 kilometers north of Thunder Bay. The name *Eabametoong* in the Anishinaabe language means "the reversing of the water place."

This phenomenon refers to the water flow from Eabamet Lake into the Albany River, which reverses each year resulting from runoff, such that water flows into Eabamet Lake from the Albany River for a short period of time, before resuming its normal flow.

The total registered population comprised about 2,500 people, of whom just over 1,500 live on-reserve. It is a member of the Matawa First Nations Management, which is a tribal council representing 10 First Nations in the Webequie and Ogoki Post area in northern Ontario. The reserve is only accessible by airplane to the Fort Hope Airport or by Winter Road that connects the community to the Northern Ontario Resource Trail.

Eabametoong originated during the fur trade era when the Hudson's Bay Company built a trading post by Eabamet Lake in 1890. The Fort Hope Band came into existence in 1905 when Treat No. 9 was signed by about 500 First Nations people.

In 1976, a cooperative store and police station were opened, and eventually, the community came under the jurisdiction of the Nishnawbe Aski Police Service. The new community of Eabametoong started in 1982, with the official name of Eabametoong First Nation being adopted in 1985.

Fort Albany (www.firstnation.ca./fort-Albany)

This First Nation is situated on the southern shore of the Albany River on Sinclair Island in Cochrane District of northeastern Ontario and named after a

Hudson's Bay Company post originally constructed in 1670. The community is only accessible by air, water, or Winter Road, and is policed by the Nishnawbe Aski Police Service.

Air Creebec provides Fort Albany residents with daily passenger flights, with connecting flights to Toronto. The majority of the population speaks Mushkegowuk Cree, although there is a mixture of languages spoken, such as French, English, and Ojibwa (Anishinaabe).

In the 1950s, the original reserve was divided into two communities along religious lines, with Fort Albany remaining largely Roman Catholic and members of the Kashechewan First Nation remaining mainly Anglican. Since the 1970s, both First Nations have been treated as separate bands with their own band councils.

In 2014, the total registered population of both First Nations (since INAC does not recognize Kashechewan as a separate First Nation) was 4,774 persons, with 3,086 of these living on the reserve. The community is a member of the Mushkegowuk Tribal Council, which represents six First Nations in the Cochrane-Moose Factory region.

Fort Hope, See *Eabametoong First Nation*
Ginoogaming (*www.ginogaming.ca*)

This First Nation, known previously as Long Lake 77, consists of one reserve located in northern Ontario, approximately 40 kilometers east of the town of Geraldton on the north shore of Long Lake, close to the town of Longlac. The total registered population consists of approximately 850 people, of which about 175 live on-reserve.

The community is within the boundaries of the territory described by the James Bay Treaty of 1905 (Treaty No. 9). The Long Lake Reserve was officially created when the band signed an adhesion to Treaty No. 9 in August 1906.

Ginoogaming First Nation is a member of the Matawa First Nations Management, which is a regional tribal council representing 10 First Nations in the Long Lac, Webequie, and Ogoki Post areas. The community's primary tribal organization is the Nishnawbe Aski Nation, which represents most of the First Nations of northern Ontario.

An important current issue for the community is the Ginoogaming Timber Claim Trust, which was established in April 2002 following negotiations and an agreement between Ginoogaming and the government of Canada for compensation resulting from the illegal taking of timber on Long Lake Reserve 77.

The overall goal of the Timber Claim Trust is to provide social, economic, and cultural benefits to all members of the Ginoogaming First Nation, no matter where they happen to live.

In conjunction with the Timber Claim Trust initiative, in January 2013 the Ginoogaming community also started the Giizhagaakwe (Cutting Wood) program in order to harvest conifer pulpwood from the Kenogami Forest, which is the second largest area of forest resources in Ontario.

Independent First Nation Alliance (www.ifna.ca)

This organization is a non-profit regional chiefs council representing Ojibwas (Anishinaabe) and Oji-Cree First Nations in northern Ontario. The council provides advisory services and program delivery to its five-member nations (kitchenuhmaykoosib Inninuwug (formerly Big Trout Lake), Lac Seul, Muskrat Dam, Pikangikum, and Whitesand First Nations).

Incorporated in 1989, this alliance is made up of a representative chief from each of the five-member communities. It provides technical advisory and community development support programs to meet the needs and aspirations of its First Nations on a collective basis, while each member First Nation maintains its autonomy.

In turn, the alliance is a member of the Nishnawbe Aski Nation, a tribal political organization representing the majority of Treaty No. 5, Treaty No. 9, and the Robinson-Superior Treaty First Nations in northern Ontario.

Indigenous and Northern Affairs Canada (www.aandc.gc.ca)

The Prime Minister of Canada changed the name of Aboriginal Affairs and Northern Development Canada (AANDC) to Indigenous and Northern Affairs Canada (INAC) in November 2015. INAC is one of the federal government departments responsible for meeting Canada's obligations to First Nations, Inuit, and Métis while also fulfilling the federal government's constitutional responsibilities in the North. INAC is one of 34 federal government departments and agencies involved in Aboriginal and northern programs and services.

The Ipperwash Inquiry was established by the government of Ontario under the Public Inquiries Act. Its mandate was to inquire and report on events surrounding the death of Dudley George, who was shot during a 1995 protest by First Nations representatives at Ipperwash Provincial Park and later died.

The inquiry was also mandated to make recommendations that would avoid violence in similar circumstances in the future. The report, containing findings and recommendations, was made public on 31 May 2007. See Hedican (2013), *Ipperwash: The Tragic Failure of Canada's Aboriginal Policy.*

Kashechewan, See also *Fort Albany First Nation.*

According to the records of the Department of Indigenous and Northern Affairs Canada, the survey information for the Kashechewan First Nation is combined with that of Fort Albany, which is located near James Bay in northern Ontario. Therefore, Kashechewan does not have a separate website or separate population totals, although they are considered locally as two separate communities. For both Fort Albany and Kashechewan First Nations, the total registered population is about 4,800 of which 3,086 live on-reserve; both First Nations share the same reserve (Albany Reserve No. 67).

A further source of confusion resulted when the name *Keeshechewan* was chosen for the name of the community, which means *where the water flows fast*. But the sign for the new post office arrived with the misspelling *Kashechewan*, which has no meaning in the Cree language. It nonetheless has become the community's official name.

Its members are represented by the Mushkegowuk Council, along with seven other First Nations in northern Ontario, and the Nishnawbe Aski Nation, which is the political territorial organization that represents the 49 First Nations that are part of the Treaty No. 9 area.

In 2007, the government of Canada signed a memorandum of agreement with the Kashechewan community for a grant of $200 million to improve and repair settlement infrastructure, housing, and flood control services.

However, in May 2014, Kashechewan residents were once again forced from their homes due to flooding, which resulted in 2,000 persons being evacuated to Thunder Bay, Kapuskasing, Timmins, and other northern locations.

Long Lake #58 (www.longlake58fn.ca)

This is an Anishinaabe (Ojibwa) First Nation situated close to Highway 11 along the northeast shore of Long Lake, adjacent to the town of Longlac, which is located 35 kilometers northeast of Geraldton. It is also immediately north of the Ginoogaming (Long Lake 77) First Nation. The total registered population is about 1,500 of which about 500 live on-reserve.

The community is associated with Matawa First Nations Management, a regional tribal council that represents 10 First Nations which are widely dispersed, from Long Lac to Webequie and Ogoki Post and other northern reserves.

This First Nation lies within the boundaries of the Robinson-Huron Treaty of 1850 and has been located on a one-square-mile tract of land since 1905, although the community contends that they have never signed a treaty with the Crown.

The surrounding territory on which the people of this First Nation have lived, hunted, and fished has been reduced considerably by railway and highway construction and the development of hydroelectric projects, which have flooded and eroded even more of the land.

Marten Falls (www.firstnation.ca/marten-falls-ogoki-post)

This Anishinaabe First Nation consists of two communities in two different districts. Marten Falls is located on the north bank of the Albany River in the Kenora District, and Ogoki Post, on the south bank of the Albany River, is in the Cochrane District.

Both communities are located about 170 kilometers northeast of Nakina, which is situated on the Canadian National Railway to the south, and about 300 kilometers northeast of Thunder Bay. The total registered population is about 750 people, of which about 375 live on-reserve.

It is a member of the Matawa First Nation Management, a regional tribal council representing 10 First Nations ranging from Long Lac to Webequie to Ogoki Post, as well as others, and is a signatory to Treaty No. 9. This First Nation is only accessible by air via Nakina Air Service. The Winter Road has not been in service since 2000.

Large freight is shipped on barges on the Albany River in the summer when water levels permit. This community has its own radio station, CKFN 89.9 FM. The on-reserve version of Children's Aid is provided through Tikinagan Child and Family Services, and the community is policed by the Nishnawbe Aski Police Service.

Matawa First Nations Management (www.matawa.on.ca)

Matawa First Nations Management was formed in 1988 to provide technical advisory services for Matawa First Nations communities situated north and northeast of Thunder Bay. The name *Matawa* was chosen by the chiefs because, in the Anishinabek (Ojibwa) and Mushkegowuk (Cree) languages, it is used to refer to the *meeting of rivers*. As such, Matawa's approach is to integrate modern social and economic development practices with traditional culture and heritage.

Mishkeegogamang (www.mishkeegogamang.ca)

In the past, this First Nation has been referred to as New Osnaburgh, Osnaburgh House, or simply as Osnaburgh. The community is located in northwestern Ontario along Highway 599, about 315 kilometers northwest of Thunder Bay and 20 kilometers south of Pickle Lake. This is the area where the Albany River meets Lake St. Joseph.

The first historical record of this First Nation dates to the founding of the Hudson's Bay Company trading post near the northeast end of Lake St. Joseph in the early 1800s. Treaty No. 9 was signed in 1905, at which time two reserves were established.

In 1954, Highway 599 was completed, from Savant Lake to an earlier mine road located several kilometers from the Osnaburgh village, so the government encouraged the people to move to the new village, known as the New Osnaburgh. Until 1993, the band was called Osnaburgh First Nation. The total registered population comprises about 2,000 people, of whom about 1,150 live on-reserve.

At one time, the community was a member of the Windigo First Nations Council, but today the band is not part of any regional tribal council, although the community retains a membership in the Nishnawbe Aski Nation. Mishkeegogamang is policed by the Nishnawbe Aski Police Service. The land base consists of two reserves, although this First Nation is made up of separate and somewhat geographically disconnected communities.

For example, on the main reserve (Reserve No. 63B) are the communities of Bottle Hill, Popular Heights, and Sandy Road. On the smaller reserve (Reserve No. 63A) which is located 24 kilometers south, is the community of 10 houses.

In addition, there are a few smaller communities such as Doghole Bay, Eric Lake, and Ace Lake, as well as a few other smaller ones. A complete history of the Mishkeegogamang First Nation, from the fur trade era until the 1970s, can be found in Charles Bishop's ethnohistorical study *The Northern Ojibwa and the Fur Trade* (1974).

Moose Cree (*www.moosecree.com*)

This First Nation is also referred to as the *Moose Factory Band* whose traditional territory is situated on the west side of James Bay. The nation has two reserves on a tract of land about 15 kilometers upstream on the Moose River on the southern tip of James Bay, which is located about 240 kilometers north of Cochrane.

The Cree had early exposure to European people with the establishment of the Hudson's Bay Company fur trading post which was located at Moose Factory in 1763. In 1905, the Moose Cree became a signatory to Treaty No. 9. The total registered population today comprises about 4,000 people, of whom about 1,700 live on-reserve.

This is an isolated community accessible via water taxi during three seasons from the town of Moosonee on the mainland. Moosonee has no road access and can only be reached by plane or train. This First Nation is attempting to diversify its economy, which presently relies on tourism, the bush economy, and seasonal construction work with the Detour Gold Company.

It has also completed the construction of an Aboriginal eco-tourist project known as Washow Lodge. The community is a member of the Mushkegowuk Tribal Council, which represents six First Nations in the Cochrane-Moose Factory region.

Mushkegowuk Council (*www.mushkegowuk.com*)

The Mushkegowuk Council represents the interests of the Cree First Nations of northern Ontario, which includes the communities of Attawapiskat, Chapleau Cree, Fort Albany, Kashechewan, Missanabie Cree, Taykwa Tagamou (New Post), and Weenusk. It is intended to respond to and carry out the collective will of all Mushkegowuk members and is committed to providing responsible and accountable political leadership.

The council's goal is to provide quality, equitable, accessible support, and advisory services to respond to and meet the social, economic, cultural, educational, spiritual, and political needs of Cree First Nations.

Muskrat Dam Lake (www.firstnation.ca/musrat-dam)

There is one reserve located in the Kenora District at Muskrat Dam Lake, which officially gained reserve status in 1976, before which this was a satellite community of Big Trout Lake. The total registered population is about 450 people, of whom 234 live on-reserve. This community is only accessible by air through the Muskrat Dam Airport and Winter Road from Red Lake and Pickle Lake.

In 2014, a business partnership was signed between Muskrat Dam and Sachigo Lake First Nations and North Star Air in order to provide more reliable air service to these two First Nations. The Muskrat Dam First Nation is part of the 1929–30 adhesion to the James Bay Treaty of 1905. The community is policed by the Nishnawbe Aski Police Service and is part of the Independent First Nations Alliance of the Nishnawbe Aski Nation.

Native Studies Review (www.publications.usask.ca/nativestudiesreview)

The Native Studies Review began publication in 1984 as a refereed bi-annual journal published by the Native Studies Department at the University of Saskatchewan. The journal's mandate is to feature original scholarly research on Aboriginal perspectives and issues in contemporary and historical contexts.

As a multi-disciplinary periodical, it publishes articles dealing primarily with a Canadian focus but welcomes submissions with an international focus.

Neskantaga (*www.neskantaga.com*)

Neskantaga was previously known as Lansdowne House which is a remote Oji-Cree First Nation situated along the shores of Attawapiskat Lake in the district of Kenora. It is a signatory to Treaty No. 9 and was originally considered part of the Eabametoong (Fort Hope) band.

The community consists of two reserves, one of which, the Summer Beaver Settlement, is shared with the Nabinamik First Nation. The other reserve, the Lansdowne House Settlement is linked to the rest of Ontario by air service at Lansdowne Airport and by winter roads to points south, via the Northern Ontario Resource Trail.

Recent resident figures indicate that the total registered population consists of 435 people, of whom 338 live on their reserve. The First Nation's Council is a member of the Matawa First Nations Management, which is a local chiefs' council consisting of 10 First Nations in the Long Lac, Webiquie, and Ogoki Post areas. It is also a member of the Nishnawbe Aski Nation, a tribal political organization representing most of the First Nations in northern Ontario.

The Neskantaga First Nation is also actively involved in the *Ring of Fire* mining development proposals. Chief Peter Moonias, for example, is quoted in a front-page article in the 14 July 2012 issue of the *Globe and Mail* entitled "Natural Resources to Define First Nations Leader's Next Term."

New Post, See *Taykwa Tagamou*
Nibinamik (*www.nibinamik.ca*)

Nibinamik, which literally means *summer beaver* in the Anishinaabe language, is a remote First Nation community in northern Ontario, which is located about 50 kilometers north of Thunder Bay. It is connected to the rest of the province by its airport and a winter/ice road that leads to the Northern Ontario Resource Trail.

The total registered population is about 440 people of whom 368 live on-reserve. It is a member of the Matawa First Nations Management, a regional chief's council, and the Nishnawbe Aski Nation, a tribal political organization representing the majority of First Nations in northern Ontario.

The community is also policed by the Nishnawbe Aski Police Service until its detachment was disbanded. The Nibinamik First Nation is located on the Summer Beaver Settlement, which it shares with the Neskantaga (Lansdowne House) First Nation.

The reason for this double occupancy of Summer Beaver is that a group of Anglican residents, related by kinship, decided to leave Lansdowne House, a Catholic settlement, in 1975.

The community had become divided along religious lines, and violence had begun to occur between the two denominational groups. Nibinamik had not been recognized as a separate First Nation until recently but is now included on the federal government's list of First Nations of Ontario.

Nishnawbe Aski Nation (www.nan.on.ca)

The Nishnawbe Aski Nation evolved out of the Grand Council Treaty No. 9, which was established in 1973 as the regional organization representing the political, social, and economic interests of the 49 First Nations in northern Ontario. They are signatories to Treaty No. 9 and Treaty No. 5. In 1982, the name changed to Nishnawbe Aski Nation.

The main objective of this organization is to represent the social and economic aspirations of all peoples living in the areas covered by Treaties No. 3 and 9 until such time as real, effective action is taken to remedy the problems and challenges experienced by the peoples of Nishnawbe Aski, and to permit the forces of self-determination to establish spiritual, cultural, social and economic independence.

Nishnawbe Aski Police Service (www.naps.ca)

This organization provides policing services to 35 First Nations in the Nishnawbe Aski Nation territory. First Nations officers are spread across an area equal to two-thirds of the province of Ontario, from the Manitoba border, along the James Bay coast east to the Quebec border.

The mission of the Nishnawbe Aski Police Service is to provide a unique, effective, efficient, and culturally sensitive and appropriate service to all of the Nishnawbe area that will assertively promote harmonious and healthy communities.

North Spirit Lake (www.firstnation.ca/north-spirit-lake)

This is a small Oji-Cree First Nation in northern Ontario located approximately 170 kilometers northeast of Red Lake, on the southwest shore of North Spirit Lake. It consists of one reserve, which is accessible only by air year-round, with services provided by Wasaya Airlines, and seasonally by a winter/ice road heading north of Red Lake, which is connected to Sandy Lake First Nation and Deer Lake First Nation.

The total registered population is about 500 people of whom nearly 440 live on-reserve. Local services include the Tikinagan Child and Family Services and the Nish Aski Police Services. This First Nation is also part of the Keewaytinook Okimakanak Council of Northern Chiefs, which represents six First Nations in the Red Lake to Fort Severn region.

This community is a signatory to Treaty No. 5, which was originally signed in 1875 with the Saulteaux and Swampy Cree First Nations of the Berens River and Norway House area of northern Manitoba, but an adhesion was made in 1908 to include First Nations in northern Ontario, which include the North Spirit Lake First Nation.

Numbered Treaties

The British North America Act (BNA), now known as the Constitution Act of 1867, conferred on the federal government the responsibility for "Indians, and Lands reserved for Indian." In other words, the First Nations peoples became wards of the Canadian federal government.

At this time, Indigenous peoples of the country were not regarded as Canadian citizens, a legal status that they did not gain until the 1960s, but were placed under separate legislation (i.e., the Indian Act of 1876), which positioned them in a different legal category.

Thus, it is fair to say the post-confederation period was one in which the First Nations peoples became increasingly marginalized in the Canadian political system, and subsequent treaties tended to solidify this situation of isolation and neglect.

For the vast territories that were surrendered by the First Nations peoples, the Canadian government tended to give little in the way of compensation, certainly nothing in comparison to the actual real estate value of the various properties involved in the treaty transactions. The Province of Ontario was created in 1867 when it entered Confederation.

At this time, the northernmost boundary of the Robinson-Superior Treaty of 1850 extended only up to the height of land which was conceived as the area just north of Lake Nipigon. In 1870, The Hudson's Bay Company relinquished its monopoly in the region, for which it was financially compensated.

The first of the so-called *Numbered Treaties* was negotiated in 1871 with the signing of Treaties Nos. 1 and 2, which mainly covered the southern portion of Manitoba and the territory to the north and west of this province. The lands between Manitoba and Lake Superior were ceded with the signing of Treaty No. 3, which focused on the Lake of the Woods or Kenora District which was an area also known as the North-West Angle Treaty.

A further *adhesion* or additional lands were also negotiated in this interprovincial area in 1929–30, thus effectively ending the treaty process in the province of Ontario, except for smaller claims that emerged in later decades.

The so-called Numbered Treaties had more specific provisions than those that were included in the Robinson Treaties. Reserve lands, for example, became more standardized, based on the granting of 160 acres per family. In addition, schools were to be established on every reserve, and an annuity of $3 per person was granted, subject to future increases when warranted.

As an example, Treaty No. 3 departed from previous treaties by allowing a reserve allotment of 640 acres for a family of five persons (see Frideres and Gadacz 2008: 194–195). As a further development, in 1889, Ontario's northern boundary was revised, extending the province to the Albany River.

Treaty No. 9 was signed in 1905 with the northern Anishinaabe and Cree, which further stretched the northern boundary of the province to Hudson Bay and James Bay. This new territory added to the province thereby allowed for the construction of the Canadian National Railway just north of Lake Nipigon in 1911. See Morris, 1880 [1979], *The Treaties of Canada with the Indians of Manitoba and the North-West Territories.*

Finally, in 1923, the Williams Treaties were signed, whereby the Anishinaabe and Mississauga Indigenous peoples of southeastern Ontario between Georgian Bay and the Quebec border were compensated for the surrender of their hunting and fishing rights.

Thus, the Williams Treaties were the last treaties negotiated in Ontario, except for the previously mentioned small plots of land that were subsequently added to Treaty No. 3 in northwestern Ontario in 1929–30.

Ogoki Post, See *Marten Falls*

Ontario Coalition of Aboriginal People (www.o-cap.ca)

The Ontario Coalition of Aboriginal People (OCAP) is an advocacy organization that represents the rights and interests of off-reserve Aboriginal peoples (such as Métis, status, and non-status Indigenous peoples) living in urban, rural, and remote areas throughout the province of Ontario. It is also an affiliate member of the Congress of Aboriginal Peoples.

According to its website, OCAP's primary goal is to create and implement a plan to restart many of the programs denied Aboriginal peoples in Ontario and secondly, to create and manage a consultation process to inform the diverse communities across Ontario about what is occurring and how to access programs and services, while gaining feedback on issues and barriers.

These goals also include organizing the various Indigenous communities in Ontario so that their members will be in a better position to respond to economic and social government initiatives that affect them.

Ontario Ministry of Indigenous Relations and Reconciliation

(www.ontario.ca/page/ministry-Indigenous-relations-and-reconciliation)

The Ontario Ministry of Indigenous Relations and Reconciliation was previously known as the Ontario Ministry of Aboriginal Affairs which underwent a change of name in June 2016. This ministry was established in 2007 as a stand-alone ministry that replaced the Ontario Secretariat of Aboriginal Affairs. The Ministry's mandate is to promote collaboration and coordination across ministries on Aboriginal policy and programs in the province.

Ontario Native Women's Association (www.onwa.ca)

The Ontario Native Women's Association is a non-profit organization that was established in 1971 to empower and support Aboriginal women and their families throughout the province of Ontario.

The organization's guiding principle is that all Aboriginal ancestry will be treated with dignity, respect, and equality, and benefits and services will be extended to all, no matter where one lives and regardless of tribal heritage. Its head office is located at Fort William First Nation near Thunder Bay.

Pikangikum (www.firstnation.ca/pikangikum)

This is an Anishinaabe First Nation situated on the eastern shore of Pikangikum Lake on the Berens River, part of the Hudson Bay drainage system, located approximately 100 kilometers north of the town of Red Lake.

A recent census of the community indicates that the total registered population was 2,689, of which 2,593 live on-reserve.

Pikangikum is one of the largest First Nation communities in northern Ontario and has the highest on-reserve population in the Sioux Lookout District. It also has an estimated 75% of the population under 25 years of age, with one-third of Pikangikum being less than 9 years of age. The population continues to grow at more than 3% annually, with the highest birthrate per capita in the Sioux Lookout zone.

Under these conditions, as could be expected, this large population of younger persons has had a significant impact on infrastructure programs and services at the community level. The local school was constructed 13 years ago and suffers from a severe shortage of classroom space.

Community-based programs are generally under-resourced, thus compromising the community's ability to provide programming that will meet its needs. As a result, the community often faces various health and social challenges. It was reported, for example, that Pikangikum suffers from one of the highest suicide rates in the world and showed a pattern of inhalant abuse by young women (see Elliot 2000).

Another notable characteristic of the Pikangikum population is that the community has a 97% retention rate of the Anishinaabe (Ojibwa) language, which is the first language of most students entering school.

In addition, the community is a signatory to Treaty No. 5 and a member of the Nishnawbe Aski Nation, a provincial-territorial organization, as well as the Independent First Nations Alliance, which represents five First Nations in northwestern Ontario. An ethnographic study of Pikangikum was conducted in the 1950s by R.W. Dunning, *Social and Economic Change among the Northern Ojibwa* (1959).

Reserves (www.ictinc.ca)

In the context of Canada's *Indian Act*, a reserve is a geographical area specifically set aside for the habitation of Status Indians and administered by the federal government through the Department of Indigenous Affairs. In other words, a reserve refers to land set aside by the Crown for the use and benefit of an Indian band as specified by various treaties signed by Indigenous people and the British Crown or representatives of the Canadian government.

Upper Canada began to experience an increasingly large influx of settlers seeking agricultural land until the end of the 1840s. This population expansion extended up to the Bruce Peninsula, north of which the climate was deemed unreliable for crop production.

However, plans were nonetheless underway for settlement of the more northerly sections of the province, not so much for agricultural reasons but because of the vast mineral resources that were presumed to exist north of Lakes Huron and Superior. As an example, by the early 1800s, prospectors had already begun to explore the mineral-rich Canadian Shield country in the Lake Superior region of northern Ontario.

However, Aboriginal peoples began to object to these intrusions into their territory because these regions had not been yet ceded to the British Crown. In one instance, violence erupted at a mining site near Sault Ste. Marie in the 1840s, which was an incident that did as much as anything else to precipitate the later treaties of the 1850s.

Prior to the 1850s, a more piecemeal approach to treaty negotiations was a common practice as the British Crown dealt with individual tribes or groups of similar tribes rather than the larger scale practice that was common with the later treaties of north and central Ontario. In other words, a more comprehensive approach to treaty negotiations began to emerge.

As a result, the Robinson-Superior and Robinson-Huron Treaties of 1850 involved extensive tracts of land, larger than any of the previous treaties combined. The area over which Aboriginal title was ceded by these treaties extended from the north shores of Lake Huron and Superior up to the height of land and the territory of Rupert's Land.

The Hudson's Bay Company held monopoly trading and administrative rights to that territory by virtue of a royal charter. The terms of these *comprehensive* treaties as they were later called were also standardized to a large extent such that annual payments or annuities were paid to the treaty signatories, with hunting and fishing rights on Crown lands extended to Indigenous community members. Also, provisions were made for the establishment of reserves for the settlement of the Indigenous populations.

Thus, the Robinson Treaties established a basic formula that would later act as a guide for additional treaties that would be negotiated in later years. For further information on individual treaties consult, Canada, 1891 [1979], *Indian Treaties and Surrenders*.

Royal Ontario Museum (www.rom.on.ca)

The Royal Ontario Museum's (ROM) diverse collections of world cultures and natural history make it one of the largest museums in North America. The ROM is also the largest field research institution in Canada, with research and conservation activities that span the globe.

It also participates in a publication program, as well as provides an online image collection of ROM artifacts and specimens. The material collections and research publications are particularly informative about the First Nations of Ontario.

Royal Proclamation

The *Royal Proclamation* of 1763 is an important factor in Canadian Indigenous history because it provided the initial foundation for the eventual treaty process, which established that the British Crown, and then later the government of Canada, would have the sole responsibility for extinguishing Aboriginal title to the lands possessed by First Nations people (see Poelzer and Coates 2015: 52, 81).

The Indigenous populations of Canada were seen as an economic asset by the first Europeans who came to North America. Later these Native populations were also eventually regarded by the British Crown as an effective military buffer in the east against further American expansion northward. This was the so-called *protectionist period* of the British colonial policy, the cornerstone of which was the *Royal Proclamation* of 1763, which stated that:

"It is just and reasonable, and essential to our interest, and the security of our colonies, that the several nations or tribes of Indians with whom we are connected who live under our Protection, should not be molested or disturbed in the Possession of such Parts of our Dominions and Territories; not having been ceded to or purchased by Us, are reserved to them or any of them as their hunting grounds."

This document could be considered the foundation of the concept of Indigenous rights because it recognized that "Indian and Inuit peoples were the original, sovereign inhabitants of this country prior to the arrival of the European colonial powers" (Canada 1975: 6).

The Proclamation also stipulated that Indigenous lands could only be bought or ceded through negotiations with the British Crown. In his regard, then the *Royal Proclamation* was also the basis for the Indian Act of 1876, as well as the legal backing for the treaty period during which reserves were created and Aboriginal peoples ceded their right to sole ownership of the territories that they inhabited (see Morse 1985; Hedican 2008:12).

Taykwa Tagamou (*www.taykwatagamounation.com*)

This is a Cree First Nation, formerly known as New Post, that consists of two separate reserves. One of these is located 14 kilometers west of the Abitibi Canyon Hydro Generation Station, between Cochrane and Moosonee. This reserve is set aside for hunting, trapping, and other subsistence-economic activities, and is not the principal settlement location.

A new reserve was created in 1984 to provide a settlement location for the Taykwa Tagamou First Nation, which is situated approximately 20 kilometers west of Cochrane. The total registered population was 516, of which 139 live on-reserve.

For many years, this community was known as New Post First Nation because of its association with the Hudson's Bay Company post located on the Abitibi River. In 1905, the community became a signatory to Treaty No. 9, also known as the James Bay Treaty. Today, it is affiliated with the Mushkegowuk Tribal Council, which represents six Cree First Nations from Cochrane to Moose Factory.

Temagami (www.temagamifirstnation.ca)

This First Nations community is located on Bear Island in the heart of Lake Temagami. The people refer to themselves as the *Teme-Augama Anishnabai*, or "Deep Water by the Shore People." In the last census, the total registered population was 816 people, of which 261 reside on-reserve. In 1943, Bear Island was purchased by the Department of Indian Affairs from the Province of Ontario for the sum of $3,000, in order to be designated as a permanent reserve.

However, official reserve status was not granted until 1971. Later, in 1988, a dispute occurred with the Ontario Ministry of Natural Resources when the expansion of the Red Squirrel logging road was approved through Temagami territory, which precipitated a series of roadblocks in 1988–89.

The Ontario government then created the Wendaban Stewardship Authority in 1991 to manage the four townships near the logging road, but a final decision on the agreement has yet to be determined.

See Matt Bray and Ashley Thomson, *Temagami: A Debate on Wilderness* (1990), and B.W. Hodgins and J. Benedickson, *Temagami Experience: Recreation, Resources, and Aboriginal Rights in the Northern Ontario Wilderness* (1989) for further details on the Teme-Augama First Nation's struggles to preserve their wilderness resources.

Treaty Indians (www.rcaane-cirnac.gc.ca)

The term Treaty Indians refers to First Nations persons, or the descendants of such people, who signed a treaty or other similar agreement with the British Crown or the later Canadian government. Usually, such a person is entitled to annuities, access to residential areas, preferred hunting rights and territories, or other benefits as stipulated in various treaties.

Truth and Reconciliation Commission of Canada (www.trc.ca)

The Indian Residential Schools Truth and Reconciliation Commission (TRC) was officially established on 2 June 2008. The TRC is part of the court-approved Indian Residential Schools Settlement Agreement negotiated between the legal counsel for former students, church members, government representatives, the Assembly of First Nations, and other Aboriginal organizations. All of the documents and research gathered by the TRC throughout its mandate will be accessible in a new national research center.

Turtle Island Native Network (www.turtleisland.org)

The Turtle Island Native Network is an independent, Aboriginal-owned and operated news and information network. Its "communities" section includes a fairly complete list of First Nations political organizations in Ontario.

It also contains a list of the Ontario Federation of Indian Friendship Centers, and various web links to many other First Nations services, training programs, and social organizations, such as the Professional Aboriginal Women's Society of Toronto, Aboriginal Legal Services of Toronto, Grand River Training and Employment, and the Ontario Aboriginal Sport Circle, to name just a few.

Union of Ontario Indians (www.anishinabek.ca)

The Anishinabek Nation incorporated the Union of Ontario Indians as its secretariat in 1949. This organization is a political advocate for the 39-member First Nations across Ontario. The Union of Ontario Indians is the oldest political organization in Ontario and can trace its roots to the Confederacy of Three Fires, which existed long before European contact.

The 39 First Nations have an approximate combined population of 55,000 citizens or one-third of the province of Ontario's Indigenous population. The Union of Ontario Indians has its headquarters located on Nipissing First Nation, just outside North Bay, and has satellite offices in Thunder Bay, Curve Lake First Nation, and Munsee-Delaware First Nation.

Wabauskang (*www.firstnation.ca/wabauskang*)

This is an Anishinaabe (Ojibwa) First Nation consisting of one reserve about 67 kilometers northwest of Dryden in northwestern Ontario near Kenora. The reserve is approximately 30 kilometers south of Ear Falls, off Highway 105, and 70 kilometers north of Vermillion Bay along the east shore of Wabauskang Lake.

It is serviced by air through Ear Falls Airport, located 13 kilometers northwest of Ear Falls. The most recent census report of this community indicated that it has a total registered population of 322, of which 137 persons live on-reserve.

The community is a member of the Bimose Tribal Council, which represents 10 First Nations in the Kenora-Dryden region, and the Grand Council Treaty No. 3. The community operates a wood products company called Makoose Wood Innovations, which is privately owned by Wabauskang members.

In important regional news regarding mining developments in the area, the *Kenora Daily Miner and News* reported on 11 March 2014, that the Wabauskang First Nation had decided to use its hearing with the Supreme Court of Canada to challenge the Province of Ontario's ability to delegate the carrying out of Aboriginal consultation to mining companies. Rather than having the Ministry of Mining and Northern Development deal with First Nations themselves.

Wabauskang was subsequently granted a hearing at the Supreme Court in October to settle its long-standing fight with Rubicon Minerals over a proposed mining project inside the First Nation's territory (see *Kenora Daily Miner*, 2014).

Webequie (www.webequie.ca)

Webiquie is derived from an Anishinaabe word meaning "shaking head from side to side." The name for this First Nation refers to a hunter who observed merganser, Webiquie's symbolic bird, trying to locate a breeze on which to take flight by shaking its head in an effort to determine the direction of the wind.

The community is located on the northern peninsula of Eastwood Island on Winisk Lake, which is situated about 540 kilometers north of Thunder Bay or 450 kilometers north of Sioux Lookout.

Webiquie is a fly-in community with no summer road access. A winter/ice road connects Webiquie to the Northern Ontario Resource Trail. Webiquie First Nation is a member of the Matawa First Nations Management, which represents 10 First Nations in the region which includes Long Lac, Webiquie, and Ogoki Post in northern Ontario, as well as a member of the Nishnawbe Aski Nation.

A recent population census indicates that the total registered population is about 877, of which 772 persons reside on the reserve. Webiquie First Nation only recently gained reserve status, because the treaty commissioners for Treaty No. 9 in 1905 erroneously designated the Webequie people as belonging to the Eabametoong (Fort Hope) First Nation which is situated approximately 80 kilometers to the southeast of Webiquie.

It was not until 1985 that the government recognized Webiquie as a distinct band, and separate reserve status was finally granted in 2001.

Weenusk (www.firstnation.ca/weenusk-peawanuck)

Weenusk, or *Winasko Ininiwak*, is a Cree First Nation consisting of one reserve on the west bank of the Winisk River at the mouth of the Asheweig River, near the southeastern shore of Hudson Bay, making it the second-most northerly First Nation in Ontario. A recent census report indicates that the total registered population is 576 persons, of whom 281 live on-reserve.

In 1986, people of the Weenusk First Nation were forced to move 30 kilometers southwest to Peawanuck, or *a place where flint is found* when spring floods swept away much of the original settlement. The Weenusk First Nation is considered an independent member of the Nishnabwe Aski First Nation but has now joined the Mushkegowuk Council, a regional tribal council.

From 1955–65, the Canadian government built 14 radar bases along the Hudson Bay coast. During this time the people of Weenusk were employed by the Canadian military.

Years later, *Wawatay News* (16 September 2010) reported that the Ontario government was planning to spend $55 million over a 6-year period to clean up 16 Mid-Canada Line sites that had been contaminated with toxic materials, such as mercury, PCBs, and asbestos, and littered with debris and derelict buildings.

Weenusk signed a 3-year, $8 million agreement with Ontario to provide and operate the base camp, while Ontario signed a 1-year, $3 million agreement with Winisk 500 Corporation, a band-based business, to do general clean-up work on Site 500, the largest abandoned radar site in northern Canada. Work on the sites was completed in 2016, with clean-up efforts continuing at five smaller sites (*CBC News* 30 May 2016).

Windspeaker (*www.ammsa.com/publications/windspeaker*)

Windspeaker, launched in 1983 and known as Canada's national Aboriginal news source, is a magazine owned and operated by the Aboriginal Multi-Media Society (AMMSA). Windspeaker magazine is published 12 times each year. Present national circulation has reached more than 24,000 with a reputed readership in excess of 140,000.

References

Acoose, J. (1995) *Iskwewak.Kah'Ki Yah Ni Wahkomakanak: Neither Indian Princess nor Easy Squaw*, Toronto: Women's Press.

Adams, A.B. (1973) *Sitting Bull: An Epic of the Plains,* New York: G.P. Putnam's Sons.

Adams, I. (1967) The Lonely Death of Chanie Wenjack. *Maclean's*, 1 February.

Adilman, S. (2002) Atanarjuat's Story No Match for its Cinema Saga: Acclaimed Inuit Movie Finally Comes Home Next Friday, *Toronto Star*, 6 April.

Aleiss, A. (2005) *Making the White Man's Indians: Native Americans and Hollywood Movies.* Westport, Conn.: Praeger.

AMMSA: The Aboriginal Multi-Media Society. (2008) Chief Dan George: Acclaimed Actor, Gentle Soul (http://www.ammsa.com/chief-dan-george, accessed 12 June 2024).

Anderson, K. (2000) *A Recognition of Being: Reconstructing Native Womanhood,* Toronto: Sumach Press.

Angilirq, P.A. (2002) *Atanarjuat, the Fast Runner*, Toronto: Coach House Press.

Armstrong, C. (2005) *Hidden in Plain Sight: Contributions of Aboriginal Peoples to Canadian Identity and Culture*, Toronto: University of Toronto Press.

Asch, M. (2014) *On Being Here to Stay: Treaties and Aboriginals Rights in Canada,* Toronto: University of Toronto Press.

Attawapiskat First Nation. (2012) Consolidated Financial Statements. accessed 19 March 2017 (www.attawapiskat.org/wp-content/uploads/2012-Consolidated-Financial-Statements.pdf)

Bailey, F.G. (1969) *Stratagems and Spoils: A Social Anthropology of Politics,* Toronto: Copp Clark Publishing.

Baldwin, W.W. (1957) Social Problems of the Ojibwa Indians in the Collins Area in Northwestern Ontario. *Anthropologica* 5: 51–123.

Banerji, A. (2012) Preventing Unintentional Injuries in Indigenous Children and Youth in Canada. *Pediatric Child Health* 17 (7): 393.

Bataille, G. and C. Silet. (1981) *The Pretend Indians: Images of Native Americans in the Movies*, Iowa City: The University of Iowa Press.

Berkhofer, R. (1978) *The White Man's Indian: Images of the American Indian from Columbus to The Present,* New York: Knopf.

Bhandari, A. (2023) Marie Clements Won't Let Canada Forget its Painful Past with Sweeping Epic Bones of Crows. *Globe and Mail*, 31 May.

Bishop, C.A. (1974) *The Northern Ojibwa and the Fur Trade: An Historical and Ecological Study*, Toronto: Holt, Rinehart, and Winston.

Boas, F. (1948) *Race, Language, and Culture.* New York: Macmillan.

Boggs, C. (1976) *Gamsci's Marxism.* London: Pluto Press.

Bonomolo, C. (2022) Marvel's Echo: Oscar Nominee Graham Greene Cast in Hawkeye Spinoff. *Comic Book*, 14 March (https://comicbook.com/tv-shows/news/marvel-echo-hawkeye-spinoff-casts-graham-greene) accessed 9 June 2024.

Borrows, J. (2002) *Recovering Canada: The Resurgence of Indigenous Law*, Toronto: University of Toronto Press.

(2010) *Canada's Indigenous Constitution,* Toronto: University of Toronto Press.

Boyden, J. (2016) *Wenjack*, Toronto: Penguin Random House.

Bray, M., and E. Epp. (1984) *A Vast and Magnificent Land: An Illustrated History of Northern Ontario,* Thunder Bay: Lakehead University.

Bray, M., and A. Thomson, (eds.) (1990) *Temagami: A Debate on Wilderness,* Toronto: Dundurn Press.

Brody, H. (1975) *The People's Land: Eskimos and Whites in the Eastern Arctic.* Marmondsworth: Penguin Books.

Brown, J.S.H. (1976) Changing Views of Fur Trade Marriage and Domesticity: James Hargrave, His Colleagues, and the "Sex." *Western Canadian Journal of Anthropology* 6 (3): 92–105.

(1980) *Strangers in Blood: Fur Trade Company Families in Indian Country,* Vancouver: University of British Columbia Press.

Brownstein, B. (2016) There's No Stopping Legendary Documentarian Alanis Obomsawin, *Montreal Gazette*, 10 November.

Bruyere, G. (2010) Review of: *Indigenous Screen Cultures in Canada*, S.B. Hafsteinsson and M. Bredin. *Choice Magazine*; accessed 29 May 2024.

Canada (1891–1979) *Indian Treaties and Surrenders.* Ottawa: Queen's Printer.

(1970) *Official Consolidation of the Indian Act.* Ottawa: Queen's Printer.

(1975) *Indian Claims in Canada.* Ottawa: Indian Claims Commission.

(2012) *Aboriginal Peoples Survey (APS).* Ottawa: Statistics Canada; accessed 23 April 2020.

(2019) *Reclaiming Power and Place: The Final Report of the National Inquiry into Missing and Murdered Indigenous Women and Girls.* 3 June. (http://www.mmiwg-ffada.ca/; accessed 30 August 2020).

Canadian Encyclopedia. (2007) Dan George. 12 August; accessed 12 June 2024). (https://www.thecanadianencyclopedia.ca/en/article/dan-george).

(2013) Jay Silverheels. 16 December; accessed 10 June 2024. (https://www.thecanadianencyclopedia.ca/en/article/jay-silverheels).

(2023) Tantoo Cardinal. 1 May; accessed 11 June 2024. (https://www.thecanadianencyclopedia.ca/en/article/tantoo-cardinal).

(2023) Alanis Obomsawin. 20 April; accessed 15 May 2024. (https://www.thecanadianencyclopedia.ca/en/article/alanis-obomsawin).

Cardinal. T. (2002) Voices from Native America. *First Nations Drum*, 28 December (www.firstnationsdrum.com/2002).

Carter, S. (1997) *Capturing Women: The Manipulation of Cultural Imagery in Canada's Prairie West,* Montreal: McGill-Queen's University Press.

CBC News. (2002) Inuit Film Earns Top Honors at Genie Awards. 8 February.

(2011) Actor Gordon Tootoosis Dies: Family. 9 July.

(2011) Margot Kidder Arrested at White House Oil Protest: Friend and Fellow Actor Tantoo Cardinal was also Taken into Custody. 23 August.

(2013) Ring of Fire Mining May Not Benefit First Nations as Hoped, Internal Memo from Aboriginal Affairs Paints Troubling Picture. 29 June.

(2014) Our Native Land: Holiday Edition. 18 December.

(2016) Clean-up of Cold War Radar Bases in Northeastern Ontario Complete. 30 May.

(2016) Alanis Obamsawin Honored with the 2016 Technicolor Clyde Gilmour Prize. 24 November.

(2017) A Perilous Pipeline: Indigenous Groups Line Up Against Keystone XL. 27 March.

(2017) Charlene Aleck on Her Grandfather, Chief Dan George. 10 October.

(2018) Gerald Stanley Acquittal Outrage Result in "Centuries of Oppression," Says Prominent Civil Rights Lawyer. 14 February.

(2018) The Horrors of St. Anne's [Residential School]. 29 March.

(2018) Radio Ad Claiming to Debunk "Myths" of Residential Schools Draws Criticism. 24 September.

(2018) Company Apologizes for Radio Ad Claiming to "debunk" Residential School "Myths." 25 September.

(2018) Ontario Will 'Duly Consult' on Resources Projects, Government Says in Wake of Landore Ruling. 28 September.

(2018) "Myths" of Residential Schools Author Stands by Article Despite Controversial Radio Ad, Criticism. 30 September.

(2019) Ottawa Trailblazer Gabrielle Fayant is the Founder of the Assembly of Seven Generations. 27 March.

(2021) On Canada Day, Thousands of Manitobans Honour Residential School Survivors, Those Who Died. 1 July.

(2021) Shingwauk Residential School in Sault Ste. Marie was Designated as a Historic Site by Parks Canada. 9 July.

(2023) CBC Arts Presentations: The 50 Greatest Films Directed by Canadians. 1 July.

(2023) Former St. Anne's Nun 8th Person Charged for Alleged Abuses at that Residential School. 19 October.

Chandler, M.J. and C.E. Lalonde. (2004) Transferring Whose Knowledge? Exchanging Whose Best Practices? On Knowing About Indigenous Knowledge and Aboriginal Suicide. In J. White, P. Maxim and P. Beavon (eds.), *Aboriginal Policy Research: Setting the Agenda for Change.* Vol 2: 111–123, Toronto: Thompson Educational Publishing.

Chronicle-Herald (Halifax, NS). (2015) Four Nova Scotians among Order of Canada Honourees. 1 July.

Christie, G. (2007) Police-Government Relations in the Context of State-Aboriginal Relations. In M.E. Beare and T. Murray, (eds.) *Police and Government Relations: Who's Calling the Shots*? Toronto: University of Toronto Press.

Churchill, W. (2001) *Fantasies of the Master Race: Literature, Cinema, and the Colonization of American Indians*, Monroe, Main: Common Courage Press.

(2007) *Pacifism as Pathology: Reflections on the Role of Armed Struggle in North America*. Oakland, CA: Arbeiter Ring Publishers (AK Press).

Churchill, W., N. Hill, and M.A. Hill. (1978) Media Stereotyping and the Native Response: An Historical Overview. *The Indian Historian* 11 (4): 46–56.

Cook-Lynn, E. (1996) *Why I Can't Read Wallace Stegner and Other Essays*, Madison, Wisc.: University of Wisconsin Press.

Cox, R. (1932) *Adventures on the Columbia River, including the Narrative of a Residence of Six Years on the Western Side of the Rocky Mountains*. New York: J & J. Harper.

CTV News. (2021) What Do We Really Know about the True History of Canada? 4 July.

Daily-Times Journal (Fort William [Thunder Bay]). (1951) Sioux Lookout Bantams Divide Exhibition Bill. 19 February.

d'Anglure, B.S. (2002) An Ethnographic Commentary: The Legend of Atanarjuat, Inuit and Shamanism. In P.A. Angilirq, N. Cohn, and B.S. d'Anglure, (eds.) *Atanarjuat: The Fast Runner,* Toronto: Coach House Books.

Daschuk, J. (2013) *Clearing the Land: Disease, Politics of Starvation and the Loss of Aboriginal Life.* Regina, SK: University of Regina Press.

Deloria, P.J. (1998) *Playing Indian*, New Haven, CT: Yale University Press.

Desjarait, R. (2017) *The Bear Walkers* (https://anishinaabeperspectives.weebly.com; accessed 22 June 2024).

Dixon, G. (2004) Greene Getting Grey Honors at Gemini Awards. *The Globe and Mail*, 17 November.

Dobbin, M. (1981) *The One-And-A-Half Men: The Story of Jim Brady and Malcolm Norris, Metis Patriots of the Twentieth Century*. Vancouver: New Star Books.

Downie, G. (2016) *The Secret Path*. (https://secretpath.ca).

Driben, P. and R.S. Trudeau. (1983) *When Freedom is Lost: The Dark Side of the Relationship Between the Government and the Fort Hope Band*, Toronto: University of Toronto Press.

Druick, Z. (2007) *Projecting Canada: Government Policy and Documentary Film at the National Film Board of Canada*, Montreal-Kingston: McGill-Queen's University Press.

Dunlevy, T. (2012) *The People of the Kattawapiskak River* Examines a Community on the Edge, *Montreal Gazette* 9 November.

Dunn, W. (1969) *The Ballad of Crowfoot*. Ottawa: National Film Board of Canada (https://pluto.tv/ca/on-demand/on); accessed 29 May 2024.

Dunning, R.W. (1959) *Social and Economic Change Among the Northern Ojibwa*, Toronto: University of Toronto Press.

Eber, D.H. (2008) *Encounters on the Passage: Inuit Meet the Explorers*, Toronto: University of Toronto Press.

Eggerton, L. (2015) Aboriginal Youth Suicide Rises in Northern Ontario. *Canadian Medical Association Journal* 187 (11): E335–6.

Elliott, L. (2000) Ontario Native Suicide Rate One of the Highest in World, Experts Says. *Canadian Press*, 27 November; accessed 19 March 2017.

Ellis, C.D. (1960) A Note on *Okima. hka. n. Anthropological Linguistics* 2:1.

Evans, A. (2010) *Chee: A Study of Aboriginal Suicide*. Montreal, PQ: McGill-Queen University Press.

Evans, M.R. (2010) *'The Fast Runner': Filming the Legend of Atanarjuat*. Lincoln, NB: University of Nebraska Press.

Evening Citizen [Ottawa]. (1951) All-Indians Beat Ottawa East Six. 17 April.

Fisher, R. (1977) *Contact and Conflict: Indian-European Relations in British Columbia, 1774–1890*, Vancouver: University of British Columbia Press.

Fleming, W.C. (2006) Myths and Stereotypes about Native Americans. *Phi Delta Kappan* 88 (3): 213–217.

Fleming, R.H., (ed.) (1940) *Minutes of Council, Northern Department of Rupert Land, 1821–1831*, Toronto: Hudson's Bay Record Society.

Forsyth, J. and M. Heine. (2008) 'A Higher Degree of Social Organization': Jan Eisenhardt and Canadian Aboriginal Sport Policy in the 1950s. *Journal of Sport History* 35 (2):261–277.

Fox, M. (2002) Inuit Movie Takes Manhattan: Atanarjuat (The Fast Runner) Surprise Hit in U.S. Art House Circuit, *Toronto Star*, 19 July.

Francis, D. (1993) *The Imaginary Indian: The Image of the Indian in Canadian Cultures.* Vancouver, BC: Arsenal Pulp Press.

Frideres, J.S., and R. Gadacz. (2008) *Aboriginal Peoples in Canada*, Toronto: Prentice-Hall.

Furnell, B. (2004) *Television Heaven* (https://televisionheaven.co.uk/reviews/wojeck).

Galbraith, J. (1949) The Hudson's Bay Company Under Fire, 1847–1962. *Canadian Historical Review* 30 (4): 322–335.

(1957) *The Hudson's Bay Company as an Imperial Factor, 1821–1869.* Berkeley: University of California Press.

Garrick, R. (2010) Martin Falls, Webequie Set Up Blockade in Ring of Fire. *Wawatay News*, 4 February.

George, Chief D. (1967) *A Lament for Confederation* (https://monova-ca/chief-dan-george-lament-for-confederation); accessed 12 June 2024).

George, Chief D. and H. Hirnschall. (2004) *The Best of Chief Dan George*, Surrey, BC: Hancock House Publishers.

Ginoogaming First Nation. (2014) Matawa Chiefs Sign Ring of Fire Framework. 26 March.

Globe and Mail [Toronto]. (1979) Matt and Jenny: On the Wilderness Trail, 20 October.

(1980) Norman Lear Buys Matt and Jenny. 7 April.

(2001) Wojeck: *CBC*, 1966–68. 31 March.

(2012) Natural Resources to Define First Nations Leader's Next Term. 14 July.

(2013) Bob Rae Jumps into Ring of Fire. 24 June.

(2017) Indigenous Rights in Canada: Significant Work Still Needed. 7 June.

(2023) 97-Year-Old Nun Charged with Historical Sexual Assaults at Residential Schools. 13 October.

Gould, L. A. (2002) Indigenous People Policing Indigenous People: The Potential Psychological and Cultural Costs. *The Social Science Journal* 39 (2):171–188.

Gover, K. (2017) Five Myths about American Indians. *The Washington Post,* 22 November.

Governor General of Canada. (2015) Graham Greene (https://www.gg.ca/en/search?t=Graham+Greene); accessed 8 June 2024.

Gramsci, A. (1971) *Selections from the Prison Notebooks*, trans. By Q. Hoare and G. Nowell-Smith. New York: International Press.

Green, R. (1984) The Pocahontas Perplex: The Image of the American Indian Woman in American Culture. *The Massachusetts Review* 16 (4): 698–714.

(1992) *Women in American Indian Society.* New York: Chelsea House.

Haas, L. R. (2021) Actor Graham Greene Reflects on His Long Career, His Latest Role as A Killer, and the Worst Films About Native Americans. *Cine Movie*, 30 July.

Hafsteinsson, S.B. and M. Bredin. (2010) *Indigenous Screen Cultures in Canada.* Winnipeg: University of Manitoba Press.

Hallett, D., M.J. Chandler, and C.E. Lalonde. (2007) Aboriginal Language Knowledge and Youth Suicide. *Cognitive Development* 35 (2):191–219.

Hallowell, A. I. (1942 [1971]) *The Role of Conjuring in Saulteaux Society.* Publications of the Philadelphia Anthropological Society, New York: Octagon Books (orig. University of Pennsylvania Press).

Harewood, A. (2003) Alanis Obomsawin: A Portrait of a First Nation's Filmmaker. *Take One*, 1 June; accessed 7 June 2024.

Harkin, M.E. and D.R. Lewis, (eds.) (2007) *Native Americans and the Environment: Perspectives on the Ecological Indian.* Lincoln: University of Nebraska Press.

Harmon-Jones, E, (2019) *Cognitive Dissonance: Re-examining a Pivotal Theory in Psychology* (Second ed.). Washington, DC: American Psychological Association.

Harper, S. (2008) *Text of Prime Minister Harper's Apology.* 11 June. Retrieved from www.ainc-inac.gc.ca.

Harris, M. (1968) *The Rise of Anthropological Theory: A History of Theories of Culture,* New York: Thomas Y. Crowell.

Hedican, E. J. (1986) *The Ogoki River Guides: Emergent Leadership among the Northern Ojibwa,* Waterloo, ON: Wilfrid Laurier University Press.

(1988) Review of: *Native American Voluntary Organizations,* in *Rural Sociology* 53 (3): 384–385.

(2001) *Up in Nipigon Country: Anthropology as a Personal Experience*, Halifax, NS: Fernwood Books.

(1991) On the Ethno-Politics of Canadian Native Leadership and Identity. *Ethnic Groups* 9 (1): 1–15.

(2008) *Applied Anthropology in Canada: Understanding Aboriginal Issues.* 2nd (ed.) Toronto: University of Toronto Press.

(2012) *Social Anthropology: Canadian Perspectives on Culture and Society,* Toronto: Canadian Scholars' Press.

(2013) *Ipperwash: The Tragic Failure of Canada's Aboriginal Policy,* Toronto: University of Toronto Press.

(2017) *The First Nations of Ontario: Social and Economic Transitions,* Toronto: Canadian Scholars' Press.

(2023) *Beyond the Beaten Path: 50 Years of Anthropology in Canada.* New York: Austin Macauley Publishers.

Hegeman, S. S. (1989) History, Ethnography, Myth: Some Notes on the 'Indian-Centered' Narrative. *Social Text* 23: 144–160.

Henderson, W.B. and C. Bell. (eds.) (2019) Rights of Indigenous People in Canada. *Canadian Encyclopedia.* 11 December; accessed 21 May 2024.

Heth, C. (1993) *Native American Dance: Ceremonies and Social Traditions.* Washington D.C.: National Museum of the American Indian.

Hilger, M. (1995) *From Savage to Nobleman: Images of Native Americans in Film,* Lanham, Maryland: Scarecrow Press.

Hiltz, R. (2018) Ontario Court Dismisses Junior Miner's Exploration Permit Over Failure to Consult. *CIM Magazine*, 8 August.

Hockey News. (1951) Twelve Little Indians Take Ottawa by Storm During Peaceful Foray. 28 April.

Hodgins, B.W. and J. Benedickson. (1989) *The Temagami Experience: Recreation, Resources, and Aboriginal Rights in Northern Ontario*, Toronto: University of Toronto Press.

Howell, P. (2002a) Inuit Director Sweeps Genies: Zacharias Kunuk's Unique Arctic Tale Takes Canadian 'Oscars' Before it Hits Theaters, *Toronto Star*, 8 February.

(2002b) Atanarjuat Exorcises the Ghost of Nanook: Innovative Inuit Film Thrills, Chills, and Uplifts, *Toronto Star*, 12 April.

(2023) TIFF 2023: The Ten (Plus) Movies Our Film Critic Can't Wait to See at Festival, *Toronto Star*, 6 September.

Hughes, K. (2023) Bones of Crows: Fact-Based Drama Depicts the Horrors of Residential Schools. *Original Cin*, 1 June; accessed 1 June 2024.

Igloolik Isuma Production. (2007) *The Legend Behind the Film: Igloolik, "Place of Houses,"* in *the Eastern Arctic Wilderness at the Dawn of the First Millennium.* 19 May (http://www.atanarjuat.com/legend/legend_film; accessed 30 May 2023).

(2008) *Interview with Paul Apak Angilirq.* 9 May (http://atanarjuat.com/production/apak_interview.php; accessed 30 May 2023).

Indian Record. (1968) Indian Magazine: Radio's Leading Role in the Quiet Revolution 31 (9): 7.

Innis, H.A. (1930 [1970]). *The Fur Trade in Canada: An Introduction to Canadian Economic History*, Toronto: University of Toronto Press.

Johnson, B.H. (1997) *The Bear-Walker,* Toronto: Royal Ontario Museum Publications.

Johnston, B. D. (1995) *The Manitous: The Supernatural World of the Ojibway*, pp. 27–35. St. Paul: Minnesota Historical Society Press.

(2002) An Arctic Masterpiece. *Maclean's Magazine*, 15 April.

(2019) Tantoo Cardinal Finally Gets the Recognition She Deserves. *Maclean's Magazine*, 3 January.

Jones, D.B. (1981) Challenge for Change: The Artist Nearly Abdicates. In Jones, D.B. ed. *Movies and Memoranda: An Interpretative History of the National Film Board of Canada*, Ottawa: Canadian Film Institute.

*Kenora Daily Miner and News. (*2014) Wabauskang to Attack Ontario's Ability to Delegate Aspects of Aboriginal Consultation to Industry at Supreme Court, 11 March.

Kidwell, C.S. (1978) The Power of Women in Three American Indian Societies. *Journal of Ethnic Studies* 5 (3):113–121.

(1992) Indian Women as Cultural Mediators. *Ethnohistory* 39 (2): 97–107.

Klein, J.Z. (2013) A Sidekick's Little-Known Leading Role in Lacrosse. *New York Times*, 31 August.

(2016) Heritage Moments: How Jay Silverheels, the Man Who Played Tonto, Got His Name. *Niagara Frontier Heritage*, 24 October.

Krech, S. (1999) *The Ecological Indian: Myths and History.* New York: Norton.

(2005) Reflections on Conservation, Sustainability, and Environmentalism in Indigenous North America. *American Anthropologist* 107: 78–86.

(2010) American Indians as the 'First Ecologists'. *The Encyclopedia of Religion and Nature*; accessed 17 April 2020.

Kumar, M.B. and M. Tjepkkema. (2019) Suicide among First Nations people, Metis and Inuit (2011–2016): Findings from the 2011 Canadian Census Health and Environment Cohort (CanCHEC), Ottawa: Statistics Canada, Cohort profile: The Canadian Census Health and Environment Cohorts (CanCHECs) statcan.gc.ca; accessed 20 May 2024.

Kunuk, Z, (2002) *Atanarjuat, the Fast Runner*, Toronto: Coach House Books.

Lamb, W.K., (eds.) (1957) *Sixteen Years in Indian Country: The Journal of Daniel Williams Harmon, 1800–1816,* Toronto: Macmillan.

Landes, R. (1937) *Ojibwa Sociology.* New York: Columbian University Press.

La Potin, A.S., (eds.) (1987) *Native American Voluntary Organizations.* New York: Greenwood Press.

LaRocque, E. (1997) Re-examining Culturally Appropriate Modes in Criminal Justice Applications. In *Aboriginal Treaty Rights in Canada: Essays in Law, Equality, and Respect for Difference.* M. Ash, ed. Vancouver: University of British Columbia Press.

Laskin, A. (2018) Ontario Court Reaffirms that the Duty to Consult Requires Real Engagement Aimed at Promoting Reconciliation, 19 July (https://jfklaw.ca/ontario-court-reaffirms-that-theduty-to-consult-requires-real-engagement-aimed-at-promoting-reconciliation); accessed 1 July 2024.

Lawrence, B. and E. Dua. (2011) Decolonizing Antiracism. In *Racism, Colonialism, and Indigeneity in Canada*. M.J. Cannon and L. Sunseri (eds.) Don Mills, ON: Oxford University Press.

Lewis, D.R. (1995) Native Americans and the Environment: A Survey of Twentieth-Century Issues. *American Indian Quarterly* 19 (3): 423–450.

Lewis, R. (2006) *Alanis Obomsawin*. Lincoln, NB: University of Nebraska Press.

Linden, S.B. (2007) *Report of the Ipperwash Inquiry*, Toronto: Publications Ontario. Retrieved from www.ipperwashinquiry.ca.

Lips, J. E. (1947) Naskapi Law (Lake St. John and Lake Mistassini Bands). *Transactions of the American Philosophical Society* 37 (4): 379–492.

Long, J. S. (2010) *Treaty No. 9: Making the Agreement to Share the Land in Far Northern Ontario in 1905*. Montreal: McGill-Queen's University Press.

Martin, D. (2007) Accountability Mechanisms: Legal Sites of Executive-Police Relations: Core Principles in a Canadian Context. In *Police and Government Relations: Who's Calling the Shots?* M.E. Beare and T. Murray, (eds.), Toronto: University of Toronto Press.

Marrubbio, M.E. (2006) *Killing the Indian Maiden: Images of Native American Women in Film*, Lexington, KY: The University Press of Kentucky.

Marrubbio, M.E. and E.L. Buffalohead, (eds.) (2018) *Native Americans in Film: Conversations, Teaching, and Theory*, Lexington, KY: The University Press of Kentucky.

Marx, K. (1978 [1852]). *The Eighteenth Brumaire of Louis Bonaparte*. Peking: Foreign Language Press.

McKiernan, M. (2012) Who Carries the Duty to Consult? *Canadian Lawyer*, 17 December; Accessed 1 July 2024.

McLaurin, V. (2019) Native American Stereotypes in Popular Media: Why the Myth of the 'Savage Indian Persists'. *Sapiens*, 27 February; accessed 24 April 2020.

Media Smarts. (2020) *Common Portrayals of Aboriginal People*; accessed 15 April 2020.

Mehl-Madrona, L. (2016) Indigenous Knowledge Approach to Successful Psychotherapies with Aboriginal Suicide Attempters. *Canadian Journal of Psychiatry* 61 (11):696–699.

Meili. D. (2010) Part-time Gig Turns to Full-time Fun for Radio Personality. 1 September, *Windspeaker*.
(2018) Obediah Johnny Yesno was Bitten by the Acting Bug. 7 April *Windspeaker*.

Melnyk, G. (2007) *Great Canadian Film Directors*, Edmonton, AB: University of Alberta Press.

Mihesuah, D.A. (2009) *American Indians: Stereotypes and Realities,* Atlanta, GA: Clarity Press.

Miller, J.R. (1996) *Shingwauk's Vision: A History of Native Residential Schools,* Toronto: University of Toronto Press.

Miller, M.J. (2008) *Outside Looking In: Viewing First Nations People in Canadian Dramatic Television Series,* Montreal, PQ: McGill-Queens University Press.

Misiak, Z. (2013) *Tonto: The Man in Front of the Mask.* Brantford, ON: Real Peoples History. MONOVA: Museums and Archives of North Vancouver. Agents of Change: Chief Dan George Legacy. (https://monova-ca/agents-of-change-chief-dan-george-legacy); accessed 12 June 2024.

Morey, W. (1968) [1893]. *Kävik the Wolf Dog.* Middlesex, Eng.: Harmondsworth.

Morris, Hon. A. (1880) [1979]. *The Treaties of Canada with the Indians of Manitoba and the North-West Territories.* Reprinted by Coles, Toronto: Belfords, Clarke.

Morrisseau, M. (2023) *'Bones of Crows': Epic Film about Canada's Residential Schools,* 2 June (https://ictnews.org/news/bone-of-crows-epic-film); (accessed 30 May 2023).

Morse, B. (eds.) (1985) *Aboriginal Peoples and the Law: Indian, Metis, and Inuit Rights in Canada,* Ottawa: Carleton University Press.

Moses, L.G. (1996) *Wild West Shows and the Images of the American Indians, 1883–1933,* Albuquerque, NM: University of New Mexico Press.

Nadasdy, P. (1999) The Politics of TEK: Power and the 'Integration' of Knowledge. *Arctic Anthropology* 36 (2):1–18.

(2005) Transcending the Debate over the Ecologically Noble Indian: Indigenous Peoples and Environmentalism. *Ethnology* 52 (2): 291–337.

Newman, P.C. (1987) *Caesars of the Wilderness: Company of Adventurers,* Vol. II, Markham, ON: Penguin Books.

News Chronicle (Port Arthur [Thunder Bay]). (1951) On the Side. 21 February.

New York Times. (1981) Chief Dan George, 82, Dies; Appeared In 'Little Big Man'. 24 September.

(2013) A Sidekick's Little-Known Leading Role in Lacross. 31 August.

Niezen, R. (2010) *Public Justice and the Anthropology of Law,* Cambridge: Cambridge University Press.

(2013) *Truth and Indignation: Canada's Truth and Reconciliation Commission on Indian Residential Schools,* Toronto: University of Toronto Press.

O'Connor, J. (2003) *Hollywood's Indians. The Portrayal of the Native American in Film*, Lexington, The University Press of Kentucky.

Odden, J. (2012) Graham Greene as Edgar Montrose References Dances with Wolves, *Way Back Machine*, 22 March accessed 9 June 2024.

Ohayon, A. (2017) *Cold Journey: A Feature on Residential Schools.* National Film Board Blog (Ivy Panda, 15 June 2023, https://ivypanda.com/essays/the-cold-journey-film-by-martin-defalco).

Olsen, K. (1989) Native Women and the Fur Industry. *Canadian Women's Studies* 10 (2–3): 55–56.

Ontario, Ministry of Natural Resources (2013) Far North Ontario: Community-based Land-Use Planning in Far North of Ontario. Retrieved from www.mnr.gov.on.ca/en/Business/Far/North.

Ontario, (1992) Akwesasne to Wunnumin Lake: Profiles of Aboriginal Communities in Ontario. Native Affairs Secretariat and Ministry of Citizenship.

Parke, H. C. (2021) From Kicking Bird to Malachi. *True West Magazine: History of the American Frontier*, 25 January.

Peterson, O. M. (1974) *The Land of Moosoneek.* The Diocese of Moosonee: The Bryant Press.

Petten, C. (2017) Jay Silverheels: TV Star Paves Way for Indian Actors. *Windspeaker*, 17 February.

Pick, Z. (1999) Storytelling and Resistance: The Documentary Practice of Alanis Obomsawin. In Banning, K. (ed.) *Gendering the Nation: Canadian Women's Cinema*, Toronto: University of Toronto Press.

Poelzer, G., and K.S. Coates. (eds.) (2015) *From Treaty Peoples to Treaty Nation*, Vancouver: University of British Columbia Press.

Ponting, J.R. (1998) Racism and Stereotyping of First Nations. In *Racism and Social Inequality in Canada: Concepts, Controversies, and Strategies of Resistance*, V. Satzewich (ed.), Toronto: Thompson Educational.

Pue, W.W. (2007) Comment on: The Oversight of Executive-Police Relations in Canada: The Constitution, the Courts, Administrative Process, and Demographic Governance. In *Police and Government Relations: Who's Calling the Shots?* (eds.) M.E. Beare and T. Murray, Toronto: University of Toronto Press.

Radin, P. (1926) *Crashing Thunder: The Autobiography of a Winnebago Indian,* New York: D. Appleton.
(1933) *The Method and Theory of Ethnology.* New York: McGraw-Hill.

Robb, P. (2015) Alanis Obomsawin: The Power of Art Revealed in Film, *Ottawa Citizen*, 19 February.

Rogers, E. S. (1965) Leadership Among the Indians of Eastern Subarctic Canada. *Anthropologica* 7: 263–284.

Rollins, P.C., and J. E. O'Connor, (eds.) (2003) *Hollywood's Indian: The Portrayal of Native Americans in Film,* Lexington, Kentucky: The University Press of Kentucky.

Ross, I. (2018) Junior Miner Ditches Duty-to-Consult Lawsuit Against Ontario. *Northern Ontario Business*, 2 March; accessed 1 July 2024.

Russell, P. H. (2010) Review of F. Widdowson and A. Howard, *Disrobing the Aboriginal Industry: The Deception Behind Indigenous Cultural Preservation* (2008), *Canadian Journal of Political Science* 43 (3): 785–787.

Sapir, E. (1917) Do We Need a Superorganic? *American Anthropologist* 19:441–447.

Saskatoon Star-Phoenix. (1951) Indian Youngsters Being Royally Treated on Tour. 15 April.

Sault Ste. Marie Star. (2021) Johnny Yesno: Survivor to Star. 5 December.

Schneller, J. (2023) Tautuktavuk's "What We See" Opening at TIFF, Explores the Persistence of Inuit Trauma. (Toronto) *Globe and Mail*, 2 September.

Schugurensky, D. (2005) Challenge for Change Launched: A Participatory Media Approach to Citizenship Education. *History of Education. The Ontario Institute for Studies in Education of the University of Toronto (OISE/UT)*. Accessed 28 May 2024.

Schwarz, M.T. (2013) *Fighting Colonialism with Hegemonic Culture: Native American Appropriation of Indian Stereotypes*, Albany, NY: State University of New York Press.

Scott, A.D. (2002) An Inuit Epic in Shades of White. *The New York Times*, 7 June.

Seton, E.T. (1900 [1987]). *The Biography of a Grizzly*. Lincoln, NE: University of Nebraska Press.

Shea, C. (2017) Graham Greene: The RD Interview. *Reader's Digest Canada*, 3 March.

Singer, B. (2001) *Wiping the War Paint off the Lens: Native American Film and Video,* Minneapolis, Minn.: University of Minnesota Press.

Skinner, A. (1911) *Notes on the Eastern Cree and Northern Saulteaux.* New York: Anthropological Papers of the American Museum of Natural History, Vol. IX, part 1.

Smith, C.C. (2006) Racial Profiling in Canada, the United States, and the United Kingdom. In *Racial Profiling in Canada: Challenging the Myth of "A Few Bad Apples."* C. Tator and F. Henry, (eds.), Toronto: University of Toronto Press.

Smith, S.L. (2000) *Reimagining Indians: Native Americans Through Anglo Eyes,* New York: Oxford University Press.

Smithsonian Institution. (2019) *Discovery Theater*, Washington, DC (https://discoverytheater.org/forms/guides/2019/nov/Hoop); accessed 19 June 2024.

Sparks, C.D. (1995) The Land Incarnate: Navajo Women and the Dialogue of Colonialism. In *Negotiators of Change: Historical Perspectives on Native American Women.* N. Shoemaker (ed.), New York: Routledge.

So today. (2021) Johnny Yesno: Survivor to Star. 5 December.

Spokesman Review (Spokane, Wash.) (1980) A Legend Dies with Jay Silverheels. 6 March.

Stanley, D. (2014) Native Performers in Wild West Shows: From Buffalo Bill to Euro-Disney. *Journal of Folklore Research* 51 (1): 24–31.

Stewart, M. (2007) The Indian Film Crews of "Challenge for Change": Representation and the State. *Canadian Journal of Film Studies* 16 (2): 49–81.

Stillman, D. (2017) *The Story of the Strange Relationship Between Sitting Bull and Buffalo Bill*, New York: Simon and Schuster.

Svetkey, B. (1991) The Breakout Stars of "Dances with Wolves." *Entertainment Weekly*, 8 March; accessed 11 June 2024.

Taylor, J. (2015) Alanis Obomsawin Passes Knowledge to Aspiring Filmmakers. *CBC News*, 14 February.

Tator, C. and F. Henry, (eds.) (2006) *Racial Profiling in Canada: Challenging the Myths of "A Few Bad Apples,"* Toronto: University of Toronto Press.

Teasdale, W. (2004) *Awakening the Spirit, Inspiring the Soul*, Toronto: SkyLight Paths Publications.

Te Hiwi, B. (2021) A 'Lack of Homelike Surroundings:' Resident Health, Home, and Recreational Infrastructure at Pelican Lake Indian Residential School, 1952–1962. *Social History* 54 (110): 99–125.

Te Hiwi, B., and J. Forsyth. (eds.) (2017) 'A Rink at this School is Almost as Essential as a Classroom': Hockey and Discipline at Pelican Lake Indian Residential School, 1945–1951, *Canadian Journal of History* 52 (1): 80–108.

Telegram (Toronto). (1951) All-Indian Team on Ice Warpath: Bantams from Sioux Lookout on Lookout for Scalps. 4 July.

Toronto Star. (1951) 'Better than Five Years in School,' Coach Says of Indian Lads' Tour. 17 April.

(1987) 10-Day-Old French Network Showing Plenty of Promise. 10 January.

Utley, R.M. (1993) *The Lance and the Shield: The Life and Times of Sitting Bull.* New York: Simon and Schuster.

Vancouver Sun. (2011a) Tootoosis Remembered for Arts, Spirituality, and Public Service. 7 July.

(2011b) Canadian Actor and First Nations Leader Gordon Tootoosis died at 69. on 9 July.

Vecsey, C. (1983) *Traditional Ojibwa Religion and its Historical Changes.* Philadelphia: American Philosophical Society.

Voyageur, C. J.; D. Beavon; and D. Newhouse. (2011). *Hidden in Plain Sight: Contributions of Aboriginal Peoples to Canadian Identity and Culture*, Volume II, Toronto: University of Toronto Press.

Wabauskang First Nation. (2014) Supreme Court Confirms Ontario Must Respect Treaty Rights. Press Release, 11 July.

Walsh, M. (2013) *Reeling Back.* 12 September (https://reeling back.com; accessed 23 June 2024).

Warren, L. (2002) The Nature of Conquests: Indians, Americans, and Environmental Histories. In *A Companion to American Indian History.* P.J. Deloria and N. Salisbury, (eds.), Malden: MA: Blackwell.

Warry, W. (2007) *Ending Denial: Understanding Aboriginal Issues,* Peterborough, ON: Broadview Press.

Washington Post. 1980. Jay Silverheels, 62, Dies. 5 March.

Watson, P. (1977) Challenge for Change. In *Canadian Film Reader.* S. Feldman and J. Nelson, (eds.), Toronto: Peter Martin Associates.

Waugh, T., M.B. Baker, and E. Winton (eds.) (2010) *Challenge for Change: Activist Documentary at the National Film Board of Canada*, Montreal-Kingston: McGill-Queens University Press.

Wawatay News. (2010) Weenusk Radar Site to be Cleaned. 16 September.

Wente, J. (2009) *Reel Injun.* (jacknilan.com/movies/reviews/reel.html); accessed 2 June 2024.

(2021) *Unreconciled: Family, Ruth, and Indigenous Resistance,* Toronto: Allen Lane Publisher.

Widdowson, F. (2019) *Separate but Unequal: How Parallelist Ideology Conceals Indigenous Dependency*, Ottawa: University of Ottawa Press.

(2021) *Indigenizing the University: Diverse Perspectives.* Winnipeg: Frontier Center for Public Policy.

Widdowson, F. and A. Howard. (2008) *Disrobing the Aboriginal Industry: The Deception Behind Indigenous Cultural Preservation*, Montreal: McGill-Queen's University Press.

Wightman, W.R. and N. Wightman. (1997) *The Land Between: Northern Ontario Resource Development, 1800 to 1990s,* Toronto: University of Toronto Press.

Windspeaker. (2016*)* Angeconeb Invested into Order of Canada 33 (10): 19.

Wong, T. (2015) ACTA Celebrates Actress Tantoo Cardinal's Four Decades of Work, *Toronto Star*, 20 February.

Yoggy, G. A. (1998) *Back in the Saddle: Essays on Western Film and Television Actors*, Jefferson, NC: McFarland Press.

Zhaawanart. (2024) *The reawakening of the Medicine People: Return of the Bear Walker*. 21 February (https://www.zhaawanart.com/post/reawakening-of-the-medicine-people); accessed 22 June 2024.